Britain in the Roman Period: Recent Trends

Edited by

R.F.J. Jones

J.R. Collis Publications
Department of Archaeology and Prehistory
University of Sheffield
1991

© Individual Authors 1991
Publisher: John R. Collis
Editor: R.B. Adams
Cover: E. Moth

Our thanks to the Pilgrim Trust for assistance in the publication
of this volume

A catalogue record of this book is available from the British
Library.

ISBN 0 906090 39 3

Copies of this volume and a catalogue of other publications by
the Department of Archaeology & Prehistory, University of
Sheffield can be obtained from:

    J.R. Collis Publications
    Department of Archaeology & Prehistory
    University of Sheffield
    Sheffield   S10 2TN

Printed in Great Britain by

    Antony Rowe Ltd.
    Chippenham

Contents

List of Figures   vi

List of Contributors   vi

Introduction   1
R. F. J. Jones

1.   Buildings   3
T. F. C. Blagg

2.   Food production and consumption - meat   15
Anthony King

3.   Food production and consumption - plants   21
Martin Jones

4.   Money in Roman Britain: a review   29
Richard Reece

5.   Britain and the Roman Empire: the evidence for regional and long distance trade   35
Michael Fulford

6.   Pottery in the later Roman north: a case study   49
Jeremy Evans

7.   The Urbanisation of Roman Britain   53
R.F.J. Jones

8.   London - New understanding of the Roman city   67
S. Roskams

9.   Lincoln   69
M. J. Jones

10.   The Romano-British countryside: the significance of rural settlement forms   75
Richard Hingley

11.   Field survey in Roman Britain: the experience of Maddle Farm   81
V. Gaffney and M. Tingle

12.   Soldiers and settlement in Wales and Scotland   85
W. S. Hanson and L. Macinnes

13.   Soldiers and Settlement in northern England   93
N. J. Higham

14.   Binchester - a northern fort and vicus   103
I. M. Ferris and R. F. J. Jones

15.   Hayling Island   111
Anthony King and Grahame Soffe

16.   Cultural Change in Roman Britain   115
R.F.J. Jones

List of Figures

Figure 1.1   Silchester, forum site.   5

Figure 1.2   Bath buildings at Silchester and Leicester.   6

Figure 1.3   Canterbury, theatre.   7

Figure 1.4   Frilford, temple sanctuary.   9

Figure 1.5   Bignor, villa.   11

Figure 1.6   Gadebridge Park villa.   12

Figure 5.1   Sources of decorated samian from London.   37

Figure 5.2   Amphora-borne commodities at Sheepen A.D. 43-61.   38

Figure 5.3   Kingsholm: Claudio-Neronian pottery supply.   39

Figure 5.4   London: Billingsgate Buildings; late first to early/mid second   40
                  century pottery supply.

Figure 5.5   Sources of imported Roman marble found in London.   42

Figure 5.6   London: New Fresh Warf; early to mid third century pottery   43
                  supply.

Figure 5.7   a) Main distribution areas of fourth century pottery.   44

                  b) Main circulation areas of barbarous radiates, Carausian coinage an issues of
                  the London mint c. A.D. 296-326.

Figure 7.1   The enclosed areas of the larger towns of Roman Britain.   57

Figure 7.2   The relationship of the areas of forum-basilica complexes to   58
                  defended areas in Romano-British towns.

Figure 7.3   Rank size curves for the planned towns of Roman Britain and   61
                  for the urbanised centres of the Trinovantes.

Figure 9.1   Roman Lincoln: land use.   70

Figure 9.2   Roman Lincoln: the sample of the archaeology investigated.   72

Figure 11.1   Maddle Farm project: sample design.   82

Figure 11.2   Maddle Farm Project: Roman pottery distributions.   83

Figure 14.1   Binchester Roman fort: the resistivity survey of the south-   104
                  eastern part of the fort, related to the excavated area.

Figure 14.2   Binchester Roman fort: Phase 8a of the commander's house and   106
                  bath suite. Mid-fourth century.

Figure 14.3   Binchester Roman fort: Phases 8b of the commander's house   107
                  and bath-suite.

Figure 14.4   Binchester Roman fort: Phases 8d of the commander's house   108
                  and bath-suite.

Figure 15.1   Hayling Island: the Iron Age and Roman temples.   112

List of Contributors

Tom Blagg	School of Continuing Education, University of Kent
Jeremy Evans	Warwickshire County Museum Service
Iain Ferris	Birmingham University Field Archaeology Unit
Mike Fulford	Department of Archaeology, University of Reading
Vince Gaffney	Department of Archaeology, University of Reading
Martin Tingle	Department of Archaeology, University of Reading
Bill Hanson	Department of Archaeology, University of Glasgow
Nick Higham	Department of History, University of Manchester
Richard Hingley	Historic Buildings and Monuments, Edinburgh
Martin Jones	McDonald Institute of Archaeology, University of Cambridge
Mick Jones	City of Lincoln Archaeological Trust
Rick Jones	Department of Archaeological Sciences, University of Bradford
Anthony King	King Alfred's College, Winchester
Lesley Macinnes	Historic Buildings and Monuments, Edinburgh
Richard Reece	Institute of Archaeology, University College, London
Steve Roskams	Department of Archaeology, University of York
Grahame Soffe	Royal Commission on Historical Monuments (England), London

Introduction

R.F.J. Jones

This book aims to provide our view of the most interesting new archaeological perspectives on the Roman period in Britain. Roman archaeologists have often seemed to exclude themselves from the changes wrought in modern archaeology over recent decades through the application of new techniques and new theories. To some of us this is a foolish waste of some of the highest quality archaeological evidence available anywhere. To me the archaeology of the Roman period is special not because of the passages of written evidence we can call in support of our interpretations, but because of its quality as archaeology. This enables us to construct interpretations through assessing evidence that is both abundant and intensively studied. That point of view arises naturally from a training as an archaeologist who specialises in the Roman period rather than as a Classical scholar who does some archaeology. It is a common approach in the contributions in this book.

If this means that we have something to say about the Roman period to other archaeologists, do we have anything to offer of broader interest? Some would say that the Roman period is a diversionary episode in the development of Britain of no lasting significance. On that view Roman Britain is no more than a peripheral and inconsequential part of a large Empire, where we can find nothing of interest to the history of that Empire and no more than a veneer of adjustment to the intruding imperialist power. This ignores the conclusive evidence for rapid and dynamic change in almost all aspects of the archaeological record over a period of some four centuries. The questions of change and mutual assimilation between native and intrusive elements are fundamental to any serious understanding of Roman Britain. Such an understanding can illuminate not only a visit to Bath or Housesteads, but more complex ideas about the nature of assimilation to external influences which are widely relevant today. What happened on the edge of the Roman Empire is also material to the Empire's rise and fall, since it was through events in provinces like Britain that it expanded and shrank. The sheer bulk of the remains of the Roman Empire and the ease of recognising fellow human beings on a tombstone or in Classical literature can make the Roman period seem sometimes too familiar. Yet the more we seem to know, the greater the danger of accepting stereotyped views of the past. The better the evidence we reliably have, the more interesting are the questions we have to tackle.

The chapters in this book are divided between general reviews and case studies. The authors were asked to present the latest ideas on their topics and to point ways ahead. There was no declared intention to publish here a collection of completely new studies. Although there is much new material here, together the chapters give an overview of the points we have reached in a wide range of aspects of the archaeology of Roman Britain. Most of the contributors still belong to what we ourselves might like to think of as the younger generation of Romano-British archaeologists. Most of us took up serious work on the subject during the 1970s. In the future we must set about conquering the peaks we can now see emerging ahead. We need to be joined in that expedition by younger enthusiasts who will ask new questions from new standpoints.

The range of people required to come together to write anything that has any aspirations to providing a general view of Roman Britain is now very large. Realising that can only increase the admiration for those scholars who have succeeded in drawing together so many threads into a coherent whole. I therefore take an editorial privilege to dedicate this collection both to Sheppard Frere, whose work has so often proved an inspiration and a sound guide, and to the new generations of scholars to come, who will overturn our cherished orthodoxies. This is offered in the hope and expectation that both will disagree with interpretations put forward here and that as a consequence both will be stirred to debate the issues further.

1. Buildings

T.F.C. Blagg

The surviving remains of Roman buildings are the most visible and enduring evidence that Britain was once part of the Roman Empire. They also mark off that period very strongly from what came before and what followed. Whatever other trading and cultural contacts there were between southern Britain and Rome before AD 43, there is as yet little sign of any Roman architectural influences on pre-conquest building. The two generations which followed the conquest saw their surroundings transformed by types of building and methods of construction which were totally new to them. After Britain ceased to be within Rome's power, c. AD 410, the decline of its Romanized culture during the fifth century included the loss of Roman constructional skills and techniques. Roman buildings could still be seen and some were still fit for use when St Augustine came to Britain in AD 597, but these were a legacy from the past, not part of a living architectural tradition.

The history of Roman buildings in Britain is therefore part of the history of a social transformation, and the buildings help to tell us about the way in which Britain adapted to being part of the Roman world, and what sort of province of the Empire it was, in what was selected or evolved there as its part of the repertoire of Roman architecture as a whole.

The following discussion will begin by considering public buildings, which will also involve examining matters relating to planning, constructional and decorative techniques and materials; it will then consider religious buildings and domestic architecture.

Public Buildings

Apart from inscriptions, and a few texts relating to the northern frontier, the only written evidence for the process of building in Roman Britain is that of Tacitus (*Agricola* 21), where he described the governor Agricola, in the winter of AD 79, as encouraging individual Britons and assisting communities to build temples, forums and houses. He was describing, in general terms, the building of new cities which were to be the administrative centres of the *civitates*. In this, the system of urban planning developed in Italy and Gaul, with a regular layout of streets intersecting at right angles, was applied to Britain. At a central intersection, a rectangular forum courtyard, with shops or offices fronted by porticoes along three sides and with a basilican hall along the fourth, provided a meeting place, a market and accommodation for the city's administration and lawcourts.

The typical Romano-British forum differs from those in Italy and Gaul in one major respect, the absence of the *capitolium* temple, which was a dominant feature in the regular forum layout which had evolved during the 2nd and 1st centuries BC (Todd 1985). In some cities in Gaul and the Alpine provinces the forum was divided by a cross-colonnade into two precincts, one around the temple and the other adjoined by the basilica (Ward-Perkins 1970). In Britain, the typical forum effectively consists of only the second of these two elements, with the main entrance to the forum in the side opposite the basilica. Silchester, Caerwent, Caistor by Norwich and London are the better-preserved examples of the type, and the main exception is Verulamium, where the forum was entered from the side, on an axis parallel with the basilica, and a building interpreted as the meeting-place of the municipal council was attached to the side opposite the basilica.

There was, however, no single blueprint for the typical Romano-British forum. Excavations during the past twenty years have revealed many variations in the detailed planning. The courtyard may be square, or an oblong parallel with or at right angles to the basilica. There are differences in the layout of the ranges of rooms around the courtyard, and in the presence or absence of porticoes along the street frontages, and of side entrances.   Despite the secondary addition to some forums (Caerwent, Cirencester and Verulamium) of buildings which have been interpreted as temples, most cities appear to have been content to do without a *capitolium*, but its absence may be the result of native religious attitudes, rather than of a military architect's failure to provide one. The arguments for regarding the Romano-British forum plan as deriving from that of the legionary *principia* are therefore not so straightforward as they may have seemed when Atkinson first elaborated them (1942:345–62). Goodchild (1946) and Ward-Perkins (1970) have preferred to consider both the forum type and the *principia* as collateral descendants of a common ancestor.   Nevertheless, the question of military assistance to early urban development in Britain remains. The army's technical skills might have been applied both in planning and in actual construction.

One recent approach has been to try to identify the units of measurement used in laying out building plots and structures.   Attempts to discriminate between the use of two standard lengths of foot, the *pes Monetalis* (0.296m) and the *pes Drusianus* (0.333m), the latter perhaps associated with the military (Walthew 1978 and 1981) have not proved statistically convincing (Millett 1982). Crummy has had more success in examining the relative dimensions of the insulae in towns (1982) and of the subdivisions of fortress plans (1985), in order to understand the mechanics of laying out a site, a process which might have several successive stages. Even when a town was built on the former site of a fortress, however, it has proved difficult to detect a 'military' planning scheme in an urban layout (Crummy 1985:85).

Rather more can be said about the nature of construction. Frere (1972:10–11) noted the resemblance between the sleeper-beam construction of the Period I timber buildings in Insula XIV at Verulamium and that at the Claudian fort at Valkenburg in the Netherlands, and he detected the work of the military carpenter, using the military stockpile of timber. Re-excavation of the Silchester forum basilica has shown that the masonry structure had a late Flavian timber predecessor (Figure 1.1), itself not the first Roman building on the site (Fulford 1985:46–9). Hassall's observation of the close resemblance in dimensions between the stone forum and basilica at Silchester and the Flavian legionary *principia* at Neuss in Germany (Hassall 1979:244–6) should perhaps be applied instead to Silchester's Flavian timber basilica. It might be argued that it was in timber rather than in stone construction that the army's assistance was influential in the towns.

So far as building in stone is concerned, there appears from an early stage to have been a clear distinction between military and civilian work in Britain (Blagg 1984). For one thing, the army in Britain was not building in stone, apart from bath-houses, until the very time when the urban buildings programme was being encouraged. The army was then heavily engaged in campaigning and building new forts and roads. It seems unlikely, therefore, that it was in a position to offer much help with the construction of masonry buildings in the towns. The army and the towns were in equal need of the services of experienced builders and stonemasons who must have come from the continental provinces. There are a few earlier instances: the legionary baths at Exeter have a close resemblance to those at the fortress of Lauriacum and the *colonia* of Avenches (Bidwell 1979:43–50); and the Neronian/early Flavian Temple of Sulis Minerva at Bath was elaborately ornamented in a manner which can be related to work in Gaul (Blagg 1979).

It was only in the last years of the 1st century and the early part of the 2nd that there was sufficient work to allow the craft of stonemasonry to become firmly established in Britain. The ornament of Corinthian capitals and cornices shows that, for the particularly skilled work, the cities of southern Britain and the fortresses and *canabae* of the military north drew on Gaulish craftsmen, but from different areas, and the schools of stonemasonry which then became established in Britain kept their their separate identities subsequently (Blagg 1984).

The regular street plans of cities and fortresses, and the forums and *principia* which stood at their respective centres, represent the institutions of Roman government and authority in architectural terms. Equally distinctive building types, the baths, the theatre and the amphitheatre, represent the social and recreational side of the Roman way of life.

At its simplest, a Roman bathhouse required a sequence of three rooms: cold, warm and hot, with a furnace to heat the air which circulated beneath the raised floors of the warm and hot rooms. An arrangement of these three rooms in line (the so-called *Reihentyp*) was typical of small bathhouses

associated with auxiliary forts. It was capable of much elaboration, by such additions as an entrance hall, a room of intense dry heat, and a forecourt for exercise, and by duplication or triplication of the main rooms. The baths at Silchester (Figure 1.2), when built in the 50s AD (Fulford 1985:56), were of this axial type, though not symmetrically arranged, and had a courtyard and portico in front. Subsequent alterations and additions produced an agglomeration of small rooms, obscuring the original axis in plan, if not in the functional progression from cold rooms to hot. The layout of the unfinished legionary baths at Wroxeter was much more symmetrical, particularly in the duplication of identical sets of rooms on each side of the entrance hall, fronting the colonnaded courtyard (Atkinson 1942). Some smaller bath-houses attached to auxiliary forts and villas have the more compact arrangement, without any axiality in their planning, characteristic of some of the earliest Roman baths, notably those at Pompeii. They represent economy and convenience rather than the intention to impress which is clearly a feature of major bath buildings.

A rather different axial symmetry, with suites of warm and hot rooms and antechambers arranged on either side of the central sequence, was a feature of the Imperial baths such as those of Titus and Trajan in Rome and the Barbarathermen in Trier. None of the Romano-British public baths had quite that degree of imposing grandeur in their planning, one function of which, in the multiplication of bath suites within one complex, may have been the provision of facilities for men and women to have bathed separately. The Jewry Wall baths at Leicester come closest to this type of plan, with three hot rooms and warm rooms side by side.

An early modification to ideas about planning major bath buildings, perhaps a concession to the British climate, was the substitution of a basilican hall for the open courtyard. The precedent set by the late Flavian legionary baths at Caerleon and Chester was followed in the 2nd-century baths at Leicester and Wroxeter, where, in the Jewry Wall and the Old Work respectively, the wall between the *frigidarium* and the basilica still stands to a height of several metres. At Wroxeter, it preserves the springing of the cross-vaults of the roof of the *frigidarium*, which spanned a width of about 30 feet (*c.* 9 metres); the walls were decorated with mosaic, a rare instance in Roman Britain. At Bath, the period III vaulting over the Great Bath, filled from the hot springs, spanned 40 feet (12 metres). Recent excavations of the reservoir of the springs (Cunliffe and Davenport 1985) have demonstrated the high degree of engineering achievement involved in the development of the site. Whether or not the Old English poem *The Ruin* refers to Bath itself (Cunliffe 1983), its description of 'the work of giants' is a suitable memorial to the fact that it was in the construction of baths that the talents of Roman builders in Britain were best displayed.

The same cannot be said of Britain's theatres and amphitheatres, which appear very provincial compared with the elaborately vaulted substructures,

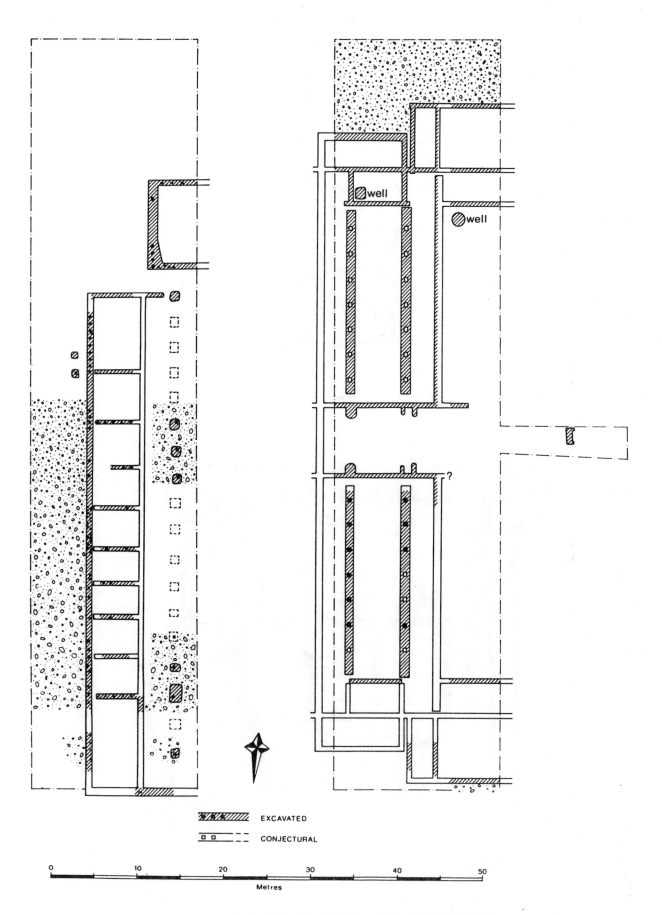

Figure 1.1   Silchester, forum site: pre-Flavian timber building (left) and Flavian basilica (right).

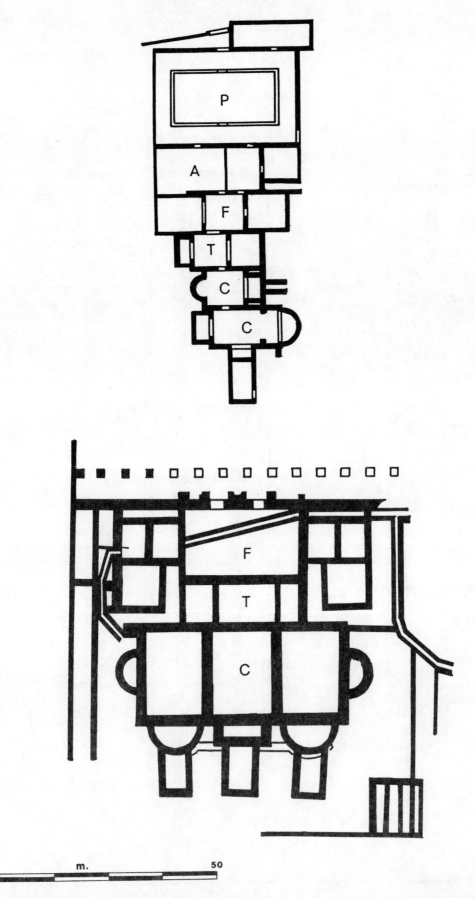

Figure 1.2   Bath buildings: above, Silchester; below, Leicester (after J.S. Wacher). A=apodyterium, C=caldarium, F=frigidarium, P=palaestra, T=tepidarium.

ornamented exteriors and stage buildings of those round the Mediterranean. Only four theatres are known from structural evidence (at Canterbury, Verulamium, Colchester, and its nearby religious sanctuary at Gosbecks), and a fifth, from an inscription at Brough on Humber. The Verulamium theatre, built in the mid-2nd century, is of the type fairly widespread in northern and central France, similar in plan to those at Drevant and Vieux, with an almost circular arena in place of the semi-circular *orchestra* of the classical Roman theatre, and a small detached stage building. The seating was carried on an earth bank contained within a buttressed external wall. The Flavian theatre at Canterbury (Figure 1.3) may originally have had an oval arena, but early in the 3rd century it was reconstructed in more classical form, with two massive concentric walls around the outside enclosing a gallery which was presumably vaulted, and semicircular counterfort walls buttressing the inner wall, a feature of some continental theatres and amphitheatres (e.g. Augst and Ribemont), as well as radial walls to support the seating (Frere 1970).

Amphitheatres are more common, but few have been excavated on any scale. The town amphitheatres

are of simpler form than those of the legionary fortresses. Maumbury Rings, outside Dorchester, was an adaptation of a Neolithic henge monument, with a seating bank made up from material excavated from the interior and retained by wooden plank walls (Bradley 1976). At Silchester, the original structure was also of timber. When rebuilt in stone, probably about the middle of the 3rd century, it had an oval arena with entrances at the ends of the long axis and two small apsidal recesses in the arena wall on the short axis (Fulford 1985). The plan has continental parallels at Augst and Martigny. The legionary amphitheatre at Chester, first constructed in wood, was rebuilt in stone about AD 100 (Thompson 1976:182). That at Caerleon appears to have been built in stone from the first, *c*. AD 80. Both have buttressed walls, are longer in proportion to their width than the civilian amphitheatres at Silchester and Cirencester, and had several subsidiary entrances in addition to the vaulted main entrance on the long axis. At none of these amphitheatres is there evidence for stone seating, so presumably it was of wood; its organization has been discussed by Fulford, in relation to the evidence from Silchester (Fulford 1985:67–8).

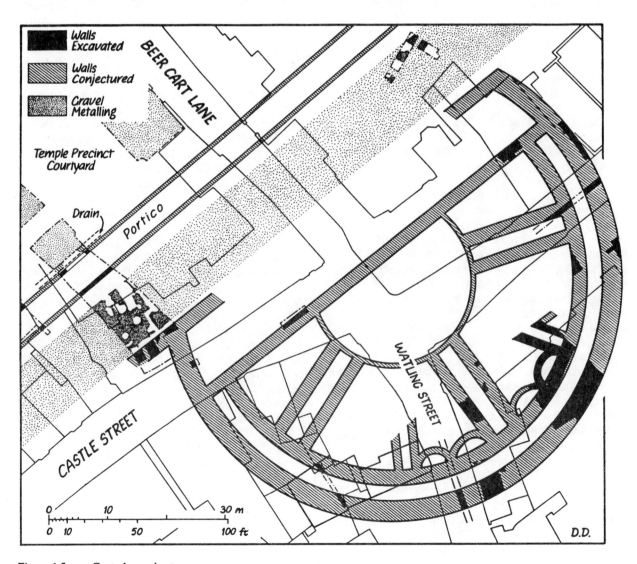

Figure 1.3   Canterbury, theatre.

Temples

Compared with the Mediterranean provinces, Britain had few temples of classical Roman type, that is, standing on a podium with steps at the front, and with a façade of columns and a pediment. It is usually accepted that the building identified as the Temple of Claudius at Camulodunum was of this form, to judge from the massive vaulted substructure of its podium, but nothing remains of its architectural ornament. At Bath, by contrast, most of a sculptured pediment and parts of the cornice and Corinthian columns of the Temple of Sulis Minerva survive to show that it was of classical appearance. Cunliffe and Davenport's comprehensive publication (1985) discusses the new evidence for the sequence of its architectural development and that of its surrounding precinct. Both these temples were built in the 1st century, in rather special contexts: the province's first *colonia*; and a spa whose early development is likely to have had official encouragement. Whether classical temples ever had a more acclimatised place in normal city architecture may be doubted. There is no positive evidence that the monumental secondary additions to the forums at Verulamium and Caerwent were actually classical temples, as is usually claimed (Lewis 1966:67–69 and 71). The imposing late 2nd-century temple in Insula VIII at Wroxeter was built in the classical manner, on a high podium at the back of an enclosed precinct, with a façade of Corinthian columns about six metres high and a decorated cornice (Blagg 1980:32), but the plan is not conventionally classical (Rodwell 1980:560). Other temples considered to be of classical type (Lewis 1966:57–72), notably those at Corbridge, are relatively modest structures.

Temples of Romano-Celtic type were a far more significant feature of the landscape, both urban and rural. The plan normally consists of two concentric squares or nearly square rectangles, the inner one forming the *cella* or cult room, the outer one defining a surrounding ambulatory. Less commonly, the plan is polygonal, as at Nettleton and Pagans Hill, or circular. The *cella* may have an apse opposite the entrance, and annexe rooms may be attached, usually as secondary additions. The materials and manner of their construction are Roman, with plastered and painted masonry walls, tiled roofs, mortar or in some cases mosaic floors, and the occasional use of stone columns. The plan, however, is not found in Roman architecture outside the Celtic provinces of the empire. The type's evolution there, as an 'adaptation of essentially Roman elements by native architects', was recognized in Wheeler's choice of the term 'Romano-Celtic' as appropriate to describe it (Wheeler 1928:316–7). Since his pioneer discussions and the more detailed analysis by Lewis (1966), two main themes have dominated discussions of these temples as buildings: the origins of the type; and how their appearance should be reconstructed, notably in Wilson's seminal paper (1975) which was fully alive to the understanding of the ritual requirements which might explain the architectural forms.

The main obstacle to defining the origin of the temple plan has been the dearth of pre-Roman Iron Age precedents, apart from the rectangular wooden structure in the village of round-houses at Heathrow which, datable to the 4th or 3rd century BC, has seemed too remote in time to be a convenient ancestor of the type. Evidence is slowly accumulating, however, for simple rectangular Iron Age structures which appear to be shrines, some of them at sites where they precede Romano-Celtic temples (Drury 1980:45–62). They stand out because they are rectangular, amid a vernacular architecture of round houses. Where such circular structures underlie Romano-Celtic temples, they cannot securely be interpreted as religious predecessors, as for example at Frilford, where Iron Age circular buildings, once regarded as ritual in purpose, are now considered to have been domestic (Hingley 1985:203). By contrast, the circular Roman temple within a square precinct on Hayling Island had a late 1st-century BC Iron Age predecessor, discussed in a separate contribution below (Chapter 15).

The sanctity of native religious sites did not depend on there being a roofed shrine. Several Romano-Celtic temples, for example those in the Gosbecks and Sheepen sanctuaries outside Colchester (Crummy 1980, Fig. 11.3) were asymmetrically placed within their precincts, and it has been suggested that a sacred tree or grove might have occupied the central position. It would seem that the form taken by Romano-Celtic temples was conditioned by existing ritual practices in the placing of votive objects and in processions around them; and that only after the conquest was it customary for them to be given the formalized setting within a building of particular type.

Until a few years ago, it was conventional to reconstruct these temples as having a tower-like *cella* surrounded on all sides by a portico of columns. It was recognized that not all temples were of this form (Wilson 1975:10) but Muckelroy, in a critical examination of the British evidence, could find only one case where it was demonstrable, and showed that in most cases where there was adequate information, it indicated that the temple ambulatories were enclosed (Muckelroy 1976). Only a small minority of British temples has in fact produced evidence of columns or other architectural embellishments, and these could have come from porches or internal colonnades rather than from external porticoes (Blagg 1980). Wilson does not accept all of Muckelroy's examples of enclosed ambulatories, while agreeing with the basic thesis, but he has also shown that when the continental evidence is examined with equal stringency, there too, open porticoes are much less usual than was supposed (Wilson 1980:25–28). He thus rejects Muckelroy's further conclusion that there was a divergence in the tradition of temple architecture between Roman Britain and the neighbouring provinces, since, as in most cases there is not enough evidence to decide what form the ambulatory took, apparent regional differences may be illusory.

Britain, however, did not copy the elaborate rural sanctuaries of northern Gaul, such as Champlieu, Ribemont and Sanxay, where a temple, a large baths building and a theatre were built in a formal axial arrangement, and many ancillary buildings accumulated alongside. Something of the idea is present at Gosbecks, outside Colchester, and at Frilford, on the boundary between the Atrebates and the Dobunni (Figure 1.4). There, in addition to temples on sites with Iron Age occupation, were built a theatre (at Gosbecks) and an amphitheatre (at Frilford), but neither site was laid out in the formally planned manner of the Gaulish sanctuaries (Crummy 1980; Hingley 1985).

Some religions of eastern origin which were introduced into Britain had distinctive cult buildings. Temples of Mithras at London and outside some of the northern forts were basilican in plan, with couches for the ritual meal in the side aisles, and an apse at the end for the cult image. Some 4th-century villas contained Christian chapels, identified as such by the subject matter of mosaics in rectangular apsidal rooms at Hinton St. Mary and Frampton in Dorset, and by wall-paintings at Lullingstone in Kent. One probable example of a church is the small building south of the forum at Silchester (but cf. King 1983), in plan a miniature version of the Constantinian basilica of St. Peter in Rome, but in general Britain did not remain a Roman province long enough to achieve significant developments in ecclesiastical architecture.

Domestic architecture

In lowland Britain the standards and types of housing were substantially transformed, in much the same way as the buildings in religious sanctuaries, by planning, materials and construction techniques in the Roman manner. The pace at which this happened varied as between town and country and, to some extent, regionally.

Fishbourne is exceptional among the houses and villas excavated within the past twenty-five years (Cunliffe 1971). The Flavian palace, with its four colonnaded wings enclosing a formal garden nearly 8000 square metres in area, and with its monumental entrance, ceremonial chambers and residential suites of rooms arranged around inner courtyards, was a magnificent building by any Roman standard. Although modest by comparison, the Neronian proto-palace which preceded it was itself a building of considerable quality in Britain for its date, with its bath suite, Corinthian columns, *opus sectile* floors, Purbeck marble decoration and Pompeian-style painted wall-plaster. It, and some comparable 1st-century villas in the southeast, at Angmering and Eccles for example, represent what may be called a grand initial stage of Romanization, which was followed by a much slower assimilation of Roman ideas in domestic housing in town and country.

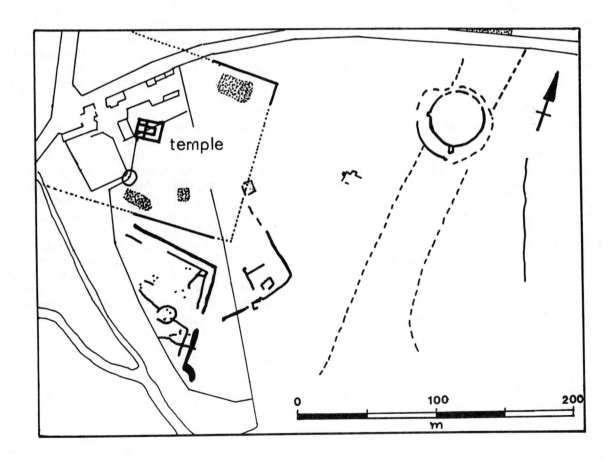

temple

0   100   200
m

Figure 1.4   Frilford, temple sanctuary (after R. Hingley).

Excavations in Verulamium, Colchester and Canterbury have produced evidence for 1st-century timber-framed rectangular structures of five or six rooms, with clay or wattle-and-daub walls and, in some cases, painted wall-plaster and mortar floors. Domestic buildings in the towns include simple rectangular strip houses, consisting of a long room or a row of rooms, usually built end on to the street, to maximise the density of occupation on the frontage; houses with one or two wings and a corridor or verandah round the front; and substantial mansions of twenty or thirty ground floor rooms, built around three sides of a courtyard. Silchester and, to a lesser extent, Caerwent, where we have the whole and two-thirds respectively of the plan, of the masonry buildings at least, still give the best overall idea of the range of houses and their distribution within a city. At Silchester, strip houses predominate on the main commercial street between the East and West Gates and in the side streets round the forum, and the twenty largest houses, with grounds which sometimes covered half an insula, were mainly located in insulae intermediate between the forum and the walls.

Only at Verulamium do we have some idea of the chronological development of the city's houses on any scale. In addition to those excavated by Wheeler in the southeast part of the city, Frere's excavations between 1955 and 1961 uncovered a number of houses of all types in the central insulae. In Insula XIV, between the forum basilica and the theatre, three periods of shop buildings were revealed in great detail, the structures being of timber in the first two periods, which were terminated by the Boudiccan and Antonine fires respectively (Frere 1972). The setback of those disasters may be one reason for the slow development of housing in Verulamium, but in any case public building seems to have taken precedence. It was only towards the end of the 2nd century that houses with more than half a dozen rooms were built, and that masonry was used in their construction. Thereafter, the picture is of healthy variety: several large houses were built in the period 215–40, some of them with cellars; even as late as *c.* 380 a courtyard house with twenty-two ground floor rooms and mosaic floors was being built, while others were being altered and extended (Frere 1983:14–23). A number of these houses have produced high quality mosaics, wall-plaster painted with architectural and floral designs, and painted plaster from a vaulted ceiling.

One useful attempt to extract some order from the varied and complex evidence for urban housing has been a paper by Walthew (1975), in which he considered in detail the similarities between town house plans and those of rural villas in Britain. He concluded that the villas set the standards, since town houses seem to have lagged behind those of the country in their development. In particular, he noted that the more sophisticated house plans are not to be found much before the middle of the 2nd century, the early 2nd-century house at Blue Boar Lane in Leicester, which had fine Pompeian-style wall

paintings in its portico, being apparently the earliest courtyard house known so far. In the *coloniae*, the situation was rather different, since both at Colchester and at Gloucester military barracks were adapted or rebuilt on similar lines as accommodation for the colonists, and only in the Antonine period were courtyard houses built on the sites (Crummy 1984; Hurst 1972).

The term 'villa' is no more precise than 'country house' in that, while it implies a building with some degree of architectural or social distinction, it can describe anything from a house of half a dozen rooms, for example Park Street, Lockleys and Hambleden in their first phases, to such palatial establishments as Bignor, Chedworth and Woodchester as they were in the 4th century. Richmond's description (1969:52–53) of the simplest form of Romano-British villa as the 'cottage' type underrates its social status. Not every senatorial aristocrat would have found their comforts adequate; but they were the country houses of the Romano-British gentry, aspiring within the means at their disposal, by the building of houses of classical Roman arrangement and construction, to the Italian Roman ideals as described by Cicero and Pliny.

Common to the planning of a great majority of them, though often elaborated, was the idea of a range of rooms in line, fronted by a corridor. The addition to the corridor side of a projecting room at each end gives the 'winged corridor' plan which has been regarded as typical of Romano-British villas, though it is equally common in northern Gaul, from where it may be presumed to have been introduced to Britain. The winged corridor frontage formed a standard type of symmetrical classical facade. The linear range of rooms was, however, the main element. Some villas never developed beyond that stage. At others, it remained the core around which extensions and additions were made: typically, wings and a corridor on the front, and the same occasionally on the back as well, as at Hambleden, or an additional row of back rooms. In the larger villas, the essence of the planning is the multiplication of linear ranges at right angles to one another, often over a long period, as Frere has now demonstrated at Bignor (Figure 1.5, Frere 1982).

Some early villas (e.g. Angmering, Eccles and Gadebridge Park in the 1st century) had separate bath buildings. Where they were built in, it was usually at one end of a range, or ranges: two at Bignor and Chedworth, three at North Leigh. Where heated bathrooms had apsidal ends, vaulted roofs may be inferred. Apart from in the baths, hypocaust heating is found in relatively few rooms, and others must have depended on portable braziers for warmth, though hearths and fireplaces are more common than is sometimes assumed (see Johnston 1978, for those in Hampshire villas).

To judge from the positions of mosaic and tessellated floors, the most important rooms in a winged corridor villa were the central room, the two projecting wing rooms and the corridor which joined them (Richmond 1969, Figs.2.1, 2.2). That corridor,

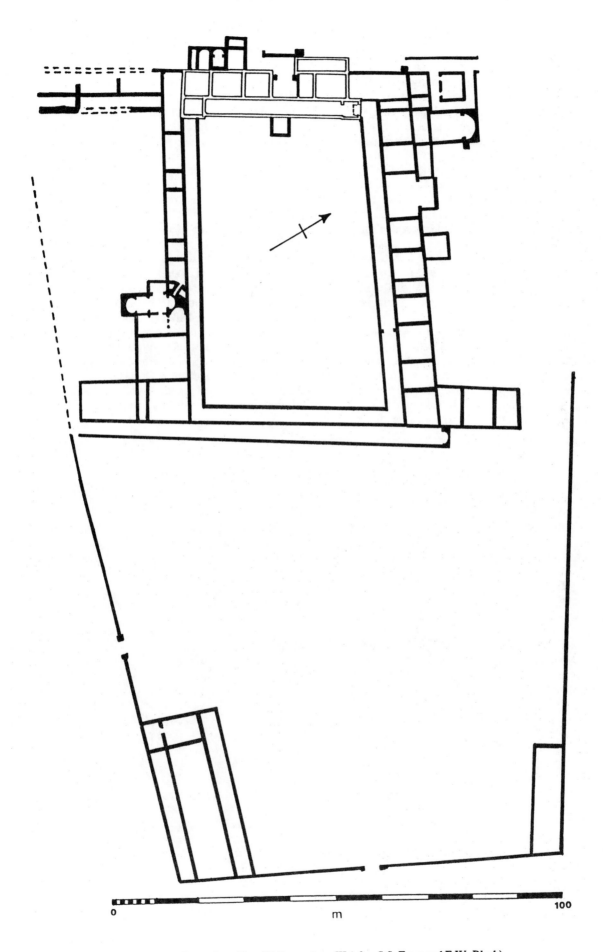

Figure 1.5   Bignor, villa: open lines, phase II; solid lines, phase III (after S.S. Frere and E.W. Black).

whether in a villa of winged or courtyard type, is often reconstructed as a portico of columns or of half-columns standing on a low wall. Actual remains of such columns, or of other decorated stonework, have been found at only a small proportion of villas, about a quarter of the number which have mosaics. Such embellishment was probably a relatively unusual feature, and many of the corridors may have been enclosed passages rather than open verandahs. Some villas, alternatively, may have had a colonnaded gallery at first floor level, as do those represented on North African mosaics. The evidence for villas having more than one storey has been discussed by Neal (1982); it is likely for those parts constructed on a steep slope, as at Gadebridge Park and Witcombe, and where more substantial foundations, particularly for rooms at the corners of a façade, suggest that there were towers (Figure 1.6). As yet, there is no certain example of a villa which was two-storied throughout, as some continental villas were.

Drury (1982b) has identified several combinations of room shapes which occur repeatedly in house plans, which can be seen as basic residential units. One such combination has a narrow room and a square room, both extending the whole width of the range, and then a pair of small rooms divided by a cross wall parallel with the long axis. In a number of late-1st/early-2nd century villas, e.g. Brixworth, Ditchley, Boxmoor and Farningham, it forms the centre of the range, with a square room added at one or both ends.

J.T. Smith (1978) had previously elaborated a discussion of the unit system, not only in relation to repeated combinations of rooms in a single building, but also to the fact that some villas effectively constitute more than one house. Chedworth began as three separate buildings, which were later extended and joined together by porticoes. Smith has interpreted this feature, which can also be seen in the Gaulish and German provinces, as explicable in terms of the continued survival of a Celtic social structure and system of land tenure, involving joint proprietorship. Not all house units in a villa group were of equal status, however. At Darenth, for example, the central house was of basically winged corridor type, but the two to each side were built, one round what Smith himself (1978:157) has likened to the Germanic 'work-hall', and the other round two large rooms which appear to have been used for storage or light industrial purposes, and each building appears to have had a different social function. Moreover, Black's attempt (1981) to work out the chronological development of the site indicates that different parts were in occupation at different times.

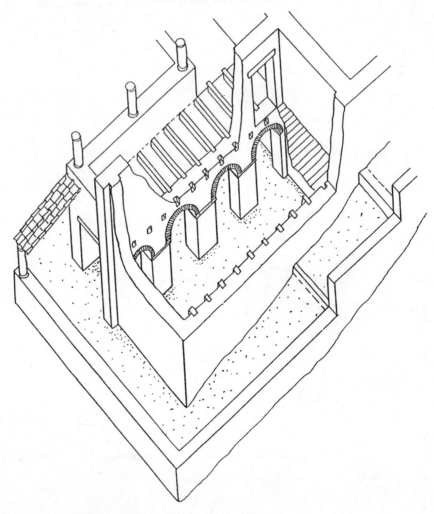

Figure 1.6   Gadebridge Park villa, reconstruction of south-east wing (after D.S. Neal).

The difference in function is more clear at sites which, unlike Chedworth and Darenth, were not given an architecturally unified façade by a portico linking the various elements. At Winterton and Gadebridge Park, for example, where the corridor villa formed the central unit, a courtyard arrangement was formed by the construction of large aisled buildings on each side (Stead 1976; Neal 1974). Such aisled buildings vary considerably in plan, and the roofs may be supported on posts, masonry walls or a combination of the two. Some were of agricultural use, as barns or for livestock, but in many cases rooms were constructed in the aisles or at one or both ends of the building to provide residential accommodation, leaving a large rectangular hall in the centre (Smith J.T. 1963; Morris 1979:55–65).

These buildings should be distinguished formally from villas which have halls behind winged-corridor façades, a type occurring mainly in Gloucestershire in the 4th century and closely related to German hall-villas (Smith D.J. 1978; Smith J.T. 1978). The social function of the halls in both types of building may, however, have been similar, and J.T. Smith (1978:358) has interpreted this as representing a social structure different from that of the inhabitants of villas with linear ranges of relatively small rooms. The frequency of aisled buildings in Hampshire and the East Midlands may be a fortuitous result of archaeological activity, or it may be connected with local abundance of the long straight timber required by the form of construction (Hadman 1978:187–8). In contrast with the hall-villas, close continental parallels for Romano-British aisled buildings are rare; it may well be that they evolved in Britain (Hadman 1978:187), and also, that the hall-houses of Saxon England were derived from them (Dixon 1982:279–82). If both propositions are true, it is an instructive comment on the history of Roman Britain that, while as the Old English poet observed 'the work of giants crumbled' (Cunliffe 1983), it was a vernacular adaptation of Roman architecture which was itself adapted, and survived. 'Ars longa, vita brevis': but for Roman Britain, art died, but life went on, so far as its architectural history is concerned.

Acknowledgements

The author is grateful to Professor M.G. Fulford and Mr. P. Bennett for supplying the illustrations for Figures 1.1 and 1.3.

References

Atkinson D. 1942 *Report on Excavations at Wroxeter (the Roman City of Viroconium) in the County of Salop, 1923–1927.* Oxford.

Bidwell P.T. 1979 *The Legionary Bath-house and Basilica and Forum at Exeter.* Exeter.

Black E.W. 1982 The Roman villa at Darenth. *Archaeologia Cantiana* 97:159–83.

Blagg T.F.C. 1979 The date of the temple of Sulis Minerva at Bath. *Britannia* 10:101–7.

Blagg T.F.C. 1980 The decorated stonework of Roman temples in Britain. In Rodwell 1980:31–44.

Blagg T.F.C. 1984 An examination of the connexions between military and civilian architecture in Roman Britain. In T.F.C. Blagg and A.C. King (eds.), *Military and Civilian in Roman Britain,* 249–63. BAR 136. Oxford.

Bradley R. 1976 Maumbury Rings, Dorchester: the excavations of 1908–1913, *Archaeologia* 105:1–97.

Crummy P. 1980 The temples of Roman Colchester. In Rodwell 1980:243–83.

Crummy P. 1982 The origins of some major Romano-British towns. *Britannia* 13:125–34.

Crummy P. 1984 *Excavations at Lion Walk, Balkerne Lane and Middleborough, Colchester, Essex.* Colchester, Colchester Archaeological Report 3.

Crummy P. 1985 Colchester: the mechanics of laying out a town. In F. Grew and B. Hobley (eds.), *Roman Urban Topography in Britain and the Western Empire,* 78–85. CBA Research Report 59. London.

Cunliffe B. 1971 *Excavations at Fishbourne. I: the site.* Oxford, Society of Antiquaries of London Research Report 26.

Cunliffe B. 1983 Earth's grip holds them. In B. Hartley and J. Wacher (eds.), *Rome and her Northern Provinces.* Gloucester.

Cunliffe B. and Davenport P. 1985 *The Temple of Sulis Minerva at Bath.* Oxford, Oxford University Committee for Archaeology, Monograph no.7.

Dixon P. 1982 How Saxon is the Saxon House? In Drury 1982a:275–87.

Drury P.J. 1980 Non-classical religious buildings in Iron Age and Roman Britain: a review. In Rodwell 1980:45–78.

Drury P.J. 1982a (ed.) *Structural Reconstruction.* BAR 110. Oxford.

Drury P.J. 1982b Form, function and the interpretation of the excavated plans of some large secular Romano-British buildings. In Drury 1982a:289–308.

Frere S.S. 1972 *Verulamium Excavations I.* Oxford, Society of Antiquaries of London Research Report 28.

Frere S.S. 1982 The Bignor villa. *Britannia* 13:135–95.

Frere S.S. 1983 *Verulamium Excavations II.* Oxford, Society of Antiquaries of London Research Report 41.

Fulford M. 1985 Excavation on the sites of the amphitheatre and forum-basilica at Silchester, Hampshire: an interim report. *Antiquaries Journal* 65:39–81.

Goodchild R.G. 1946 The origins of the Romano-British forum. *Antiquity* 20:70–77.

Hadman J. 1978 Aisled buildings in Roman Britain. In Todd 1978a:187–95.

Hassall M.W.C. 1979 The impact of Mediterranean urbanism on indigenous nucleated centres. In B.C. Burnham and H.B. Johnson (eds.), *Invasion and Response,* 241–53. BAR 73. Oxford.

Hingley R. 1985 Location, function and status: a Romano-British 'religious complex' at the Noah's Ark Inn, Frilford (Oxfordshire). *Oxford Journal of Archaeology* 4(2):201–14.

Hurst H. 1972 Excavations at Gloucester, 1968–1971: first interim report, *Antiquaries Journal* 52:24–69.

Johnston D.E. 1978 Villas of Hampshire and the Isle of Wight. In Todd 1978a:71–92.

King A.C. 1983 The Roman church at Silchester reconsidered. *Oxford Journal of Archaeology* 2:225–37.

Lewis M.J.T. 1966 *Temples in Roman Britain.* Cambridge.

Millett M. 1982 Distinguishing between the *pes monetalis* and the *pes drusianus*: some problems. *Britannia* 13:315–20.

Morris P. 1979 *Agricultural Buildings in Roman Britain.* BAR 70. Oxford.

Muckelroy K. 1976 Enclosed ambulatories in Romano-Celtic temples in Britain. *Britannia* 7:173–91.

Neal D.S. 1974 *The Excavation of the Roman Villa at Gadebridge Park, Hemel Hempstead, 1963–8*. Oxford, Society of Antiquaries of London Research Report 31.

Neal D.S. 1982 Romano-British villas: one or two storied. In Drury 1982a:153–71.

Richmond I.A. 1969 The plans of Roman villas in Britain. In A.L.F. Rivet (ed.), *The Roman Villa in Britain*. London, 49–70.

Rodwell W.J. 1980 (ed.) *Temples, Churches and Religion: Recent Research in Roman Britain*. BAR 77. Oxford.

Smith D.J. 1978 Regional aspects of the winged corridor villa in Britain. In Todd 1978a:117–147.

Smith J.T. 1963 Romano-British aisled houses. *Archaeological Journal* 120:1–30.

Smith J.T. 1978a Villas as a key to social structure. In Todd 1978a:149–85.

Smith J.T. 1978b Halls or yards? A problem of villa interpretation. *Britannia* 9:351–8.

Stead I.M. 1976 *Excavations at Winterton Roman Villa and other Roman Sites in North Lincolnshire, 1958–1967*. London.

Thompson F.H. 1976 The excavation of the Roman amphitheatre at Chester. *Archaeologia* 105:127–239.

Todd M. 1978a (ed.) *Studies in the Romano-British Villa*. Leicester.

Todd M. 1978b Villas and Romano-British society. In Todd 1978a:197–208.

Todd M. 1985 Forum and Capitolium in the early Empire. In F. Grew and B. Hobley (eds.), *Roman Urban Topography in Britain and the Western Empire*. 56–66. CBA Research Report 59. London.

Walthew C.V. 1975 The town house and the villa house in Roman Britain. *Britannia* 6:189–205.

Walthew C.V. 1978 Property-boundaries and the sizes of building-plots. *Britannia* 9:335–50.

Walthew C.V. 1981 Possible standard units of measurement in Roman military planning. *Britannia* 12:15–35.

Ward-Perkins J.B. 1970 From Republic to Empire: reflections on the early provincial architecture of the Roman west. *Journal of Roman Studies* 60:1–19.

Wheeler R.E.M. 1928 A 'Romano-Celtic' temple near Harlow, Essex, and a note on the type. *Antiquaries Journal* 8:300–26.

Wilson D.R. 1975 Romano-Celtic temple architecture. *Journal of the British Archaeological Association* (3rd series) 38:3–27.

Wilson D.R. 1980 Romano-Celtic temple architecture: how much do we actually know?. In Rodwell 1980:5–30.

2. Food Production and Consumption – Meat

Anthony King

Students of Roman Britain are relatively well served with animal bone reports, both when compared with other periods in British archaeology and with other provinces of the Roman Empire. Although many reports are about small assemblages, they are from a wide range of sites throughout the non-acidic soil areas that came under Roman control. There are also some notable large assemblages from certain towns, villas and forts, that have allowed for more profound study of those aspects that require substantial samples of bones, e.g. ages-at-death, metrical analysis, etc. Therefore, the opportunity exists to draw out the implications of the osteological evidence for the economic and cultural history of Roman Britain, on a province-wide basis, and also using the more detailed focus that the larger assemblages provide. (See the Bibliographic Orientation at the end of the article for references.)

Animal Husbandry and the Meat Diet

The orientation of animal bone studies for the Roman period has undergone a shift in emphasis in recent years. During the 1970s bones were analysed largely to establish economic inferences, using theories and techniques developed primarily for prehistoric assemblages. Minimum number of individual estimates were used to provide a basis for discussing the animal husbandries of individual sites, which were usually considered implicitly as isolated units. However, the study of large urban bone deposits, and the development of an inter-site comparative framework had induced a move away from purely animal husbandry concerns towards recognition of the complexity of factors that bear upon the composition of assemblages. Such complexity is due both to the developed nature of Romano-British social structure and to the realisation that assemblage formation processes, both pre- and post-deposition, are affected by a much wider spectrum of activities than simply the husbandry of the animals.

A particular strand of study that has arisen from this has been the analysis of diet. For a complex society, animal bones have a greater relevance when studied in terms of diet, butchery practices, rubbish disposal practices, etc., than in terms of animal economies, since trade and the movement of livestock have a limiting effect on the inferences that can be made in the latter sphere. This is not to say that husbandry and related concerns are no longer discussed by Romano-British archaeozoologists – some types of site, particularly rural sites, yield good evidence in this respect.

Notions of Region, Identity and Status in the Study of Animal Bones

An emphasis upon bones primarily as evidence for diet has allowed some of the more recently developed theoretical issues to be brought to bear upon animal bone studies. These principally revolve around explorations of the dynamics of cultural change, a matter which is very apposite to the understanding of Roman Britain, since the major feature of the period is the interaction, peaceful or otherwise, of diverse cultural groups.

i) Because Roman Britain appears to have relatively clear *status differentiation* visible in its sites and building types, it is appropriate to question whether similar differences can be observed in bone assemblages, e.g. whether 'rich' sites such as villas conform to a dietary pattern that can be considered as reflecting a high-status diet, while the un-romanised settlements are tied more to a subsistence-based, low-status diet.

ii) Related to this are *acculturation* and change of *ethnic identity*, which may be reflected in animal bone groups in the form of romanised sites having a more 'foreign' (i.e. Mediterranean-style) element in their meat diet than un-romanised sites.

iii) Particular groups within society, too, may maintain their *group identity* by differentiating their diet. For Roman Britain, the major group that can be examined from this point of view is the army, which is sufficiently distinctive to be recognised easily in archaeological terms.

iv) Closely related to the notion of dietary identity is that of the *dietary region* – a mapable area displaying distinctive characteristics. A group with its own dietary identity moving to a new region may find that geoclimatic constraints force a modification of that identity. Regionalism in the diet develops, and eventually contributes to a refocussing of the group's general cultural identity.

The exploration of these notions is undertaken primarily via the evidence of the animal bones themselves, but also includes provenance and taphonomic studies, and a certain amount of data from other faunal remains (e.g. excreta, preserved soft tissues, pathological conditions in human bones, etc.). The information which can be extracted from the animal bones centres upon counts of fragments and estimates of numbers of animals. These give basic inter-site comparative data, although it should be realised that comparisons are not always easy, due to considerable variations in assemblage size and state of preservation, and also the range of counting methods used by bone analysts. Further relevant information is gained from the study of butchery and age-at-slaughter patterns at individual sites, which give a valuable insight into the quality of meat consumed and the degree of selectivity involved.

Also useful are biometrical data and non-metrical bone morphology in assessing sex-specific and regional traits in animal populations, as a contribution to understanding the breeds of domestic stock present and the introduction/ development of new varieties. These aspects, together with palaeopathological studies, to assess the state of health of the animal population, bring animal husbandry concerns into the realm of study, and provide a useful link between the dietary emphasis of current work and more traditional evaluations of animal economies.

Chronological Trends

The Late Iron Age

The prevalent view of Iron Age agriculture is that sheep were the main focus of the livestock economy, for their wool primarily, but also their meat. This view has arisen because of the concentration in earlier years on sites on the lighter soils, predominantly the southern chalklands. Fortunately, the widening database of bone assemblages from a greater variety of localities in recent years has allowed more precision to be given to this picture.

On the chalkland and limestone areas, sheep is usually the most common domesticate in terms of numbers of bones, but the age-at-death evidence does not incline towards a specifically wool-orientated sheep husbandry, but a more generalised pattern of slaughter with a relatively high proportion of juveniles being killed. This pattern would in fact put the stress as much on milk and meat as on wool. Cattle are more common on these sites than might be expected, usually being 30 - 45% of bones of the three main domesticates, and rarely below 20%. This implies that beef was probably the most common meat consumed, given the relative weights of the carcasses of the food animals. However, it should be noted that Iron Age animals were significantly smaller than their modern counterparts, so the size and weight differential would not have been so marked. The cattle were usually slaughtered fairly young, suggesting milk production or a preference for tender meat, for instance on higher status sites such as hillforts.

In other parts of Britain cattle were more important in the diet, particularly in the highland areas of Wales and the north, where their bones may constitute up to 70% of the three main food animals. This is interesting in light of the modern pattern in these areas, where sheep are now by far the most common animal, and it probably reflects a more sheltered landscape in Iron Age (and Roman) times; a suggestion supported by the amount of woodland cover inferred from palynological analysis.

Pigs do not form a large percentage of the bones on Iron Age sites, with one important exception. At certain Late Iron Age sites in the southeast, pig bones are in the range 20 – 50% of the three main food species. The sites are all high status, usually oppida, and have artefacts such as amphora, denoting trade links with the Roman province of Gaul. These

links may explain the relatively good representation of pig bones, since Gallic sites of the same date also display similar percentages. The Roman world, and, it seems, the Gaulish élite in the Late Iron Age, valued pork as a delicacy and a high status meat. This preference was emulated by Britons in those areas where contact with the continent was strongest, and in general terms, this can be interpreted as pre-Roman adoption of a 'romanised' or 'gallicised' diet, probably by the élite as a facet of their display of control over information and resources not generally available. Interestingly, the size of the pigs on these sites is slightly higher than the average for the period, which may be a result of the introduction of new stock, and thus relatable to other changes in agriculture now thought to have taken place at the end of the Iron Age.

Other species exploited for food in the Iron Age are few. Goats are not common, as might be expected in a north European region, and this continues to be so throughout the Roman period. Chicken does not appear until fairly late in the Iron Age, and is also rare. Horse was probably eaten, but not in any great numbers, and dog also may have figured occasionally in the diet. More surprising is the very low representation of wild animals in the diet. Although land clearance for agricultural purposes had reduced wild habitats, especially in the southeast, there were still large tracts where deer and other game could live, as is clear from the late Roman period (see below). Other factors, perhaps primarily religious or status-related, may have restricted the exploitation of what should have been an obvious food resource.

Early Roman Period

The invasion of AD 43 marks a clear change in the power structure of Britain in political and social terms, but many other aspects of life would have continued relatively unaltered for some time after the conquest. Such is the case with the meat diet, for it is not until the spread of Romanisation in, roughly, the Flavian period, that changes can be detected in the archaeological record. Even Roman military bases reflect local dietary patterns initially, no doubt because local animals were effectively the only available source. However, it was probably army personnel and other Roman officials who were the main agents in the dietary changes from the late 1st century onwards. Military sites, especially legionary fortresses, and the more highly romanised towns such as the colonies and municipia show a pattern that has relatively few sheep bones, and high percentages of pig and cattle bones. Cattle bones, indeed, can be particularly common, more than 90% on some sites, which must have represented an almost unrelieved diet of beef as far as the meat component was concerned.

To explain this pattern, it can be observed that it has some similarities with the late pre-Roman one from southeastern high-status sites (see above), but the percentage of cattle bones is often higher. Also, the military/urban high ox and pig assemblage is known to occur in analogous continental deposits. In all probability, therefore, a process of 'romanisation/gallicisation' took place, whereby incoming groups – the army, officials and traders, primarily from the northwestern provinces – set the dietary norms that local people proceeded to emulate. Viewed in this light, the pre-Roman high-status pattern can be seen to be the *avant-garde* of dietary change, and it was probably the native British élite groups that continued to provide the impetus to more widespread change.

The impact of change can be clearly seen when the full range of site types in the early Roman period is considered. At villas and what might be termed the provincial romanised sites such as civitas capitals and vici (i.e. not so thoroughly 'Roman' as legionary fortresses or colonies), the cattle- and pig- dominated pattern is not so marked, nor is the age-at-death pattern for cattle (see below). In fact, there is a gradient from legionary sites with their distinctive high pig and ox assemblages, through urban sites, villas and vici, to the non-romanised settlements which continue the Iron Age pattern of relatively high sheep percentage. Effectively, the more romanised the site, the less likely it is to have a diet high in sheepmeat. In Empire-wide terms, the non-romanised dietary pattern is very distinctive, not occuring in other western provinces where the osteological evidence is adequate.

There was also a change from the Iron Age in the age-at-death pattern for cattle. Adult animals are more common, especially on military and urban sites, where occasionally there are no juveniles at all. This implies, in all probability, a specialised consumption pattern, perhaps connected with the sale or movement of animals from the producing sites, e.g. the villas. There is a certain amount of evidence from the butchery marks on cattle bones from urban sites of apparently well-ordered butchery, and hence possibly organised supply of live animals and carcasses.

The trend towards cattle does not mean that sheep were ignored by these people who lived on romanised sites, since there were also changes in the overall age-at-death pattern for sheep. More animals were killed when sub-adult or adult than in the Iron Age, which probably implies a husbandry system that emphasised meat and wool production. There was perhaps surplus production that was traded to the towns. An interesting implication of the tendency for sheep and cattle to be slaughtered at a more advanced age than in the Iron Age is that farming communities in general must have been richer, since more live animals were occupying the land at the same time, consuming valuable pasture and fodder. Animal husbandry would have been a more 'visible' part of the agricultural system.

Associated with the foregoing changes was a trend to increasing variation in the size-range of domestic stock. Larger animals can be detected in the osteological record, especially for pigs and horses, but also for cattle, sheep and dogs. Smaller individuals are still present, particularly in the peripheral parts of the province such as the southwest, where the Iron Age size-ranges are more-or-less perpetuated. Size changes are most marked in the southeast (the most highly romanised area) and the north (the most militarised area). On some sites, distinct dual size ranges have been observed, but it is disputed whether this represents breed differences or sexual dimorphism. The reasons for the presence of larger animals during the Roman period are also disputed, for although the obvious explanation may be the importation of new stock, perhaps from the Mediterranean area where larger animals certainly existed at this time, there is also a case for improvements due to selective breeding of existing stock, because this a subject that is clearly referred to by the ancient agronomists. In fact, both explanations may be relevant, since larger animals could have been introduced specifically for interbreeding with native types, with a view to their improvement.

Amongst the minor changes in the early Roman period is the apparent ending of consumption of horsemeat, since butchery marks are not found on horse bones. However, the evidence is ambiguous, because the great majority of horse bones are found disarticulated in food refuse deposits, and are often broken, which may imply a method of food preparation that did not involve the butchery marks usually associated with the cattle bones in the same deposits. Other changes include the increasing consumption of chicken, and the eating of oysters. There is little evidence for oysters on Iron Age sites, even in proximity to the southeast coast where these shellfish were to be found in profusion at the time, but from the early Roman period they became quite common as a food item, first of all on coastal sites, then much further inland, implying an organised transport system.

Late and Post–Roman Periods

After the diversification of the diet in the early Roman period due to the changes outlined above, the late Roman period sees a homogenisation, and a general drift towards higher cattle and pig percentages. In this respect, Romanisation has clearly had its effect by this time and most types of site are influenced. Even in areas like the Cotswolds, which in the Iron Age (as in the medieval period) was strong sheep-rearing territory, cattle and pigs are more in evidence. Rural sites occupied throughout the Roman period quite frequently show a trend to a more romanised diet by the 4th century, accompanied by development of romanised architecture and a villa-type layout. A weak converse trend can be observed in the towns, where late Roman de-urbanisation brings about bone assemblages in the towns having a slaughter pattern for cattle akin to that of the rural sites, rather than the apparently specialised pattern visible earlier.

Both urban and rural sites have generally adult bovine and caprovine ages-at-death, perhaps reflecting the development of a milk and wool economy. Wool products from Britain are specifically referred to in late Roman documents such as Diocletian's Price Edict, and two factors probably coincided to make Britain stand out in this respect; the distinctive complexion of British animal husbandry, with a high level of sheep rearing, as reflected particularly on the un-romanised sites, and the well-known prosperity of Britain in the early 4th century, especially visible in the villas. Villa economies may well have been slanted towards wool, even if the bones from these sites reflect the romanised style of diet. This can be explained in terms of the inhabitants being rich enough to select their diet, which therefore tended towards a socially acceptable (i.e. romanised) pattern, while inhabitants of un-romanised sites, probably also involved in wool production in a subsidiary and dependent capacity, did not have the economic freedom to choose their diet, which consequently more nearly reflects the actual proportions of animals husbanded.

Another way in which villa sites display their prosperity is by the increasing variety of meats in the diet. Hunted species become a more significant component, with the result that more sites have cervid bones, especially red deer, but also roe deer (and perhaps fallow deer, but the evidence for this species is not clear-cut). Hare is also found quite frequently in bone assemblages. There may be a religious dimension to this phenomenon, if the suggestion made earlier that there were restrictions in exploiting wild animals during the Iron Age and early Roman period is correct. Celtic and Romano-Celtic religion was predominant in the earlier period but by late Roman times other cults were becoming quite common. In the villas in particular there is evidence for sophisticated worship of eastern cults and Christianity, which may have contributed to the decline of any 'taboos' that may have existed about the consumption of certain animals.

For the period after the collapse of Roman rule, sites with bone assemblages are rare. However, it is apparent the early Saxon bone groups do not differ markedly from late Roman ones. Proportions of the main food species remain the same until the late Saxon period, when signs emerge of a developing sheep-dominated wool economy and accompanying change in diet. Slaughter patterns and animal sizes in the post-Roman centuries are also similar to the immediately preceding period, and it seems likely that there was a measure of continuity in diet and animal economies. A new development from the Saxon period onwards is the increasing consumption of fish, a resource that had clearly, and surprisingly, been under-exploited in Roman Britain.

Prospects for Future Work

The study of animal bones from Roman sites is now firmly established as a facet of modern excavation research design. So much so, in fact, that there are considerable quantities of bones awaiting analysis, and it is inevitable that sampling techniques will be increasingly applied to cope with the backlog. However, there are still many gaps in the overall picture, particularly from the very late Roman and post-Roman periods and from sites in the highland areas where preservation is poor. More attention also needs to be paid to intra-site spatial variation and to taphonomic processes affecting bone preservation. As far as inter-site comparative work is concerned,

measurements, age-at-death patterns and pathology are all subject areas where the increasing database will allow for more accurate assessment of trends in the future. Finally, of course, there is the matter of funding. The growing complexity of osteological analysis means that current levels of funding will not be adequate in future to deal with assemblages to the standard expected. In addition, there is a need for the development of more infrastructure than exists at present – a centralised and freely accessible archaeo-zoological archive would be a step in the right direction.

Bibliographic Orientation

General works on archaeozoology are not given here, but for 'nutrition anthropology' as a theoretical framework see Goody 1982 and Fieldhouse 1986.

Surveys of bone reports and comparative studies on Roman assemblages include King 1978, 1984; Maltby 1981a; Luff 1982 and Noddle 1984. The *Agrarian History of England and Wales* also has general discussion in Applebaum 1972 and Ryder 1981, but is now somewhat out-of-date.

Specific themes: military sites, Davies 1971; villas, King 1988a; Wessex, Coy & Maltby 1987; Cotswolds, King 1986; deer, Grant 1981; dogs, Harcourt 1974; pigs, Coy 1985; sheep, Ryder 1983; cattle, Noddle 1983; birds, Coy 1983; butchery, Aird 1985; Maltby 1985a.

Recent individual reports worth consulting:

a) Iron Age; Danebury, Grant 1984; Gussage All Saints, Harcourt 1979; Winnall Down, Maltby 1985b; Old Down Farm, Maltby 1981b; Ashville Trading Estate, Wilson *et al*. 1978; Skeleton Green, Ashdown & Evans 1981; Thorpe Thewles, Rackham 1987; comment on late Iron Age high-status sites, King 1988b.

b) rural sites, including villas; Frocester Court, Noddle 1979; Barnsley Park, Noddle 1985; Barton Court, Wilson *et al*. 1986; Shakenoak, Cram 1973; 1978; Fishbourne, Grant 1971; Rudston, Chaplin & Barnetson 1980; Old Winteringham & Winterton, Higgs & Greenwood 1976; Whitton, Kinnes 1981; Maxey, Halstead 1985; Grandford, Stallibrass 1982.

c) towns; Exeter, Maltby 1979; London, Armitage 1980; West unpub; Colchester, Luff 1982; 1985; Canterbury, King 1982; Rielly forthcoming; Cirencester, Thawley 1982; King 1986; Levitan 1986; Ilchester, Levitan 1982; York, O'Connor 1988.

d) vici; Chelmsford, Luff 1982; Baldock, Chaplin & McCormick 1986; Braughing, Fifield 1988; Staines, Chapman *et al*. 1984; Neatham, Done 1986.

e) forts and military vici; Vindolanda, Hodgson 1977; Watercrook, Fifield 1979; Castleford, Taylor 1985; Caerleon, O'Connor 1986; Cirencester, Thawley 1982; Brancaster, Jones *et al*. 1985.

f) late and post-Roman; Portchester, Grant 1975; 1976; West Stow, Crabtree 1985; general survey of Saxon assemblages, Clutton-Brock 1976.

References

Aird P.M. 1985 On distinguishing butchery from other post-mortem destruction: a methodological experiment applied to a faunal sample from Roman Lincoln. In N.R. Fieller *et al.* (ed.), *Palaeobiological Investigation*, BAR S66. Oxford, 5–17.

Applebaum P. 1980 Roman Britain, *The Agrarian History of England and Wales*. Cambridge, 1, ii:3–277.

Armitage P. 1980 Mammalian remains. In D.M. Jones, *Excavations at Billingsgate Buildings, Lower Thames Street, London, 1974*. London & Middlesex Archaeological Society Special Paper 4. London, 149–61.

Ashdown R. and Evans D.C. 1981 Animal bones. Part 1: mammalian bones. In C. Partridge, *Skeleton Green*. Britannia Monograph 2. London, 205–35.

Chaplin R.E. and Barnetson L.P. 1980 Animal bones. In I. Stead, *Rudston Roman Villa*. Leeds, 149–61.

Chaplin R.E. and McCormick F. 1986 The animal bones. In I.M. Stead and V. Rigby, *Baldock: the excavation of a Roman and pre-Roman settlement, 1968–72*. Britannia Monograph 7. London, 396–415.

Chapman J., Wolfe S., Woodedge W. 1984. Animal and human bone. In K. Crouch and S. Shanks. *Excavations in Staines, 1975–6*. Dorking, 115–23, MF 44–52.

Clutton-Brock J. 1976 The animal resources. In D.M. Wilson (ed.), *The Archaeology of Anglo-Saxon England*. London, 373–92.

Coy J. 1983 Birds as food in prehistoric and historic Wessex. In C. Grigson and J. Clutton-Brock (ed.), *Animals and Archaeology: 2 Shell Middens, Fishes and Birds*. BAR S183. Oxford, 181–95.

Coy J. 1985 Assessing the role of pigs from faunal debris on archaeological settlements. In N.R. Fieller et al. (ed.), *Palaeobiological Investigations*. BAR S266. Oxford, 55–64.

Coy J. and Maltby M. 1987 Archaeozoology in Wessex. In H. C. M. Keeley (ed.) *Environmental Archaeology: a regional review II*. HBMC Occasional Paper I:204–251.

Crabtree P. 1985 The faunal remains. In S. West, *West Stow: the Anglo Saxon village*. East Anglian Archaeology 24. Ipswich, 85–96.

Cram C.L. 1973 Animal bones. In A.C. Brodribb *et al*, *Excavations at Shakenoak Farm, near Wilcote, Oxfordshire: IV*. Oxford, 145–64.

Cram C.L. 1978 Animal bones. In A.C. Brodribb *et al.*, *Excavations at Shakenoak Farm, near Wilcote, Oxfordshire V*. Oxford, 117–60.

Davies R.W. 1971 The Roman military diet. *Britannia* 2:122–42.

Done G. 1986 The animal bones from Areas A and B. In M. Millett and D. Graham, *Excavations on the Romano-British Small Town at Neatham, Hampshire, 1969–1979*. Hampshire Field Club Monograph 3. Gloucester, 141–7.

Fieldhouse P. 1986 *Food and Nutrition: customs and culture*. London.

Fifield P.W. 1979 The animal bones. In T.W. Potter, *Romans in North-West England*. Kendal, 299–311.

Fifield P.W. 1988 The faunal remains. In T. Potter and S. Trow, Puckeridge-Braughing, Herts: the Ermine Street excavations, 1971–72. *Hertfordshire Archaeology* 10:148–153.

Goody J. 1982 *Cooking, Cuisine and Class: a study in comparative society*. Cambridge.

Grant A. 1971 The animal bones. In B.W. Cunliffe, *Excavations at Fishbourne, 1961–1969 II, The Finds*. Soc. of Antiqu. Research Report 27. London, 377–88.

Grant A. 1975 The animal bones. In B.W. Cunliffe, *Excavations at Portchester Castle I, Roman*. Soc. of Antiqu. Research Reports 32. London, 378–408, 437–50.

Grant A. 1976 The animal bones. In B.W. Cunliffe,

Excavations at Portchester Castle II, Saxon. Soc. of Antiqu. Research Report 33. London, 262–87.

Grant A. 1981 The significance of deer remains at occupation sites of the Iron Age to the Anglo-Saxon period. In M. Jones and G. Dimbleby (ed.), *The Environment of Man: the Iron Age to the Anglo-Saxon period*. BAR 87. Oxford, 205–13.

Grant A. 1984 Animal husbandry. In B.W. Cunliffe, *Danebury: an Iron Age hillfort in Hampshire*. CBA Research Report 52. London, 496–548, MF 16:A2–17:E9.

Halstead P. 1985 A study of mandibular teeth from Romano-British contexts at Maxey. In F. Pryor *et al.*, *Archaeology and Environment in the Lower Welland Valley*. East Anglian Archaeology 27. Cambridge, 219–24.

Harcourt R.A. 1974 The dog in prehistoric and early historic Britain. *J. of Archaeol. Sci*. 1:151–76.

Harcourt R.A. 1979 The animal bones. In G.J. Wainwright, *Gussage All Saints: an Iron Age settlement in Dorset*. DOE Archaeol. Report 10. London, 150–60.

Higgs E.S. and Greenwood W. 1976 Fauna. In I.M. Stead, *Excavations at Winterton Roman Villa*. DOE Archaeol. Report 9. London, 301–3.

Hodgson G.W. 1977 *Vindolanda II, The Animal Remains 1970–1975*. Hexham.

Jones G., Jones R., Longley P. and Wall S. 1985 Zoological evidence. In J. Hinchcliffe and C. Sparey Green, *Excavations at Brancaster 1974 and 1977*. East Anglian Archaeology 23. Gressenhall, 129–75.

King A.C. 1978 A comparative survey of bone assemblages from Roman sites in Britain. *Bull. Inst. Archaeol. London* 15:207–32.

King A.C. 1982 The animal bones. In P. Bennett *et al.*, *Excavations at Canterbury Castle*. Maidstone, 193–205.

King A.C. 1984 Animal bones and the dietary identity of military and civilian groups in Roman Britain, Germany and Gaul. In T. Blagg and A. King (ed.) *Military and Civilian in Roman Britain*. BAR 136. Oxford, 187–217.

King A.C. 1986 Animal bones from site DE/DF. In A. McWhirr, *Houses in Roman Cirencester*. Cirencester Excavations III. Cirencester, 142–52.

King A.C. 1988a, Villas and animal bones. In K. Branigan & D. Miles (ed.) *Villa Economies*. Sheffield, 51–59.

King A.C. 1988b A comment on the animal bones. In T. Potter and S. Trow, Puckeridge-Braughing, Herts: the Ermine Street excavations, 1971–72. *Hertfordshire Archaeology* 10:144–5.

Kinnes I.A. 1981 The animal bones. In M.G. Jarrett and S. Wrathmell, *Whitton, an Iron Age and Roman Farmstead in South Glamorgan*. Cardiff 232–8.

Levitan B. 1982 The faunal remains. In P. Leach, *Ilchester I, Excavations 1974–5*. Bristol, 269–85.

Levitan B. 1986 The vertebrate remains from site CQ and CX/CY. In A. McWhirr *Houses in Roman Cirencester*. Cirencester Excavations III. Cirencester, 133–41.

Luff R.-M. 1982 *A Zooarchaeological Study of the Roman North-Western Provinces*. BAR S137. Oxford.

Luff R.-M. 1985 The fauna. In R. Niblett, *Sheepen: an early Roman industrial site at Camulodunum*. CBA Research Report 57. London, 143–9, MF 4:A2–E7.

Maltby J.M. 1979 *Faunal Studies on Urban Sites: the animal bones from Exeter, 1971–1975*. Sheffield.

Maltby J.M. 1981a Iron Age, Romano-British and Anglo Saxon animal husbandry; a review of the faunal evidence. In M. Jones and G. Dimbleby (ed.), *The Environment of Man: the Iron Age to the Anglo-Saxon period*. BAR 87. Oxford, 155–203.

Maltby J.M. 1981b Animal bone. pp. 147–53 and various short sections of text in S.M. Davies, Excavations at Old Down Farm, Andover, II: Prehistoric and Roman. *Procs. of the Hants Field Club and Archaeol. Soc.* 37:81–163.

Maltby J.M. 1984 Animal bones and the Romano-British economy. In C. Grigson and J. Clutton-Brock (ed.), *Animals and Archaeology: 4 Husbandry in Europe.* BAR S227. Oxford, 125–38.

Maltby J.M. 1985a Assessing variations in Iron Age and Roman butchery practices: the need for quantification. In N.R. Fieller *et al* (ed.) *Palaeobiological Investigations.* BAR S226. Oxford, 19–30.

Maltby J.M. 1985b The animal bones. In P.J. Fasham, *The Prehistoric Settlement at Winnall Down, Winchester.* Hants Field Club Monograph 2; Gloucester, 97–112.

Noddle B.A. 1979 The animal bones, pp. 51–62. In H.S. Gracie and E.G. Price, Frocester Court Roman villa. Second report 1968–77: the courtyard. *Trans. Bristol and Glos. Archaeol. Soc.* 97:9–64.

Noddle B.A. 1983 Size and shape, time and place: skeletal variations in cattle and sheep. In M. Jones (ed.), *Integrating the Subsistence Economy.* BAR S181. Oxford, 211–38.

Noddle B.A. 1984 A comparison of the bones of cattle, sheep and pigs from ten Iron Age and Romano-British sites. In C. Grigson and J. Clutton-Brock (ed.) *Animals and Archaeology: 4, Husbandry in Europe.* BAR S227. Oxford, 105–23.

Noddle B.A. 1985 The animal bones, pp. 82–97 In G. Webster *et al* The excavation of a Romano-British rural establishment at Barnsley Park, Gloucestershire, 1961–1979: part III. *Transactions of the Bristol and Gloucestershire Archaeological Society* 103:73–100.

O'Connor T.P. 1986 The animal bones. In J.D. Zienkiewicz, *The Legionary Fortress Baths at Caerleon II, The Finds.* Cardiff, 225–48.

Rielly K. forthcoming. The animal bones. In K.M. and P. Blockley, *Excavations in the Marlowe Car Park and Associated Areas.* Maidstone.

Ryder M.L. 1981 Livestock, *The Agrarian History of England and Wales.* Cambridge, I,i:301–410.

Ryder M.L. 1983 *Sheep and Man.* London.

Stallibrass S. 1982 The faunal remains. In T. and C. Potter, *A Romano-British Village at Grandford, March, Cambridgeshire.* London 98–122.

Taylor F.J. 1985 *Investigations into Meat Supply to the Roman Fort at Castleford, West Yorkshire, c. AD 75–85.* Unpublished MA thesis; University of Sheffield.

Thawley C. 1982 The animal remains. In J. Wacher and A. McWhirr, *Early Roman Occupation at Cirencester.* Cirencester Excavations I. Cirencester, 211–27.

West B.A. unpublished *The Roman Buildings West of the Walbrook Project: human, animal and bird bones.* Level III archive. Museum of London.

Wilson B., Hamilton J., Bramwell D. and Armitage P. 1978 The animal bones. In M. Parrington, *The Excavations of an Iron Age Settlement, Bronze Age Ring-Ditches and Roman Features at Ashville Trading Estate, Abingdon, Oxfordshire 1974–76.* CBA Research Report 28. London, 110–39.

Wilson B., Wheeler A., Bramwell D., Harcourt R., Armitage F. and Cowles G. 1986 Faunal remains: animal bones and marine shells. In D. Miles (ed.), *Archaeology at Barton Court Farm, Abingdon, Oxon.* CBA Research Report 50. London, MF 8:A1–G14.

3. Food Production and Consumption – Plants

Martin Jones

Introduction

An understanding of the production, distribution and consumption of the basic food plants of a community must underpin any understanding of its economy. In Roman Britain we have a database that lends itself particularly well to an investigation in this field. We are, for example, able to detect a wide range of sites corresponding to various stages in the sequence of the food plant economy, and it seems that carbonised plant food remains are more or less ubiquitous on those Romano-British sites that have been systematically sampled for such remains. In addition, the existence of wells on many Romano-British urban and rural sites, and the low-lying nature of many urban sites has allowed the record from charred plant remains to be greatly enhanced by the record from waterlogged plant remains.

The physical evidence for different aspects of the food plant economy is also relatively rich for the Roman period in the form of implements, structures, buildings, fields and traces of cultivation. Finally, there is a wealth of contemporary literature from Southern Europe, particularly the works of Cato, Varro, and Columella, dealing with the methods and practice of estate farming, admittedly within a climatic regime very different from that of Britain.

We are a long way from realising the rich potential of this database, and the reasons are various. First, the number of excavated sites receiving comprehensive environmental analysis remains disappointingly small. Secondly, we still lack sufficient survey data to speak with confidence on the relative place within the agrarian landscape of the different categories of Romano-British rural settlement. Thirdly and linked to this last point, we have yet to establish the role and relative importance of 'villas' on the one hand, and of contemporary estates on the other, within these rich and diverse landscapes. Fourthly, we have tended to be imprecise about how exactly our data relates to the production, distribution, storage or consumption of food plants. In an economy in which the bulk movement of food plants, sometimes over long distances, is a critical aspect, we should be wary of such imprecision.

I have argued in two earlier reviews that the inclusion of parts of Britain into the Roman Empire marked the beginnings of a period which leaves evidence, not of innovation, but of stagnation in the sphere of agricultural production (Jones 1981, 1983). The evidence is essentially two-fold. On the one hand, those new metal implements that may be directly related to cereal production are not found in Britain prior to the late 3rd century. On the other hand, the botanical evidence itself, both from individual sites such as Barton Court Farm (Jones 1986) and collated from regions such as the southern chalklands (Green 1981), point to a change in the later Roman period.

Novel aspects of the early Roman period in relation to crop usage, such as storehouses, mechanical mills, and exotic species, concern the handling and movement of crops rather than their production. It was only from the later 3rd century AD, that existing archaeological and environmental evidence could be linked to innovation in the methods of agricultural production. While evidence of such innovation is, in a number of cases, associated with villa sites or field systems around villas, it involved methods appropriate to temperate Europe, and rather different from those applicable to the Mediterranean (cf. White 1970).

In this chapter I shall review the evidence for the production, distribution, and consumption of food plants, such as it exists for Roman Britain, and point to some ways in which our understanding of these processes could be improved.

Lines of Evidence

Fields, Plots and Cultivations

There is undoubtedly a whole series of surviving field boundaries, lynchets and cultivation traces that preserve evidence of Romano-British agriculture. The problem in their analysis is one of chronology. Many relict field-systems were in use for thousands of years, and accumulated relatively little dating evidence in the process. The problems of isolating a 400 year time-span within them are consequently great. A few examples illustrate possibilities and problems.

Bowen (1962) tentatively associated a block of elongated plots on Martin Down in Hampshire with a nearby Romano-British settlement. He linked their elongated shape with cultivation by heavy plough, in contrast to the small square fields that apparently underlay them, better suited to cross cultivation in the later Bronze Age. These dates derive from loose association with nearby sites, and an assumption of two discrete phases of enclosure rather than organic development of the system through time.

Riley (1980) has extensively photographed a complex and extensive system of land enclosure lying more or less between Doncaster and Nottingham. Settlements within this system which have been excavated have been found to be of approximately 3rd century AD date. We can therefore presume that these fields were in use during that period. Towards the north of the system however, the enclosures are cut across by a Roman road which appears to be respected by a Roman fort near Rossington, implying that the enclosures predate the settlement. In fact the closest structural parallels to such coaxial systems of enclosure come from the Bronze Age.

Other studies of Romano-British field systems, such as on Bullock Down in Sussex (Drewett 1982), have shown them to be reworked and extended prehistoric landscapes, rather than pioneer systems. So, as the landscapes farmed in the Roman period were already 'old', we should be cautious about interpreting their shapes as if they were pioneer landscapes. Within these constraints, however, a detailed examination of field systems, closely co-ordinated with fieldwalking evidence, may provide valuable insight into the Roman countryside in the context of a much longer timescale, as illustrated by the work of Williamson (1984) in East Anglia (see also Fleming 1987).

For stratigraphically more secure evidence from these field systems, we can examine field-edge lynchets and sealed cultivation marks, a range of which can be assigned to the Roman period (see below). In addition to cultivated fields, a variety of smaller plots, gardens and enclosures has come to light that may be linked directly with Roman towns and villas, providing an impression of intensive food-plant production in restricted areas.

Structures and Artefacts

A considerable body of crop-related evidence of this type exists for Roman Britain, from harvesting and cultivation equipment, grinding implements and storage vessels, to granaries, threshing floors and the so-called 'corn-drying ovens' (Rees 1979; Morris 1979). Where such artefacts can be related to particular parts of the economic sequence, they provide a potential database for elucidating that sequence. Such interpretation, however, requires care. While it is clear that cultivation and harvesting equipment relates to production, the great majority of such items derive from metal hoards gathered together for reworking (cf. Rees 1979). Only where they are apparently lost or abandoned can we make a clear association with their primary agricultural context.

A number of structures, though clearly *in situ*, lack an unequivocal association with any particular stage within the economic system. The obvious example is storage facilities, that may be established at a point of production, distribution or consumption. The thing that can be gleaned from remnants of storage provision in Roman Britain is an understanding of the stage or stages at which crops were being handled in large quantities.

A more difficult situation arises with the sunken ovens generally referred to as 'corn-driers'. Reynolds and Langley (1980) have produced experimental evidence that their function may be for other than drying corn, and involve such processes as malting. This latter possibility has been corroborated by finds of germinated grain within some of these ovens, for example at Barton Court Farm, Oxon (Jones 1986) and Catsgore, Somerset (Hillman 1982).

Quernstones and grinding equipment have been associated with sites of consumption rather than

production (e.g. Wacher 1975; Lloyd Jones 1984). This is of course not a necessary association, but one that is reasonable wherever botanical evidence indicates that cereals were reaching urban settlements and other consumer sites as whole grain.

Each of these points brings us to the botanical evidence that is associated with these structures and artefacts, and which may considerably aid our understanding of their usage.

Staple Crop Remains

Detailed ethnographic studies by Hillman (1981, 1984) and G. Jones (1984) have laid the basis for linking different stages in the food plant economy with different kinds of crop debris, in the form of seeds of crops, of various types of weeds, and various forms of chaff.

Hillman's own approach to the analysis of production and consumption involves a qualitative consideration of particular forms of chaff, in relation to an assumed pattern of removal at production and consumption sites.

I have attempted a similar approach (Jones 1985) emphasising the quantitative aspects of crop debris at different categories of site. This approach depends on the systematic application of a probabilistic sampling strategy over a range of contemporary sites (Jones 1979) within the context of independent environmental data.

The botanical material most usually subjected to such analysis is carbonised remains, as these are generally dominated by crop processing debris. Waterlogged plant remains augment the picture by providing information about the immediate environment of a site, structure or artefact, which is often fundamental to an understanding of its place within the economic sequence.

It is worth emphasising in this context that high levels of cereal pollen in an archaeological context are more likely to derive from crop processing, when the cereal florets are beaten open, than from crop growth, when, with the exception of rye, very little pollen is released from the plant (Vuorela 1973).

Exotic Food-plant Remains

Alongside the movement of large volumes of staples, the 'delicatessen' trade in towns has left numerous fragments of exotic crops that had travelled long distances, presumably in much smaller quantities than the staples (e.g. Grieg 1976; Willcox 1977; Kenward and Williams 1979; Murphy 1984:40). Perhaps the furthest travelled were the dates from 1st century Colchester (Murphy 1984), followed by the figs and grapes that seem ubiquitous in Romano-British towns.

Having considered the various lines of evidence available, we can now move to a summary of the inferences we may draw from them.

Production

Methods of Cultivation

The traditional bow ard, sometimes with an iron

share-tip, undoubtedly continued in use from the Iron Age into the Roman period. The wooden share of a Donnerupland-type bow ard was recovered from a 3rd century well at Abingdon, Oxon (Fowler 1978). This would have been supplemented, and in some parts replaced, by manual cultivation with spades, mattocks and hoes (Rees 1979). The ridging observed as 'cord-rig' in Scotland (Halliday and Reynolds 1984), and along the surface of an urban allotment in Roman Colchester (Crummy 1984:138–141), are believed to result from manual cultivation.

Alongside these tools, the Roman period saw a series of developments associated with cultivation to greater depth than was usually achieved with a simple ard. Two poorly dated models showing shares have been tentatively placed in the 2nd or 3rd century AD (Rees 1979), corresponding presumably to what Palladius described as:

'Ploughs: simple, or, if the open nature of the terrain permits, eared, so that with the latter it may be possible to raise up the plants on a deeper furrow to counteract the high water table in winter' (O.A.I:XLIII:I, K.D. White's translation)

Certain of the wooden shares of the preceding Iron Age could also feasibly have had wings connected (Rees 1979).

A greater depth still could be reached by running a coulter through the soil prior to the share, thereby creating a cut into which the share could bite. A number of coulters survive from the late 3rd and 4th centuries AD (Rees 1979). As they are found dismantled from the implement of which they were part, we cannot be certain what type of share was mounted with them, if a share was mounted at all. However the same period sees the appearance of asymmetrical shares such as would be expected to tip a true mouldboard plough, and it therefore seems that this implement made its first appearance in Britain in the late Roman period.

We can also consider these developments in relation to the cultivation marks they leave behind. The traces of cross-cultivation may be associated with shallow ard ploughing; one-way cultivation marks may tentatively be linked with slightly deeper cultivation, perhaps with a winged share; one-way marks together with inverted furrows may be confidently associated with mouldboard ploughing, just as ridge-and-furrow can be associated with repeated systematic mouldboard ploughing.

Cross-cultivation marks are widespread in contexts belonging to the last three millennia of prehistory. One-way cultivation marks are known from Romano-British contexts at Slonk Hill and Newhaven, both in Sussex (Bell 1976; Hartledge 1978), at the villa sites of Latimer in Buckinghamshire (Branigan 1971), and Gadebridge Park in Hemel Hempstead, Herts (Neal 1974), and sealed beneath Rudchester fort on Hadrian's Wall (Breeze 1974).

Inverted furrows and ridge-and-furrow have not been found in secure Romano-British contexts.

Staple Crops

The point has already been made that the first 200 years of Roman rule were not characterised by change and innovation in the sphere of agricultural production, which instead continued the pattern established in the later Iron Age. In a sister volume to this I have attempted a description of Iron Age crop production in greater detail (Jones forthcoming). Here I shall provide a briefer outline.

The major crops in evidence were: spelt wheat, *Triticum spelta*; and hulled six-row barley, *Hordeum vulgare*. These were accompanied by: emmer wheat, *Triticum dicoccum*, principally in the southwest and far north; celtic beans, *Vicia faba* var. *minor*; peas, *Pisum sativum* ; perhaps vetch, *Vicia sativa*; possibly 2-row barley, *Hordeum distichon* (Murphy 1985); and on an increasing number of farms, particularly in the later Roman period: bread/club wheat, *Triticum aestivum/ compactum*; rye, *Secale cereale*; and oats, *Avena spp.* (Green 1981; Jones 1981).

Particularly in the later stages, two extremes of field cultivation would have been in view. In some places spelt wheat and/or six-row barley would have been seen, sometimes in mixtures, in fields shallowly cultivated with a wooden ard, thick with wild grasses and other weeds. Some of the larger weeds, such as fat hen and chess, would have been frequently harvested and eaten with the cereal crop. In other places we might have seen fields more deeply cultivated with ploughs with metal parts. In them would be bread/club wheat perhaps in a maslin with rye, oats and beans, growing in fields much cleaner of weeds, and with some hitherto quite rare species of weeds in evidence.

Already by the end of the Iron Age this contrast between two cropping systems could be drawn; a low-risk system involving a very broad range of crops and weeds that could be relied upon to produce something edible whatever the growing conditions, and an intensive system focussing on more deeply cultivated, relatively clean fields, and crops, such as bread wheat, that are responsive to these methods. From the botanical and artefactual evidence, it would seem that such intensive cultivation became more prominent on land associated with large Roman villas during the late 3rd and 4th centuries.

One area of plant resource management in which the lack of early Roman innovation may not hold true is in hay-cropping. There is an increasing body of evidence for Romano-British hay cropping, comprising hay-cutting scythes dating back to the 1st century AD (Rees 1979), waterlogged evidence of hay meadow plant communities (Lambrick and Robinson in press), charred material (Murphy 1985), and pieces of organic material preserved in wells, interpreted as 'fodder' (Wilson 1981).

Horticulture

A feature that becomes evident, particularly in the later Roman period, is the existence of small plots of land given over to intensive cultivation. One group is characterised by a simple, unornamented arrangement of planting holes, originally filled with nutrient-rich debris. Examples include the planting ditches at North Thoresby in Lincolnshire (Webster *et al.* 1967), the planting pits in association with the

Roman villa at Ditchley, Oxon (Applebaum 1972), and those within the walls of Roman Wroxeter (Wacher 1975).

A second group is characterised by levels of 'dark earth' in urban contexts. Macphail (1981) has argued on the basis of micromorphological evidence that at least some dark earths were made up deposits which were subsequently cultivated, and Crummy (1984:138–141) has examined such a deposit that clearly forms part of an urban allotment at Colchester. The allotment from the Culver Street site in Colchester retains cultivation ridges running parallel to each other at two metre intervals.

It is not at all clear what was being grown within these plots, and it is worth emphasising that our archaeological means of detecting vegetable crops, as opposed to seed and grain crops, are particularly inadequate. The work of the Environmental Archaeology Unit at York on the identification of waterlogged stem and leaf tissue may provide one direction forward. From the seed evidence, we can however detect the presence of some herbs and spices, such as the coriander and dill at Barton Court Farm (Robinson and Jones 1986).

It is equally difficult to determine whether such plots relate to production for subsistence or for the market. Either way, the extent of such plots, particularly in late Roman towns, and the intensity with which we would presume they were worked, implies horticultural production on a considerable scale.

Distribution

As our appreciation of the diversity of Romano-British settlement increases, so the possible routes of crop movement from points of production to points of consumption increase. Among current projects that are examining such movements, we may draw attention to the Stonea project, examining the workings of what may be a large imperial estate (van der Veen, 1988a and in preparation); the Holme-on-Spalding Moor project, investigating the relationship between agricultural and industrial production in the form of pottery manufacture (Millett and Halkon 1988); and the Essex coastal survey, tying together resource utilisation on agricultural land and on the coast (Wilkinson and Murphy 1986a and b).

While the study of these interrelationships develops, two major axes of crop movement in Roman Britain have already received a great deal of consideration: movement to the developing urban centres, and to the military posts.

Mobilisation to the Urban Centres

As urbanised Britain was preceded by a landscape which, at least in the south and east, was already organised around focal sites, we might consider the case for an organic development of crop mobilisation into towns, from their Iron Age forerunners.

An Iron Age site that has been examined in some detail in relation to crop movement is the hillfort at Danebury in Hampshire (Cunliffe 1985). Here I have argued that cereals were brought in from the

surroundings of the site, sometimes from several kilometres away. They appear to have been brought in in an unprocessed state, and much of the plant debris within the fort derives from the cleaning, processing and storage of these crops (Jones 1985b). It is quite feasible that processing was strictly controlled within the hillfort, in order that tribute could be collected. There is no evidence of food plants moving in from beyond the immediate catchment of the individual fort, if we define the 'immediate catchment' in terms of Thiessen polygons with neighbouring hillforts in contemporary use.

During the Late Iron Age, the site of Hengistbury Head also displays a range of crop-processing debris similar to the Danebury material, and we might infer a similar relationship to crop movement (Nye and Jones 1987). In addition, exotic crops are reaching the site from some distance. For this there is the indirect evidence of Mediterranean amphora, and the direct evidence of waterlogged fig seeds (Robinson in press).

There are currently few sites that can generate such information, but the impression gained from these two sites alone is of a long, late prehistoric tradition of crop mobilisation from scattered farms to centralised point of consumption. In the Early and Middle Iron Age, the spatial scale of this movement may have been relatively restricted, but by the Late Iron Age, the focal sites were located with access to waterways and food plants were travelling long distances. In other words, by the time of the Roman occupation, a suitable pattern of mobilisation of plant produce from scattered farms to central positions in the landscape was already in existence. Several Roman towns developed nearby, and, in some cases, within earlier focal sites, and a continuity in relation to food movement seems not unreasonable.

A few points of contrast may be made between Roman towns and their Iron Age predecessors. First, the range of 'delicatessen' crops moved over long distances is much greater in the Roman period (see above). This difference may of course disappear, or be back-dated to the Late Iron Age, once more Late Iron Age sites have been examined for plant remains.

Secondly the scale of movement clearly increases, such that stored crop infestation by beetles becomes a serious problem during the Roman period. This point is graphically illustrated by the evidence from the Coney Street warehouse in York (Kenward and Williams 1979).

Thirdly, while cereals were reaching the two Iron Age sites mentioned in an unprocessed state, there is some evidence that grain was moving into urban sites in a fully cleaned state (e.g. Murphy 1985). If the speculation that processing was centrally controlled proves to be correct, then this would represent an interesting shift. The transport of cleaned grain also links in with the increasing popularity during the course of the Roman period of bread wheat, a cereal which is most easily dehusked at source (cf. Green 1981).

Mobilisation to a Standing Army

In contrast to the supply of towns, the supply of the

24

army could not, at least in its early stages, have developed organically from preceding modes of distribution. The Roman army was sizeable, at times probably constituting one to two per cent of Britain's resident population, and required feeding as soon as they arrived, that is long before the existing agrarian system could be modified in any way.

We must presume that, in whatever way the grain was initially extracted from native farmers, and bearing in mind the possibility of supplementation by long distance import (cf. van der Veen 1988b), the impact must have been similar to a series of bad years climatically, with many of the native population resorting to famine foods and eating into their seed corn.

In the longer term, mobilisation could have worked in a number of ways. The cultivation of land in the vicinity of the standing army could have been greatly extended. More intensive farms could have responded to the monetary stimulus to produce crops. The area from which grain was drawn could have been sufficiently large such that extraction was possible without any significant change in productivity.

The possibility of localised intensification can be examined in relation to the evidence of pollen and buried soils. A number of small excavations along the line of Hadrian's Wall have revealed cultivation marks beneath the structure (e.g. Breeze 1974), clearly demonstrating that crop production in the military zone was well established by the early 2nd century AD. Such pollen diagrams as have been radiocarbon dated from east of the Pennines suggest that the major phase of clearance for agriculture preceded the military presence by 30–150 years, suggesting that the army moved into the productive area, rather than stimulating production afresh (Bartley *et al.* 1976; van der Veen 1985).

There is, however, evidence for continued agricultural expansion during the course of the Roman period, and Turner (1981) suggests that this may apply west of the Pennines, tying in with rural sites which Higham (1981) has suggested are Romano-British. Both pollen and sites are however in need of more secure dating than exists at present.

The possibility of a direct monetary boost to production can be examined in relation to the evidence of plant macrofossils, artefacts and structures on individual sites. As implied above, these data do not as yet provide support for agricultural intensification within individual farms during the first 200 years of Roman rule.

We have seen how methods do intensify within such farms from the later 3rd century. There is also during this period some evidence of a greater pooling of crops at the producer, rather than the consumer end. This is in the form of an elaboration of harvesting equipment (cf. Rees 1979) and provision of large granaries within villas (cf. Morris 1979).

From the Late Iron Age harvests had been taken with either a short crescent sickle, or a slightly larger balanced sickle. During the later Roman period these are joined by very large scythes, and possibly an animal driven harvester known as the *vallum*, though

evidence of these is restricted to continental Gaul (White 1967). These implements are not known after the demise of Roman Britain, and we can presume that they were either no longer economically viable or economically relevant.

In a survey or Romano-British farm buildings, Morris (1979) records eight of the substantial 'military style' granaries in association with villas. Of these only one can be securely placed before the 3rd century. The existence at all of massive granaries in the early Roman countryside reflects some pooling by producers, but such large scale handling nevertheless seems to be more characteristic of the later Roman period.

The fact that during the earlier period, the large granaries are found away from such points of primary production lends support instead to mobilisation of existing surpluses over a very wide area, rather than any more localised intensification.

Consumption

As far as the biological evidence is concerned, food plants become markedly less discernible in archaeological terms during the stages immediately preceding consumption. The major group of food plants, cereals, may be consumed whole, or alternatively cracked, rolled or milled. They may be eaten green, fully ripe, or germinated, and the latter state is of course a precursor to brewing. Of these various states, some are more easily discerned than others.

Germinated grains can easily be distinguished from ungerminated grains, and have often been encountered in Romano-British contexts (e.g. Hillman 1982; Murphy 1985; Jones 1985). Green corn, which can be used in soups and stews in the manner of pearl barley, may char to produce morphologically distinct specimens, and as such have been recognised in archaeological contexts (e.g. Knörzer 1979). However, charred seeds generally include a range of deformed specimens whose abnormal shape could be attributed to various pre- and post-depositional factors other than an unripe state.

For the same reasons, fragmented charred grains cannot necessarily be associated with rolled, cracked or milled cereals, and these are difficult to detect with certainty. The milling of cereals however will release bran fragments that are discernible in the waterlogged state, and have been recovered from well deposits (Hall pers. comm.) and from the stomach of Lindow Man (Stead *et al.* 1986).

Bran and chaff may also survive within coprolite deposits, as in the ditch fill from the Antonine fort at Bearsden, near Glasgow, which has been subjected to detailed analysis (Knights *et al.* 1983).

Some material evidence exists for these processes of food preparation. The Roman period sees the earliest British examples of fragments of mechanical milling equipment. These may be found in association both with forts, for example, at Chesters on Hadrian's Wall and in such towns as London, Canterbury and Lincoln (Wacher 1975). In terms of baking, a large iron slice believed to be for turning loaves was recovered from Verulamium, and a cake-mould was found at Silchester (Wacher 1975). The possible link between T-shaped sunken ovens and brewing has been discussed above. A further item that may await recognition among assemblages of Roman stonework is the large stone mortar, which Hillman (1981) argued would be used for pounding such cereals as spelt wheat to release them from their chaff.

Concluding Points

Having briefly reviewed in this chapter the approaches to, and evidence for, food plant production, distribution and consumption, a few themes may be drawn from the evidence as it stands.

In terms of food plant production, the Roman period is immersed within a longer period of expansion of the agricultural landscape. As far as we can tell from the better dated pollen diagrams, imperial expansion follows the major wave of agricultural expansion, rather than vice versa, but such expansion continues in various parts of the country during the Roman period.

Agricultural methods are also changing in the longer term, and there do seem to be periods in which that change seems particularly pronounced. Within the Roman period such changes seem concentrated in the late 3rd and 4th centuries, when some large villa estates are making extensive use of metal agricultural implements, farming cereals more intensively, and moving into horticulture.

By contrast, the large scale movement of crops is a feature of the early stages of the Roman period, and may have its roots in the Late Iron Age. I would suggest that consumption in early towns, villas and military sites was made possible by this capacity for extraction from large areas rather than by more local agricultural intensification, but for clarification we await more comprehensive environmental analyses of sites of the early Roman period.

Acknowledgements

I am grateful to Martin Millett, Peter Murphy, and Marijke van der Veen for reading through and commenting on earlier drafts of this paper.

References

Applebaum S. 1972 Roman Britain. In H.P.R. Finberg (ed.) *The Agrarian History of England and Wales* i(ii) Cambridge University Press, 1–277.

Bartley D.D., Chambers C. and Hart-Jones B. 1976. The vegetational history of parts of south and east Durham. *New Phytologist* 77:437–468.

Bell M. 1976. The excavation of an early Romano-British site and Pleistocene landforms at Newhaven, Sussex. *Sussex Archaeol. Colls.* 144: 218–305

Bowen H.C. 1961. *Ancient Fields*. British Association for the Advancement of Science, London.

Branigan K. 1971. *Latimer*. Chess Valley Archaeological and Historical Society.

Breeze D.J. 1974. Plough marks at Carrawburgh on Hadrian's Wall. *Tools and Tillage* 2:188–190.

Crummy P. 1984. *Colchester Archaeological Reports 3: Excavations at Lion Walk, Balkerne Lane and Middleborough*. Archaeological Trust, Colchester.

Cunliffe B.W. 1984. *Danebury: an Iron Age hillfort in Hampshire*. CBA Research Report London.

Drewett P. 1982. *The Archaeology of Bullock Down, Eastbourne, East Sussex: the development of a landscape*. Sussex Archaeol. Soc., Lewes.

Fleming A. 1987. Coaxial field systems: some questions of time and space. *Antiquity* 61:188–202.

Fowler P.J. 1978. The Abingdon ard-share. In M. Parrington (ed.), *The Excavation of an Iron Age Settlement, Bronze Age Ring Ditches and Roman Features at Ashville Trading Estate, Abingdon (Oxfordshire) 1974–76*. CBA Research Report 28, London, 83–88.

Green F.J. 1981. Iron Age, Roman and Saxon crops: the archaeological evidence from Wessex. In M.K. Jones and G.W. Dimbleby (eds.) *The Environment of Man: the Iron Age to the Anglo-Saxon period*. BAR 87. Oxford, 129–153.

Grieg J. 1976. The plant remains. In P.C. Buckland (ed.) *The Environmental Evidence from the Church Street Roman Sewer System*. The Archaeology of York 14/1:23–28.

Haarnagel W. 1979. *Feddersen Wierde. Die Ergebnisse der Ausgrabung der vorgeschichtlichen Wurt bei Bremerhaven in den Jahren 1955–1963*. Band 1. Wiesbaden.

Hartledge R. 1978. Excavations at the prehistoric and Romano-British site at Slonk Hill, Shoreham Sussex. *Sussex Archaeol. Colls.* 116:69–141.

Halliday S.P. and Reynolds D.M. 1984. *Cord Rig in Southeast Scotland: Field Survey Programme 1983–4*.

Higham N.J. 1981. The Roman impact upon rural settlement in Cumbria. In P.A.G. Clack and S. Haselgrove (eds.), *Rural Settlement in the Roman North*. CBA Group 3, Durham, 105–122.

Hillman G.C. 1981. Reconstructing crop husbandry practices from charred remains of crops. In R. Mercer (ed.), *Farming Practice in British Prehistory*. Edinburgh University Press, 123–162.

Hillman G.C. 1982. Evidence of spelt-kilning at Catsgore in Somerset. In R.H. Leech (ed.), *Excavations at Catsgore*. Western Archaeological Trust, Bristol.

Hillman G.C. 1984. Interpretation of archaeological plant remains: the application of ethnographic models from Turkey. In W. van Zeist and W.A. Casparie (eds.), *Plants and Ancient Man*. A.A. Balkema, Rotterdam, 1–41.

Jones G.E.M. 1984. Interpretation of plant remains ethnographic models from Greece. In W. van Zeist and W.A. Casparie (eds.), *Plants and Ancient Man*. A.A. Balkema, Rotterdam, 43–61.

Jones M.K. 1978. Sampling in a rescue context: a case study from Oxfordshire. In J.F. Cherry, C. Gamble and S. Shennan (eds.), *Sampling in Contemporary British Archaeology*. BAR 50. Oxford, 191–205.

Jones M.K. 1981. The development of crop husbandry. In M.K. Jones and G.W. Dimbleby (eds.), *The Environment of Man: the Iron Age to the Anglo-Saxon period*. BAR 87. Oxford, 95–127.

Jones M.K. 1984. The plant remains. In B.W. Cunliffe (ed.) *Danebury: an Iron Age hillfort in Hampshire*. Vol. 2. CBA Research Report London 483–495.

Jones M.K. 1985. Archaeobotany beyond subsistence reconstruction. In G. Barker and C. Gamble (eds.) *Beyond Domestication in Prehistoric Europe*. Academic Press, London, 107–128.

Jones M.K. forthcoming. Iron Age plant exploitation. In T.C. Champion and J.R. Collis (eds.) *The Iron Age in Britain and Ireland–recent trends*. Sheffield

Kenward H.K. and Williams D. 1979. *Biological evidence*

from the Roman warehouses in Coney Street. CBA York.

Knights B.A., Dickson C.A., Dickson J.H. and Breeze D.J. 1983. Evidence concerning the Roman military diet at Bearsden, Scotland, in the 2nd century AD. *Journal of Archaeological Science* 10:139–52.

Knörzer K-H. 1979. Verkohlte Reste von Viehfutter aus einem Stall des römischen Reiterlagers von Dormagen. *Rheinische Ausgrabungen* 20:130–137.

Lambrick G. and Robinson M.A. in press. The development of floodplain grassland in the Upper Thames Valley. In M.K. Jones (ed.) *Archaeology and the Flora of the British Isles: human influence on the evolution of plant communities.* Committee for Archaeology, Oxford.

Macphail R. 1981. Soil and botanical studies of the 'dark earth'. In M.K. Jones and G.W. Dimbleby (eds.) *The Environment of Man: the Iron Age to the Anglo-Saxon period.* BAR 87. Oxford 309–331.

Millett M.J. and Halkon P. 1988. Landscape and economy: recent fieldwork and excavation around Holme-on-Spalding-Moor. In J. Price, P. Wilson and S. Briggs (eds.) *Roman Yorkshire: studies presented to Mary Kitson Clark.* BAR 193. Oxford, 37–47.

Morris P. 1979. *Agricultural buildings in Roman Britain.* BAR 70. Oxford.

Murphy P.L. 1984. Carbonised fruits from building 5. Carbonised cereals and crop weeds from buildings 38, 41 and 45. In P. Crummy (ed.) *Excavations at Lion Walk, Balkerne Lane and Middleborough.* Archaeological Trust, Colchester, 40,105,108,110.

Murphy P.L. 1985. *Culver Street, Colchester, Environmental Studies.* Ancient Monuments Laboratory Reports HBMC, London.

Neal D.S. 1974. *The Excavation of the Roman Villa in Gadebridge Park, Hemel Hempstead, 1963-8.* Society of Antiquaries: London.

Nye S. and Jones M.K. 1987. The carbonised plant remains. In B.W. Cunliffe (ed.) *Excavations at Hengistbury Head.* Oxford University Committee for Archaeology Monograph 13. Oxford, 323–9.

Rees S. 1979 *Agricultural Implements in Prehistoric and Roman Britain.* BAR 69. Oxford.

Reynolds P.J. and Langley J.K. 1980. Romano-British corn-drying ovens, an experiment. *Archaeol. J.* 136:27–42.

Riley D.N. 1980. *Early Landscapes from the Air.* Dept of Prehistory and Archaeology, Sheffield.

Robinson M.J. 1987. The waterlogged plant remains. In B.W. Cunliffe (ed.) *Excavations at Hengistbury Head.*

Robinson M.J. and Jones M.K. 1986. The crop plants. In D. Miles (ed.) *Archaeology at Barton Court Farm, Abingdon, Oxon.* Oxford Archaeological Unit and CBA, London.

Stead I.M., Bourke J.B. and Brothwell D. 1986. *Lindow Man: the body in the bog.* British Museum Publications, London.

Turner J. 1979. The environment of northeast England during Roman times as shown by pollen analysis. *J. Archaeol. Sci.* 6:285–290.

Turner J. 1981. The vegetation. In M.K. Jones and G.W. Dimbleby (eds.) *The Environment of Man: the Iron Age to the Anglo-Saxon period.* BAR 87. Oxford, 53–56.

van der Veen M. 1988a. Natives, Romans and cereal consumption. Food for thought. In R.F.J. Jones *et al.* (ed.) *First Millennium Papers.* BAR S401, pp.99–107. Oxford.

van der Veen M. 1988b. Carbonised grain from the granary at South Shields North East England. In (ed.) *Der prähistorische Mensch unnd seine Umwelt. Festschrift U. Ködrber Grohne.* Stuttgart.

van der Veen M. in preparation. The plant remains. In R.P.J. Jackson and T.W. Potter, *Excavations at Stonea, Cambs. 1980–1984.* British Museum Publications, London.

Vuorela I. 1973. Relative pollen rain around cultivated fields. *Acta Botanica Fennica.* 192:1–27.

Wacher J. 1975. *The Towns of Roman Britain.* Batsford, London.

Webster D., Webster H. and Petch D.F. 1967. A possible vineyard of the Romano-British period at North Thoresby, Lincolnshire. *Lincolnshire History and Archaeology* 2:55–61.

White K.D. 1970. *Roman Farming.* Thames and Hudson, London.

Wilkinson T.J. and Murphy P.L. 1986a. Archaeological survey of an intertidal zone: the submerged landscape of the Essex Coast, England. *Journal of Field Archaeology* 13(2):177–194.

Wilkinson T.J. and Murphy P.L. 1986b. *The Hullbridge Basin Survey.* Interim Report No.6. Essex County Council, Chelmsford.

Willcox G.H. 1977. Exotic plants from Roman waterlogged sites in London. *J. of Archaeol. Sci.* 4:269–282.

Williamson T.M. 1984. The Roman countryside: settlement and agriculture in northeast Essex. *Britannia* 15:225–230.

Wilson D.G. 1981. The plant remains. In M.G. Jarrett and S. Wrathmell (eds.) *Whitton, an Iron Age and Roman Farmstead in South Glamorgan.* University of Wales Press, Cardiff, 240–243.

4.   Money in Roman Britain: A Review

Richard Reece

The subject of Money in Roman Britain contains three main strands: what coins were used and how they were supplied; where the coins were used and lost; and how Britain compares with the Empire in the subject of coin use. With the almost complete absence of written texts relating to Roman Britain it is no surprise that the subject of money has to be tackled completely from an archaeological or material starting point; we know nothing about the supply of money to the province, or the use of the money supplied, other than that which we gain archaeologically. In Palestine the subject can be approached through the Gospels of Matthew, Mark and Luke, in Italy from the Satyricon of Petronius, and in North Africa there is some help from the Golden Ass of Apuleius. These texts can give us a general introduction to the Roman and Romanizing use of money (summary in Reece 1981a), but to apply what they say to Britain directly would be to fall into the trap of assuming that coin use in the Empire was uniform and hence of ruling out the study of Britain versus the Empire.

The study of this subject is therefore closely related to any other archaeological study of material, but it has certain advantages. Roman coins were produced by the million, and there is more than enough evidence that such numbers are direct statements rather than vague generalizations. They appear in definite forms, which, to the specialist, are clearly indentifiable, and these forms have been well-organized into works of reference. The specialist working with Roman coins can describe his material, and communicate his observations to others with a low probability of error and a reasonably high objectivity; when two people identify coins from a site the two lists produced are usually very similar and discrepancies can usually be discussed and eliminated. The specialist can therefore produce a list of reliable reference numbers which will communicate to any other worker what has been found, and the result is a sequence of artefacts, whose production is dated perhaps to within five years and from known provenances up to 2,000 miles away from the site. Add to this the knowledge that in the 4th century AD the whole of the Empire seems to have been an inter-related trade area and the potential for study becomes obvious. But we must return to one small part of the whole.

This standard of excellence can be upheld so long as the coins found are products of the official mints of the Roman Empire, but Britain has a particularly high incidence of irregularly produced coins, probably made in the province, and possibly to supplement the regular supply from some way away. Apart from the short life of the mint in London from 286 to about 326, all regular coinage had to be sent from the mainland of Europe; in the 4th century the nearest mints were Trier and Lyon. An excellent survey of these irregular coins which supplement the

regular issues in large numbers can be found in Boon 1988. The study of regular and irregular coins gives two sets of information which are partly complementary. The regular coins in their numbers and conditions show how far Britain was a part of the financial life of Europe; the irregular coins show the points at which Britain diverged, either by choice or necessity, from that life. Study of the regular coins as objects of production in themselves says little about Britain, but could say a lot about Imperial coin production, while study of the locally produced copies can tell us about the economy, skills and trade networks of Britain. This is not the point to review the work on copies because there are at least three studies in progress and results are at present unofficial and unpublished but it is well worth pointing out that the next few years will see a study by Robert Kenyon on copies of coins of Claudius I (AD 43 to about 64), by John Davies who has taken the highly courageous step of trying to organize the copies of radiate coins (Barbarous Radiates c. AD 260 to 300?), and by Mike Hammerson who has already looked at the earlier copies of the House of Constantine, AD 330 to 348 (Hammerson 1980). The later copies AD 350 to 360 have been published by Richard Brickstock (1987). A useful summary may be found in Crummy 1987. In each case these studies are showing an organised production in which the moderate or minimal artistic competence contrasts with a large scale and possibly centralized undertaking. This comes as an important corrective to the idea that copies of coins are household production made, community by community, in the toolshed.

One theme in common in these studies is the difficulty of recognition of the copies and the problematical borderline separating the regular coin from its local imitation. At all dates there are obvious copies which give no specialist any trouble, but at most dates there are borderline products whose full identification is at present almost totally subjective. This state of affairs should change with the publication of the studies mentioned above.

This leads us back to the more general topics of coin finds throughout Britain. It immediately becomes necessary to divide 'Roman coins' up into manageable groups for there is little point in comparing the crude numbers of coins found on different sites. Such a procedure may do no more than compare the different areas excavated or the relative efficiency of the excavators. But once the coins are split up into early, middle, later and latest it is possible to begin analysis. It has been accepted, since numerical work on coin finds began, that any division into chronological groups should come from the changes in the coinage produced rather than from historical sources, numerically equal groups, or any other source. So the early system of coinage, settled by the first Emperor Augustus, can be used as a unit until the system itself fell apart in the middle of the 3rd century. Phase A runs from 27 BC to AD 259 and includes a whole period of coin use in which well known denominations such as the denarius and the sestertius continued in use and maintained their relative values. Phase B is a phase of change in which a very base silver coinage forms the only denomination available apart from the gold piece; it runs from 259 to 294, and every coin found tends to show the emperor wearing a crown of the sun's rays – hence the radiate period. Great reforms came under Diocletian in 294 and a fairly simple system of bronze coinage, with occasional silver and constant, but rare, gold continued to the end of large scale production in the western mints around AD 400; this is divided into an earlier phase, with generally larger, and therefore rarer, coins from 294 to 330, phase C, and the latest phase from 330 to 402, phase D. The distribution of coins within these periods is not uniform in sites in Britain. A generalisation can be made which divides sites into two groups; the first group (group 1) contains most of the large towns and a few of the smaller towns in the east of the country, the second group contains the other sites which range from the smaller towns down to single farmsteads in the countryside, but also includes religious, military and defended sites (Reece 1980a, 1987). A mean value for the two groups can easily be given in coins per thousand:

		Group I urban	Group II rural
Phase A	27 BC to AD 259	223	75
Phase B	259 to 294	387	186
Phase C	294 to 330	53	59
Phase D	330 to 402	342	683

Several points at once become apparent. The early coinage is more common in towns than in rural sites, whereas rural sites have far more late coinage than towns. Within sites, the towns tend to have roughly the same amount of phase B and phase D whereas the rural sites tend to have about three time as many coins in phase D as in phase B. At this point it may be helpful to look further afield. If we compare British coin finds with those of France and Italy it becomes obvious that British Group I is the more typical distribution of finds in Europe. British towns are a little low in early coin loss compared with towns nearer the centre of the Empire, and do have a surprising number of late coins compared with the continent, but they are in general comparable. Judged on this same basis British rural sites are most atypical of coin loss in Europe (Reece 1988c). As a general guide, metropolitan coin loss, as judged by Italy, can be described as a constant loss of coins with about 5% of the total being lost in each twenty year period of the 400 years of the Empire (Reece 1984a). Historical and numerical workers would no doubt join in judging this a reasonable model against which to judge peripheral provinces.

On these terms coin loss in Britain is fairly easy to describe. The towns approximate best to Roman coin loss, but they show lamentably few losses in the early period. Phase A is over 60% of the time scale, yet it accounts for only 22% of the coin loss, whereas in Italy it accounts for that 60%. There is a small number of coins lost in Britain, and therefore perhaps, used in Britain, before AD 259. The tempting conclusion is that coin use on the Roman model was slow to catch on in Britain. This is not because coinage came as a novelty to Britain with the Roman armies of AD 43; on most estimates coins had been produced, and presumably used in some way, in Britain for a century before that (Kent 1981). Coin loss from 259 to 294 is unusually high compared with Europe, and the 4th century is totally peculiar. The simplest interpretation would be that after a slow start coin loss, a reflection of coin use, took off in the middle of the 3rd century, and by the 4th century coin use in Britain was considerably in excess of that in Italy and France.

What seems at first a simple point is capable of almost infinite complication. A first step must be to look at *what* coins were being lost. In Britain the majority of the coins lost after 259 are rubbish – in so far as any money can properly be called rubbish; the finds in Italy are of much higher quality. One of the main differences is the proliferation in Britain of the Barbarous Radiate copies and the non-appearance of the good regular coins issued in Italy and Gaul between 274 and 294. The impression given by Italian finds is of coin loss as a result of constant coin use; in Britain the impression is of a considerable rise in use and coin loss as the face value of the coins, even the official issues, slid quickly from 260 to 270. There is a remarkable coincidence in the drop of silver content in coins in that decade from perhaps 10% silver to less than 1% silver and a rise in the numbers of site-finds from perhaps 1 coin per thousand to 10 or 20. This is before the main spate of copying. This seems to be co-terminous with the reform of the coinage in 273–4 by which the silver content was raised to around 4% and the weight of the coin was more than doubled. The purchasing power of these new coins must have been at least ten times that of the worst of the old coins and they are rarely lost in Britain. Instead there is the great period of imitation of the older, less valuable coins and the simplest interpretation is that the new reformed coins were either not sent to Britain or were just too high in value to be relevant to the majority of British purchases.

The same sort of process can be seen in the comparison between the larger better coins of 294 to 330, all with detectable silver content, and the smaller coins struck after 330 with less silver. The numbers lost in Britain change in the opposite way. After the reform of 294 and the apparent disappearance of Barbarous Radiates the only coin commonly lost was a good large coin of high value; it is lost in very small numbers. That coin gradually decreased in standard, and correspondingly higher numbers are lost and found (Ryan 1988). By 330 the standard is almost back to the standard of 270 and the numbers lost are similar. Meanwhile in Italy a more or less constant coin loss has been going on (Reece

30

1973). The implication seems to be that coin use in Britain is thriving when the face value of the coins are suitable; and this in turn seems to imply that, for full use of coins, smaller values were needed in Britain than in the centre of the Empire. This corresponds with the observation (Reece 1985a) that when there are two denominations of coin issued simultaneously from the mints in the 4th century the larger denomination is more common in Italy and the centre, and the smaller preponderates in Britain. A parallel might be usefully drawn between this state of affairs and the action of the British mint in the early 19th century when half and third farthings were minted in London solely for use in Malta and the West Indies: the needs of the Colonies were for lower value coins than in the centre.

This might lead us on to consider the relationship between coinage in Roman Britain and the economy. The problem is the lack of proper synthesis for trade and industry in Britain so that the fluctuations in the coinage have to be compared with rather vague generalizations on the economy derived from one or two industries such as pottery which are not necessarily good indicators of business in Roman Britain as a whole.

Put in a very simple, if not simplistic, way, coinage in Roman Britain seems to be a particular feature of the late 3rd century and the whole of the 4th century. There are more later coins than earlier coins. This compares with the growth of the villa economy as judged by newly built villas, re-built villas, and the installation of mosaic pavements (Rivet 1969, Todd 1978) but it does not compare well with the decline which all commentators see in the towns of the 4th century, some (Reece 1980a, 1988b) more than others (Salway 1981). Economists, sociologists and economic historians are very unhappy with the idea that a movement of decentralization, from larger towns to more and smaller towns, from town to country, and from a clear hierarchy to a much more equal spread of only moderately organized settlements which come on the border of towns and villages, can correspond to a rise in prosperity. They seem to have as an article of belief the necessity of hierarchy and complexity for the existence of prosperity. I have no such belief and I am delighted when I find evidence of the opposite state of affairs.

My biased view of the connection between coins and the economy is therefore as follows: the economy of Roman Britain at the time of the Roman conquest was flourishing, but coins played a small part in the transactions that went on. Prices were lower than on the mainland of Europe and the value of coins was such that the majority of transactions were below the range of the coins commonly supplied (see Reece 1984a for a study of denominations). By the late 3rd century home production was booming, as seen in the pottery industries and the success of villa farms, and at the same time the value of each coin dropped to a point at which it was relevant to the majority of British transactions. Within this context of military and administrative connections with the outer world, the obviously greater use of coins is a true reflection of the buoyant nature of the British economy in the 4th century. Both aspects – supply and use – changed suddenly around AD 400 when coins were no longer supplied and the military and administrative links were broken. Unfortunately the lack of coin supply means that we cannot follow any further the split between the fortunes of the town and the farms.

The division which has been made between town sites and rural sites may appear to some people to be inexact and capable of much greater refinement. In practice any attempt further to subdivide the groups has not worked. The town sites such as the different excavations at Lincoln (Mann and Reece 1983) or Verulamium (Reece 1984b) form groups in which the Lincoln sites are most like other Lincoln sites, and the Verulamium sites are most like other Verulamium, but both Lincoln and Verulamium keep to the rough equality between phase B (259–294) and phase D (330 to 402) and so diverge strongly from villas, forts of the Saxon Shore, temples, and small settlements, which have many more coins of phase D than phase B (Reece 1980a). But temples do not diverge clearly from 'villas', and neither group is clearly separable, judging solely by coin loss, from Saxon Shore forts or small settlements. It is not purely to cause trouble that I have suggested recently that these groupings of late settlements are a product of our over-analytical imaginations and that the coin evidence gives us a true lead into settlement in the 4th century (Reece 1988a).

Thus the basic coin distribution in the 4th century is either the large settlement, the town, which, on coin evidence is clearly either in serious decline, or, at best, less successful than it was in the 1st and 2nd centuries, and the small settlement. The small settlement may be either a group of obviously separate dwellings or farms or cottages, in which case it is called a village; or it is a planned group of such dwellings in an architectural ensemble, in which case it is called a villa; or it is inside defences intended from time to time as a military depot and refuge, in which case it is called a late fort; or it is a transient occupation, every second Friday in the month as a market at a focus of some religious cult, and it is called a temple (Reece 1987). My suggestion is simply that the coin use in each of these cases is similar and our different names for the types of settlement reflect realities other than those economic and the use of money.

Before looking more closely at the actual mechanisms of supply of this coinage whose loss I have been describing, a different category of coin find ought to be mentioned. I have emphasized that the site-find is the result of casual loss, and have even referred to such coins as rubbish. This may be overstating the case, but it is generally agreed that the less valuable a coin that is lost, the less effort will be put in to finding again and therefore the more likely it is to be available to the modern archaeologist. Site-finds are biased towards worthlessness. But there is the valuable coin which is hidden away and never recovered, the hoard, which is also available to the modern observer. The hoard is biased in favour of value because is best stored in the form which will be most likely to keep its value. The use of hoards by the numismatist and the archaeologist is a dangerous business (Reece 1988c, Kent 1988, Robertson 1988, Aitchison 1988). A hoard must be one of the most unusual forms of archaeological evidence, for, to be available to us, it must have failed. Our sample of ancient hoards is not just 'rather biased', it is totally biased. Every hoard we know of is a failed hoard, every hoard which exists to be known about is a failure, and in strict logic such a peculiar sample, which cannot by definition contain a single successful hoard, cannot tell us anything about coin hoarding in Roman Britain. We must, I think, assume that the majority of hoards were successful and were recovered so reason tells us that we really know nothing about the overall pattern of this activity and yet, of course we all write about the pattern of coin hoards. What we mean is the pattern of unrecovered coin hoards, and this is where the difficulties start. The most obvious interpretation is that every coin hoard was buried or hung in the roof, or hidden in the wall, with the intent to recover it; if it is still there the depositor was prevented from recovering his hoard; and the most obvious cause of failure to recover a hoard is the violent death of the depositor (Reece 1988e, Aitchison 1988).

This sequence of thought is reasonable and even useful so long as it is not used as a reverse argument to the exclusion of all other possible reasons for the non-recovery of hoards. Thus while the violent death of the person who buried the hoard may well lead to its remaining buried, the existence of a hoard in the ground does not prove the violent death of its owner. The coinage in circulation in the Roman Empire changed quite substantially, and sometimes quite suddenly, and it is reasonable to assume that in at least some cases coins were demonetized or re-tariffed at highly unfavourable rates. But the reaction of the man in the street to such an official dictate is not always to trade in his old coin when he is told to, or to trade it in while he can, even if the rate is unfavourable, he tends to put it away in the hope that things will get better. The many changes in modern currencies have perhaps made the modern archaeologist more aware of this factor than the student in the 19th century, to whom money was an almost unvariable commodity so that silver of George III (of around 1800) was still to be found in circulation in the 1950s in Britain. At times of change in the Roman coinage we must at least allow the possibility that some hoards which have never been recovered were buried with sighs and pious hopes but little expectation that they would ever see the market place again. This is particularly true at a peak time of hoarding in Britain, by which of course we mean a peak time of non-recovery of buried hoards, in the period 260 to 300. Some of the largest coin hoards belong to this period, and the hoards buried in these years are probably the most numerous class in Britain (Robertson 1988). But this has already been mentioned as a time of fast change in the coinage, of fast loss of silver content, and a major reorganisation through a final reform in 294, so it is just the time when coins might be collected together

and put away in the hope of future use, and the fact that they were not recovered need not tell of rape, pillage and plunder. There is a strong temptation to use this argument of sudden death, because this outcrop of unrecovered coin hoards in Britain corresponds to a period of major trouble in Gaul and Germany caused by invading Germans. But there is no evidence of such trouble in Britain and the archaeological record, especially in the countryside, is of building, re-building and expansion.

Many commentators have suggested that there are different types of hoard and that deeper analysis and classification will tell of savings, petty cash, or instant money gathering due to imminent disaster. It is a truism, but worth insisting upon, that if the different motives of hoarding lead to different sorts of hoard, then these different sorts of hoard must be distinctively different. They are not. This does not mean that the different motives were not at work but that no one has yet shown (a) how these different types of hoard *might* be different in theory, or (b) *that* there are in fact distinguishably different types of hoards. One hoard which was held to be evidence of slow saving, or slow circulation north of the frontier, was the Falkirk hoard; it is indeed a very odd hoard when judged solely by the date of the latest coin in it, but that is because it is an old hoard, topped up with a few current coins on its final burial (Reece 1980b). In general hoards seem to be remarkably uniform and variation within types of hoards seems to depend mainly on the number of coins in the hoard (Reece 1981b).

The reasoning behind this makes good sense when put out in detail, for, whatever the motive of the hoarder, he or she could only collect coin that was available and the contents of every hoard are therefore more dependent on what coinage was supplied to the province than the likes and dislikes, requirements and hopes of the person salting the money away. At present we have not got a detailed enough picture of the coinage which was supplied to be able to detect deviations from this general coinage pool and hence follow up deviations from a general norm.

A general commentary on the unrecovered coin hoards of Britain cannot yet be written for two reasons. Firstly, Professor Anne Robertson is just about to bring to a conclusion her life's study of coin hoards in Roman Britain, and we eagerly await this publication; secondly, there are few summaries of coin hoards outside Britain with which to compare our insular offerings. The great series of the Fundmünzen der römischen Zeit in Deutschland will eventually give us details of German hoards, and the workers in France are making great strides with the new Corpus des Trésors Monétaires Antiques de la France, which will list all the known Roman hoards in France. There are a few major points of difference which are already clear from the works that have been published. Hoards of late silver coins (356 to 400) seem to be almost confined to Britain; at best they are extremely rare on the continent, even though all the coins were minted in Trier, Lyon, Arles, Aquileia or Rome. Gaul and much of Germany lack the great number of rubbishy late bronze hoards which occur so commonly in Britain. And Britain lacks the rashes of closely dated hoards which crop up in Germany during the invasions of the 230s and the 350s. If coin hoards really do tell of pillage and plunder then Britain here acts as a tranquil norm against which the odd happenings in Germany stand out as something most unusual. Conversely there seem to be no really strange happenings in Britain which stand out from the continental norm.

Before dealing with the cessation of supply to Britain, we ought to spend a little more time on that process of supply itself. Since Britain is an extreme part of the western Empire, the whole of supply in the period up to 250 depends on the mint of Rome which was the only western mint in production. There is no subject worth the study of differential coin supply so far as the mint of origin is concerned at this period. But it has very recently become clear that there is a differential supply to Britain in terms of which of the coins minted were sent to Britain. This will hardly seem surprising, for it is almost impossible that coin produced could have been mixed to a uniform consistency of reverse types at the mint before being sent out. Any practical scheme of supply would be to send out sacks of newly minted coin as and when produced, as and when needed. Yet David Walker's demonstration that certain reverse types of Hadrian and Antoninus Pius (117–138 and 138–161) seem to have been sent exclusively to Britain must rank as one of the most exciting studies in the subject recently carried out (Walker 1988). Malcolm Todd pointed out some time ago (Todd 1966) that the issue of Antoninus Pius with a reverse of Britannia seated on a rock was more commonly found in Britain than elsewhere, and while being regarded as an important observation this occasioned little surprise, on account of the reverse. Now we can see that this is only part of a wider system of supply whose other parts have no obvious reverse type connection to Britain at all.

Britain diverged from the coin of the continent in the early part of the 3rd century when sestertii, the largest bronze coins, seem not to have entered the country. These sestertii of emperors such as Severus Alexander (222–235) and Gordian III (238–244) are often the most commonly found coins on continental sites but they are extremely rare in Britain. Hoards of sestertii including coins of Postumus (259–68) and therefore buried after 260 contain numbers of worn sestertii of the 2nd century, so there can be no doubt that the coin was still in use at the time, and we might fairly presume that if new coins had been available they would have been used (Reece 1988d).

Coin supply is complicated between 259 and 274 by the existence of the Gallic Empire based in Cologne which produced its own coinage and held sway over Britain in opposition to the Central Empire based in Rome. Unfortunately the Gallic Empire was able, year by year, to keep up a better silver standard than the Central Empire so that it is not surprising that it is the worse coins of the Central Empire that are lost in greater numbers than the better coins of the Gallic Empire. It would be fascinating to be able

to study the coin loss of this period on the basis of politics, but the differences of the coinages make this impossible. From 286 to 296 an emperor, first Carausius and then Allectus (286–293 and 293–296) governed from Britain, though there was soon little else *but* Britain that he was allowed to claim. This was the start of the short life of the mint of London and a second mint which signs itself CL, or, as Andrew Burnett recently suggested, GL; his suggestions seems to me to make excellent sense and would allow the two provinces of southern Britain which emerge in the 4th century to mint coins from their respective capitals at London and Glevum (Gloucester). This would transfer the accepted seat of the second southern capital from the assumed Cirencester to the nearby Gloucester.

Diocletian, on his recovery of the province in 296 kept the mint of London working as part of his great reorganisation but it succumbed to Constantine the Great's megalomania in about 326 when it may have furnished part of the staff required for the new mint at Constantinople. For the short period from 296 to 326 we have the chance to study the workings of a mint to furnish with copper coin an island unit; no one has yet taken up this challenge. Later in the 4th century Trier, the nearest mint, seems to have been mainly responsible for supply until about 356; production at Trier then declines sharply and most of the coins minted between 356 and 402 come from Lyon and Arles. The mechanism of supply, or drift, is intriguing, but several studies have so far come to no firm conclusions (Fulford 1978; Reece 1982a, 1982b, 1984c). The only point which seems to have emerged with relative clarity is the supply of bronze coinage in greater quantities to frontier provinces (Reece 1979), and the suggestion that this is mainly because it is supplied as bait to attract back to the treasury the gold paid out to the frontier concentrations of the army (Reece 1978). John Casey has pursued the problem of the connection between the supply of coinage and the requirements of the military (Casey 1988, 1979, 1986) but the problem as always in Britain is complicated by the absence of clear evidence on the exact presence and strength of army units at any given time.

The end of Roman coinage in Britain is at present reasonably clear. Andrew Burnett has recently made out a very strong case for the cessation of silver coinage by about 410 to 415, and it seems most unlikely that copper coinage could continue at a token value in the absence of an enforcing administration and a total absence of bullion coinage of intrinsic value (Burnett 1984). Without the bullion the copper coinage can have had no appeal at all. This means that the latest coins to be issued, around the year 400 were probably no longer used by about 420. The record of coinage in Britain, apart from five or six examples of strays in gold or silver from the continent and a few gold pieces in jewellery in Saxon graves, is a blank until the start of Saxon gold coinage in the 7th century. There are no coins known which are available to fill this gap, for all the putative coinages of the Dark Ages such as Barbarous Radiates are now proved to belong earlier in the sequence through die-linking; and the archaeological record is eloquent in its silence, for deposits of the 5th and 6th centuries just do not contain coins which are unknown at other dates.

One of the most interesting points about the total death of coinage is the absence of copying which was endemic in the 3rd and 4th centuries (Boon 1988). In some way the need to produce copies, or the chance of profiting by producing copies, must depend on the integration of Britain into the continuously coin-using society and administration of the Mediterranean world (Reece 1985b). Once separated from that society Britain found no use for coins and went its own de-romanised way.

References

Aitchison N. 1988 Roman wealth, native ritual. *World Archaeology* 20–2:270–284.

Boon G. 1988 Counterfeit coins in Roman Britain. In Casey and Reece 1988:102–188.

Brickstock R. 1987 *Copies of the Fel Temp Reparatio Coinage in Britain*. BAR 176, Oxford.

Burnett A. 1984 Clipped siliquae and the end of Roman Britain. *Britannia* 15:163–8.

Casey J. 1979 The coins. In J. Dore and J. Gillam, *South Shields*. Newcastle upon Tyne, 79–97.

Casey J. 1986 *Understanding Ancient Coins*. London.

Casey J. 1988 The interpretation of Romano-British site-finds. In Casey and Reece 1988:39–56.

Casey J. and R. Reece (eds.) 1988 *Coins and the Archaeologist*. Second edition. London.

Crummy N. (ed.) 1987 *The coins from the Excavations in Colchester 1971–1979*. Colchester Excavation Reports 4. Colchester.

Cunliffe B. (ed.) 1981 *Coinage and Society in Britain and Gaul*. CBA Research Report 38. London.

Fulford M. 1978 Coin circulation and mint activity in the later Roman Empire. *Archaeol. J.* 135:67–114.

Hammerson M. 1980 *Copies of Constantinian Coins, 330–348*. M Phil Thesis, University of London.

Kent J. 1981 the origins of coinage in Britain. In Cunliffe 1981:41–43.

Kent J. 1988 Interpreting coin finds. In Casey and Reece 1988:201–217.

Mann J. and R. Reece 1983 *The Roman Coins from Lincoln 1970–1979*. The Archaeology of Lincoln, Vol. 6, Fasc. 2. London.

Reece R. 1973 Roman coinage in the western Empire. *Britannia* 4:227–51.

Reece R. 1978 Coins and frontiers or supply and demand. In J. Fitz (ed.), *Limes*. Budapest, 643–6.

Reece R. 1979 Economic history from Roman site-finds. In T. Hackens and R. Weiller (eds.) *Actes du 9e Congrès Internationale de Numismatique*. Luxembourg, 495–502.

Reece R. 1980a Religion, coins and temples. In W. Rodwell (ed.) *Temples, Churches and Religion in Roman Britain*. BAR 77. Oxford, 115–28.

Reece R. 1980b The Falkirk Hoard reconsidered. In W. Hanson and L. Keppie (ed.) *Roman Frontier Studies 1979*. BAR 71. Oxford, 119–29.

Reece R. 1981a Roman monetary impact on the Celtic world. In Cunliffe 1981:24–28.

Reece R. 1981b The normal hoard. In C. Carcassonne and T. Hackens (eds.) *Numismatique et Statistique*. PACT 5. Strasbourg, 299–308.

Reece R. 1982a Roman coinage in the western Mediterranean. *Opus* I Fasc 2:341–50.

Reece R. 1982b A collection of coins from the centre of Rome. *Papers of the British School at Rome* 50:116–45.

Reece R. 1984a The use of Roman coinage. *Oxford Journal of Archaeology* 3–2:197–210.

Reece R. 1984b The coins. In S.S. Frere *Verulamium Excavations*. Vol. 3. Oxford 3–18.

Reece R. 1984c Mints, markets and the military. In T. Blagg and A. King (eds.), *Military and Civilian in Roman Britain*. BAR 136. Oxford, 143–60.

Reece R. 1985a Coin finds and coin production. In G. Depeyrot (ed.) *Rhythmes de la production monétaire*. Paris, 208–13.

Reece R. 1985b Rome in the Mediterranean world, the evidence of coins. In C. Malone and S. Stoddart (eds.), *Papers in Italian Archaeology 4* BAR S246; Oxford, 85–98.

Reece R. 1987 *Coinage in Roman Britain*. London.

Reece R. 1988a Coins and villas. In K. Branigan and D. Miles (eds.) *The Economy of the Roman Villa*. Sheffield, 34–41.

Reece R. 1988b *My Roman Britain*. Oxbow, Oxford.

Reece R. 1988c Clustering of coin finds in Britain, France and Italy. In Casey and Reece 1988:73–85.

Reece R. 1988d Numerical aspects of Roman coin hoards in Britain. In Casey and Reece 1988:86–101.

Reece R. 1988e Interpreting Roman hoards. *World Archaeology* 20–2:261–9.

Rivet A. (ed.) 1969 *The Roman villa in Britain*. London.

Robertson A. 1988 Romano-British coin hoards. In Casey and Reece 1988:13–38.

Ryan N. 1988 *Fourth Century Coin Finds from Roman Britain*. BAR 183. Oxford.

Salway P. 1981 *Roman Britain*. Oxford.

Todd M. 1966 The Romano-British mintages of Antoninus Pius. *Numismatic Chronicle* Series 7, No. 6:47–53.

Todd M. (ed.) 1978 *Studies in the Romano-British Villa*. Leicester.

Walker D. 1988. The Roman coins. In B. Cunliffe (ed.) *The Temple of Sulis Minerva at Bath*. Vol. 2:281–358. Oxford.

5. Britain and the Roman Empire: The Evidence for Regional and Long Distance Trade

Michael Fulford

This contribution is concerned with setting out the evidence for economic relations between Britain and the rest of the empire, rather than within Britain.[1] Archaeology provides our most important source because, though partial through the differential survival of artefacts, it is considerably richer than the limited – and virtually finite – written sources of the period. Artefacts can be divided between those which can be grouped together on the basis of style and those which, in addition to stylistic arguments, can be attributed to source, either because manufacturing detritus is abundant or because scientific methods of analysis allow accurate provenancing. In effect this means a division between objects of glass and metal and those of stone and ceramics. The place of manufacture may be suggested for a particular metal or glass artefact on the basis of the distribution of known examples, but new discoveries may completely alter the basis for the attribution in question; establishing the origin of the metals themselves is even more difficult. We should not overlook perishable artefacts of wood or textiles, where the type of wood or material, such as silk, may be foreign to Britain, even if we cannot be more specific about source and place of manufacture. The chief limitations of archaeological evidence include, on the one hand, the relationship of what survives in the archaeological record with what was originally traded and, on the other, the comprehension of the systems responsible for the movement of goods. Written evidence may be more useful here, but there is insufficient to attempt to characterise the period as a whole. It also suffers from its very general character, lacking information about volume, value, origins, destinations and duration.

As far as Britain's economic relations with the rest of the Roman world between the Late Iron Age and the end of the Romano-British period are concerned, there has been an enormous advance in our knowledge over the last two decades. On the one hand more extensive excavations have provided us with larger quantities of finds which have called for systematic and specialist treatment, while, on the other, associated research on individual categories of finds has led to a much greater understanding of their affinities and place of manufacture. Quantification of artefact types and assemblages has been an integral part of these developments and its results are beginning to revolutionise old interpretations based on qualitative assessments.

In this survey our first concern must be with the long distance contact established between Britain and the Mediterranean in the later Iron Age. Although written evidence suggests that tin was being sought from south-western Britain during the Hellenistic period (Todd 1987:185–88), the earliest convincing archaeological evidence for Roman involvement dates from the later 2nd or early 1st century BC. Hengistbury Head in the middle of the south coast of England has produced a minimum of about thirty Italian Dressel IA wine-amphorae dating up to the mid-1st century BC (Cunliffe 1987). In addition to the amphorae, the site produced considerable quantities of Armorican pottery as well as some imported glass and metal. Cunliffe suggests that all these goods were exchanged for metals, such as tin, lead and silver, for which there was evidence of processing on site, as well as slaves and agricultural produce (1987:339–42). The Armorican material, as well as similar wine jars from the coast of Brittany, suggests that Hengistbury formed part of an Atlantic trade-network (Galliou 1984; Fitzpatrick 1985). This earliest phase of contact lasted up to about 50 BC and seems to have involved small amounts of traded goods as can be seen from the comparative scarcity of imported objects inland (Cunliffe 1987:340–45). Consequently there is little evidence to suggest that this trade had much impact on British society (cf. Cunliffe 1984a).

The Roman conquest of Gaul saw a significant change in the direction and character of trade across the Channel. Firstly, Caesar tells us that the Belgic tribes sought help from Britain (*de Bello Gallico* iv, 20) and Kent (1981) has argued persuasively that the occurrence of both the Belgic war coinage (Gallo-Belgic E) and the typologically earlier Gallo-Belgic C in southeastern England can be explained as payment for the help provided. Gallo-Belgic A and B need not have arrived much earlier. In this case, the written evidence offers a political interpretation for the pattern of coin finds; but whether we can assume that social relations continued to underpin cross-channel relations after the war is uncertain. Certainly to begin with, the volume of traffic, as evidenced by Dressel 1B amphorae, fine Roman metalwork and Gaulish coins, does not appear large and may well be consistent with the meeting of obligations between related leaders and groups on each side of the channel (Haselgrove 1984:18–23). Alternatively, if the Roman conquest of Gaul had severely damaged those relations, the pattern of imports may be attributable to a low volume of entrepreneurial trade, independent of social ties. This could equally well have originated in north-western Gaul, which shares a similar range of traded items whose ultimate origin was the Mediterranean. The contexts of the amphorae and metalwork are largely confined to burials in southeast Britain, until the last two decades of the 1st century BC when they become more

---

1 A complementary paper has appeared in M. Todd (ed.) *Research on Roman Britain: 1960–1989*. Society for the Promotion of Roman Studies Monograph 11 (1989).

common on major settlements (Fitzpatrick 1985). This kind of evidence makes clear the prestige attached to imported luxuries and the continued association of the objects of long distance trade with an élite minority in southeastern Britain emphasizes the importance attached to its control (Haselgrove 1982). Trade to Hengistbury and the south coast continued into the second half of the 1st century BC, but on a reduced scale (Cunliffe 1987). Clearly the conquest of Gaul marked the beginning of a permanent shift in the orientation of trade; the longer and more dangerous west coast routes appear to have declined as internal routes and markets within Gaul became secure (Cunliffe 1984b).

A change of tempo in the volume of traffic can be detected during the principate of Augustus from between 20 and 10 BC. This can be measured by the appearance of a wider range of artefacts, which are now found commonly in settlement as well as grave contexts in southeast Britain. Skeleton Green in Hertfordshire may serve as an example of a settlement which has produced such a range of imports from this period (Partridge 1981). These include amphorae carrying olive-oil and fish-sauce from Italy and southern Gaul, other table ware from central (micaceous) and northern Gaul (Gallo-Belgic wares) and cooking pots from central Gaul. Glass and some metalwork, such as a variety of brooches, were imported. This material comes from a small part of a major Late Iron Age settlement at Braughing whose development takes off at about the time the new range of imported goods start to arrive. Similar finds have been recorded at the better known Late Iron Age sites or oppida of Camulodunum (Hawkes and Hull 1947), Verulamium (Wheeler and Wheeler 1936) and Calleva (Boon 1969; Fulford 1987a), which also seem to develop rapidly from the last two decades of the 1st century BC and which eventually became important Roman towns. What prompted the surge in trade at this time?

Two interlocking explanations seem the most likely: the commencement of the Augustan campaigns into Germany and the Romanisation of central and northern Gaul, witnessed by the laying out of roads and the establishment of towns (Drinkwater 1983; Wightman 1985). Both are likely to have stimulated demand for the kind of raw materials and foodstuffs that Strabo attests Britain exported: 'corn, cattle, gold, silver, iron, hides, slaves and hounds' (*Geogr.* IV.v, 2–3). Amber, glass and other manufactured goods, Strabo records, were received in exchange. The fact that the imported artefacts are common to northern Gaul means that it is uncertain how much, if any, of the trade involving Britain originated in the Mediterranean. As earlier, items of long distance trade could have been redistributed from within northern Gaul.

While increased trade may be attributable to new demands caused by Augustan activity in Gaul and Germany, a third possibility needs to be considered. Although not directly attested in the written sources, the visits of British leaders, like Tincommius, to Rome about AD 6 – 7 would be consistent with regular diplomatic contacts between southern British

leaders and Rome (Frere 1967:41–5; Todd 1981:31–3). Exchange of gifts may have formed part of the protocol and the payment of subsidies to British leaders may have formed part of treaty arrangements. A deliberately contrived rivalry between the Atrebates and the Catuvellauni has been suggested as one of the objects of Augustan diplomacy (Frere 1967:42). However that may be, the origin of the gold and silver employed to produce the dynastic and tribal coinages of the period between Augustus and Claudius remains to be established. Clearly some will have been derived from coinage imported at the time of the Gallic wars, but some of the bullion must have been new to Britain. Although an origin is traditionally sought within the British Isles, the lack of evidence for production and for exchange relations on any scale with western Britain where the ores are to be found, combined with the southeastern findspots of most of the precious metal in question, argue against such an interpretation (Tylecote 1986). Gold and silver arrived either as part of the payment for goods, etc., just as at the time of the Gallic wars, or as imperial subsidies of the kind paid to the German leader Vannius by Tiberius, or both (Todd 1981:32–3). This seems to contradict the testimony of Strabo (above), but not necessarily; he could well be describing the re-export of gold and silver. Whereas the pre-Caesarean trade does not seem to have had a significant impact on British communities, the correlation between the increase in trade from 20 – 10 BC with the emergence of the southeastern oppida and the evidence for increased and aggressive competition among the élites of southeastern Britain seems more than coincidence. The most powerful group, the Catuvellauni, at the time of Claudius' invasion also displays the most wealth in terms of its coinage (Allen 1975) and imported luxuries.

The impact of the Claudian invasion on cross-Channel traffic is not immediately apparent. This is because much the same range of goods (that survives in the archaeological record) continued to be imported after AD 43 as before and so it is only at newly founded sites, almost invariably forts, that the character of post-conquest trade can be determined. Considerable variation between individual sites means that it is difficult to ascertain general trends. However, the quantitative evidence of stamped and decorated sigillata goes some way towards providing this (Marsh 1981). At those sites, principally towns and forts, where the evidence has been assembled, the graph shows a steep rise in the amounts of sigillata (South Gaulish) to a peak in the third quarter of the 1st century AD (Figure 5.1). This may be taken as a crude indicator of an overall and rapid rise in imported goods after AD 43, where the distribution is largely confined to towns and military sites.

The origin of imports is extremely varied as the two maps indicate (Figures 5.2–3). On the one hand the evidence for the volume of wine, olive-oil, salazones (*garum*, etc.) and *defrutum* syrup calculated by Sealey (1985) to have been carried in the sample of amphorae excavated at Sheepen,

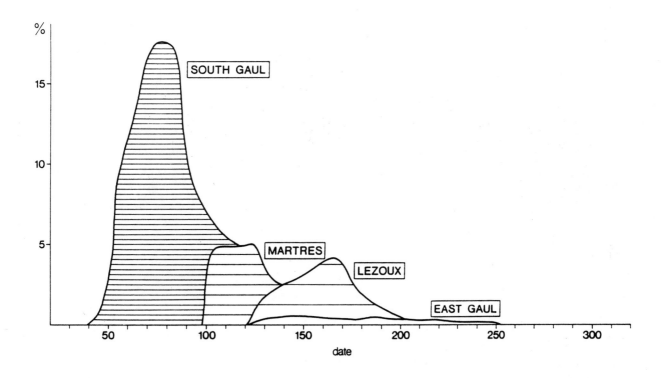

Figure 5.1   Sources of decorated samian from London (after Marsh 1981. Fig. 11.7). The graph is similar for other urban and military sites in southern Britain.

Colchester in 1970 has been presented on Figure 5.2. The material is dated between AD 43 and 61 and shows the overall importance of the Spanish provinces which supplied 66% of all amphora-borne commodities. On the other hand, the second map shows all the known sources of all types of imported pottery found at the Claudio-Neronian fort at Kingsholm, just outside Gloucester (Hurst 1985). Here, the size of symbol represents the number of sherds of the ware in question as a percentage of all the stratified sherds, both imported and British, in the entire assemblage. Although no single ware accounts for even as much as 10% of the assemblage, imports as a whole amount to 53%. In the context of all the pottery, the Spanish provinces (7.3%) supply considerable less than central and southern Gaul (16.2%). As at Colchester there is considerably representation of Rhodian wine and also ?Palestinian 'carrot' amphorae. Although the evidence of the varied and remote sources of imports to pre-Flavian Britain is derived from ceramics, it is not unreasonable to suppose a similar diversity of sources for the entire range of imported goods. The

Gaulish material may be the first indication of the arrival of commodities in perishable containers, like barrels, in significantly greater quantities than those carried in amphorae from the Mediterranean region. While Kingsholm is unequivocally military, it is not otherwise yet possible to distinguish between military and civilian patterns of supply. High proportions of imports do, however, appear to be confined to larger military sites and the major towns. At Chelmsford, which may have had a post-Boudiccan garrison, imports in the period of AD 60 – 80 amount to less than 2% of the assemblage (Going 1987). At the former oppidum of Calleva, where substantial military occupation has yet to be established, the proportion of imports in all pre-Flavian groups is 22% (Fulford 1984a). Finds from rural settlements are generally rare. Increased traffic can be attributed to a number of factors. First, there was the need to supply the army which may have numbered as many as 40,000 men. We need not suppose that this depended solely on amphora-borne commodities and a variety of pottery types, which we happen to be able to relate to a specific source. The

37

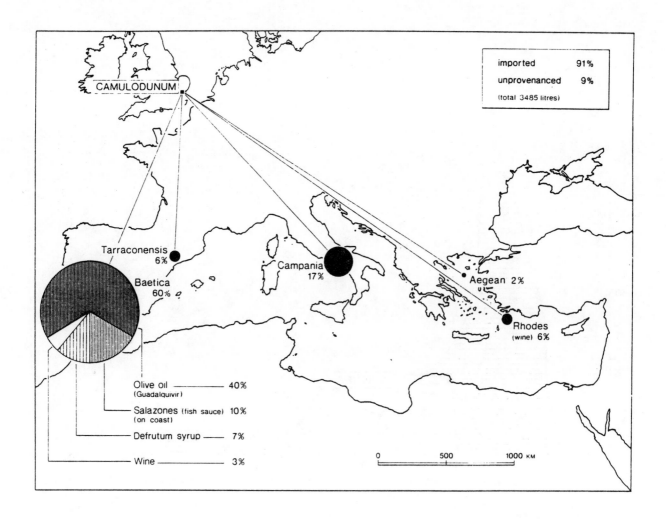

imported   91%
unprovenanced   9%
(total 3485 litres)

CAMULODUNUM

Tarraconensis
6%

Baetica
60%

Campania
17%

Aegean 2%

Rhodes
(wine) 6%

Olive oil ————— 40%
(Guadalquivir)

Salazones (fish sauce) 10%
(on coast)

Defrutum syrup ——— 7%

Wine ————————— 3%

0   500   1000 KM

Figure 5.2   Amphora-borne commodities at Sheepen A.D. 43-61 (extracted from Sealey 1985). Sample of 3485 litres; calculated from the estimated capacity of the amphora present.

range and volume of raw materials, foodstuffs and manufactured goods was probably very great and the importance of access to the sea is shown by the location of the major pre-Flavian fortresses like Colchester, Chichester, Exeter, Kingsholm and Usk. The rapid rise of London from the early 50s as the major port of the province also demonstrates the importance of the province's overseas connections. What the archaeological record reveals as imported represents the tip of the iceberg and much of it may have been of secondary importance, carried along by a stream of strategically essential materials. Occasionally, evidence for the importation of basic foodstuffs, such as cereals comes to light, as in pre-Boudiccan London (Straker 1987) and, later, at Caerleon (Helbaek 1964). Although it has been argued by some that Britain was able to feed and supply the invasion force with most, if not all of its essentials, the opposing case for considerable dependence on basic supplies has been made elsewhere (Fulford 1984b). The serious famine which followed the Boudiccan rebellion reminds us of how precarious conditions were at that time

(Tacitus, *Ann.* xiv, 38.).

The pay of the soldiers themselves will have been another source of payment for imports. Indeed much of what is recovered in the archaeological record, like minor metalwork and pottery, was probably bought by individuals, while the legions took care of strategic supplies. That pay would have been supplemented by the sale of booty, of which slaves were probably the most valuable element. The natives themselves provided a third source of imports. Given the demands imposed on the province by the presence of the army, it is difficult to see what scope there was for continued exports of the kind that Strabo described for the pre-conquest period. However this loss would have been compensated for by the payments received for goods and foodstuffs supplied to the army over and above what was made over as tax. In addition some of the traffic would have been sustained by the credit said by Seneca to have been advanced to members of the British aristocracy. Thus, apart from the unquantifiable number of slaves and other booty, imports to Britain would have been paid for by coin.

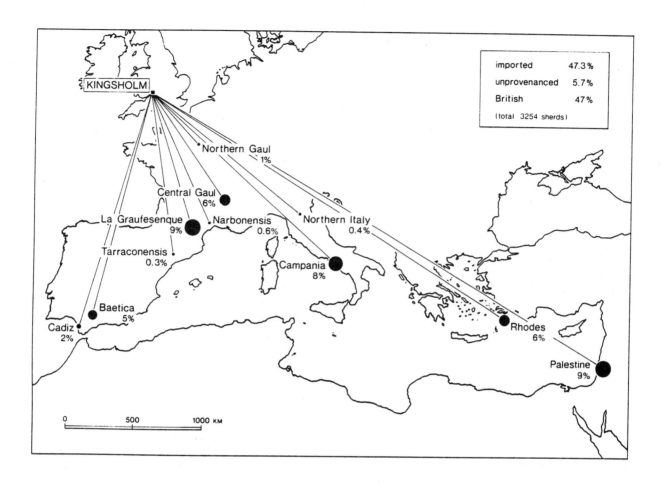

Figure 5.3   Kingsholm: Claudio-Neronian pottery supply. All types of imported pottery expressed as percentages of stratified sherds (T=3254 sherds) (calculated from Hurst 1985).

The export of metals is different because until mines were leased out, all the income would have accrued to the emperor and so helped to offset the costs of the army. Given the distances over which those imports which survive in the archaeological record have travelled, it does seem likely that their unit costs were kept low by a greater volume of traffic in goods which are archaeologically invisible. The correlation between the behaviour of long distance trade with Britain and the reduction in both military activity and the size of the garrison will be explored further below.

Thus the evidence from early Roman Britain fits Hopkins' model (1980) of the rich inner provinces of the empire recovering the cash with which to pay their taxes by trading with the periphery on which much of the tax revenue was being expended. The exploitative, colonial core-periphery model explored by Hingley (1982) does not fit so well, unless the sense of core is limited to the army of occupation and imperial support of the Romanization of the province. Otherwise the core, meaning the physical centre of the empire, would (*contra* Hingley) have

derived little or no economic gain (but considerable political advantage) from the conquest of southern Britain. The range and volume of imports is not, therefore, so much a reflection of the intrinsic wealth of the country, but of the scale of expenditure on the army and the conquest (cf. Willems 1984 for a similar view of the lower Rhineland).

With some minor changes, which see the origins of imported items from the Mediterranean provinces largely confined to sources in southern Spain and Narbonensis, trade continued essentially unaltered into the Flavian period when the frontier was pushed forward into Scotland. As the army established itself in new forts and fortresses in the north, so complementary efforts were made to organise self-governing civitates in the south, each with its own urban centre. The combination of an aggressive forward policy and expensive urban building in the south rather suggest that the character of cross-Channel trade remained much as before, with little available for export.

If the evidence for the changing supply of sigillata (Figure 5.1) holds good for trade as a whole, then the end of the 1st century marks a sharp drop in traffic. This coincides with the decline of the South Gaulish workshops and the start of major production in Central Gaul, first at Les Martres de Veyre in the Trajanic period and then at Lezoux from about AD 120. At the moment no other changes have been observed in the pattern of cross-Channel trade to correlate with those recorded in the sigillata industry. It is possible that the failure of the South Gaulish workshops was due to internal reasons; it can scarcely be attributed to competition because the output of Les Martres de Veyre was so much less than that of La Graufesenque, etc. However, if the pricing of South Gaulish sigillata was only made reasonable because the *negotiatores* handling it were able to exploit a supply system which was paid for, directly or indirectly, by the imperial government, then any major changes in the organisation of official requisition would have a disastrous effect on a parasitic trade like that of sigillata (Middleton 1979). It has been suggested elsewhere that the change in the supply of sigillata also broadly coincides with a period of major relocation and reduction of the garrisons of Britain and Germany (Fulford 1984b). In effect, by the early 2nd century these had been halved, and the consequences for patterns of trade and supply are obvious.

The overall range of imported goods in the 2nd century does indeed appear to be less varied than in the 1st (Figure 5.4). This is particularly noticeable with the amphorae which are dominated by the Baetican olive-oil (Dressel 20) and southern Gaulish wine carriers (Gauloise 4) (Peacock and Williams 1986). The former has an extensive distribution across Britain and is not uncommon in small quantities on rural settlements. The proportion of amphorae by sherd count or vessel count is never more than a few percent, even on urban sites (e.g. about 6% in late 1st to mid 2nd century contexts at Billingsgate Buildings, London (Green 1980)). Whether more use was being made of barrels, particularly to carry wine, is unclear because these only survive in wet conditions. Interestingly the majority of barrels reused as well-linings in London is of 1st and 2nd century date (Willmott 1982). These can be shown to have been imported by the type of wood used, larch or silver fir. The shipping of wine alongside drinking and table wares may explain the extraordinary success of the Central Gaulish sigillata industry. Given the distance of the kilns from Britain, compared with that of the East Gaulish workshops, it is remarkable that Central Gaulish sigillata should be so much more common than the East Gaulish products (A. King 1981). The

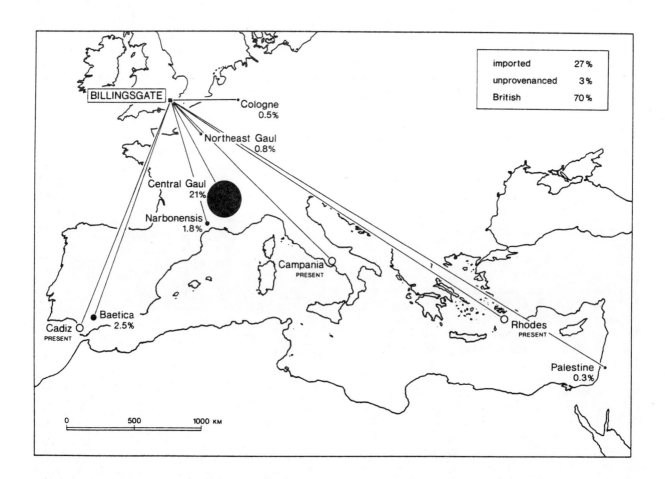

Figure 5.4   London: Billingsgate Buildings; late first to early/mid second century pottery supply. All types of imported pottery expressed as percentages of EVE's (estimated vessel equivalents) (calculated from Green 1980).

overall distribution in relation to the kilns is also unusual with the latter located at the southern extremity. These characteristics may best be accounted for if the pottery accompanied other cargoes, including wine, requisitioned supplies etc. However, in terms of the stamped and decorated ware, the volume of imports appears much reduced from the peak of South Gaulish sigillata for those sites where a quantified assessment has been made (Figure 5.1). This picture may be deceptive and relate mainly to urban sites, because it should not be forgotten how relatively common 2nd century Central Gaulish sigillata is on rural sites across lowland Britain (cf. Millett 1980). Similarly the ratio of unstamped to stamped plain-ware and decorated vessels may increase in the 2nd century. As examples of the ratio of imported to British pottery we may cite the example of Chelmsford, where the percentage rises to 8% in groups dated to the period of AD 80 – 120/25, falls to 5% in groups of AD 120/25 – 160/75 and then rises to 11% in groups dated AD 160/75 – 200/10 (Going 1987). These figures compare favourably with small groups of a similar date-range from Silchester, while contrasting with a figure of 29% for all imports in late 1st to mid 2nd century deposits at Billingsgate Buildings in London (Green 1980). The latter is almost certainly influenced by the proximity of the quays, but serves to remind us of the continuing importance of London as a port.

We have already drawn attention to the problem of how imports were paid for in the 1st century; in the 2nd century the problem, if not so acute, still remains. Was there scope for the export of agricultural produce of any kind? This still seems unlikely, given the overall level of military activity with three legions and their auxiliaries, the investment in frontiers and civil developments. Although more than 40% of textiles recovered from London's waterfront are believed to be imported (Milne 1985:117), the 2nd century may see the start of the export of the woollens which later receive mention in panegyrics and Diocletian's Price Edict (Fulford 1977:62–3). This may have been the concern of the two *negotiatores vestiarii* trading with Britain and recorded on inscriptions from Cassel and Marsal in Gallia Belgica (Hassall 1978). They are not independently dated, but probably belong to the 2nd or 3rd century. Presumably, as wars continued on the northern frontier, booty, including captives, was exported from the province.

Of mineral exploitation and export we can say very little. Despite the advance of analytical procedures, there are still serious obstacles in the way of the successful attribution of metals in manufactured objects to their original sources. Lead mining seems to have been of considerably greater importance than the extraction of tin, copper or gold (Tylecote 1986:61–70). Along with the traces of ancient workings, the finds of stamped and unstamped lead pigs hint at the scale of the enterprise. The latter range in date from the reign of Claudius to Marcus Aurelius and are almost entirely confined to Britain in their distribution. The examples from St. Valéry-sur-Somme, Châlons-sur-Saône and, possibly,

Lillebonne (Gowland 1901:379) attest export out of Britain but do not help us to determine the overall volume of traffic. On the basis of the lead pigs, a case could be made out for the greater part of the output to have been consumed in Britain, although finds clustering around ports like Clausentum and Brough-on-Humber may well have been destined for export. Given the lack of lead naturally occurring in northern Gaul, we might reasonably expect Britain to have been a major supplier there. Except for those instances where mines were leased out and some profit would have accrued to the lessee, all revenue reverted to the emperor. Whether the end of the practice of stamping the lead pigs had implications regarding the scale of exploitation rather than the organisation of the industry, it is difficult to say. The continuity of some lead and tin extraction is implicit in the prevalence of pewter, lead coffins, etc. in the later Roman period.

A case has also been made out for the export of iron from the Weald, where production, partly under the control of the *Classis Britannica*, seems to peak in the 2nd century (Cleere and Crossley 1985:57–86). Although iron ores occur commonly in lowland Britain, the scale of working in the Weald suggested to Cleere that some of the output was exported. By the mid 3rd century production in the Weald appears to have ceased.

But for some evidence of mineral export, war booty, and a small quantity of pottery and other artefacts, the question as to how Britain paid for its imports in the 2nd century remains unresolved. The re-export of precious metal as coinage remains the most likely explanation. If any kind of credit system operated within the trading networks of the western empire, it might account for the relative scarcity of higher value denominations of coins lost in Britain, when compared with Gaul, Germany and Italy (Reece 1973) – the implication being that accounts were settled before coinage was despatched to the province. Like in the 1st century, the volume of trade, as measured by the archaeological record, and the distance over which large numbers of relatively low value goods travelled in the 2nd century is in excess of anything registered in Britain until the early modern period. Ultimately this can, in large part, be attributed to the revenue spent on Britain, rather than on the wealth created by the province.

How then was this trade organised? A number of inscriptions consisting, firstly, of a large group from the mouth of the Scheldt at Colijnsplaat and Domburg and, secondly, of several individual finds from Britain, Gaul and Germany record *negotiatores* involved with Britain (Hassall 1978; Bogaers 1983). They can be divided into two groups, one which describes the trader simply as Britannicianus, the other, the type of trade in which the *negotiator* specialised. So we have two examples of *negotiator cretarius Britannicianus* and two of *negotiator vestiarius a* or *ex Britannia*. The first group of six inscriptions records four different individuals (*negotiatores* at York and Cologne are also mentioned at Colijnsplaat) and presumably refers to traders concerned with the general range of goods and commodities traded with Britain, while the second comprises specialist merchants. One more can be added to the general group from Colijnsplaat; Valerius Mar......, interpreted as trading with Kent and Boulogne (Bogaers 1983:13–15). The York find is the only one of these inscriptions to have been found in Britain and all, except for the second inscription of C. Aurelius Verus from Cologne and the *negotiatores vestiarii* have been found at port or temple locations. Tentatively, we may infer a broad division in the organisation of trade between those merchants who plied the Channel, North Sea and Atlantic coasts, usually with general rather than specialist cargoes, and those who operated in Gaul and Germany as far as the coast and tended to specialise in particular goods and commodities. The careful examination of shipwrecks will shed further light on organisation. Central Gaulish sigillata, brick and tile have been recovered from the Pudding Pan sands off the north Kent coast, but there has been no systematic investigation to identify the actual wreck, if it survives, and so learn more about the ship and the composition of the rest of the cargo (Smith 1907; 1909).

The scope of the *Classis Britannica's* role in the supply of the northern frontier is unclear. The association of C L B R tiles with iron-making sites in the Weald suggests an official involvement in the extraction of iron, while its presence in the north is attested by an inscription from Hadrian's Wall (Cleere and Crossley 1985). Likewise both Agricola's campaigns in the north in the 1st century and Severus' in the 3rd were facilitated by the fleet, but we cannot begin to gauge the importance of its contribution compared with the role of private merchants.

Although by the later 2nd century the reduced long distance links were largely limited to Gaul, Germany and Spain, study of the imported marble (used principally for decorative veneers, rather than for columns, capitals, etc.) shows that small amounts continued to be drawn from as far afield as Egypt and the east Mediterranean (Pritchard 1986) (Figure 5.5). Quantities are such that the trade could well have been organised through marble yards in provinces bordering the west Mediterranean. Nevertheless, the fact that other exotic goods such as the silk in the Holborough tumulus (Wild 1965) continued to reach Britain in the 3rd century shows that long distance trade continued to survive, even if the volume of traffic was greatly reduced.

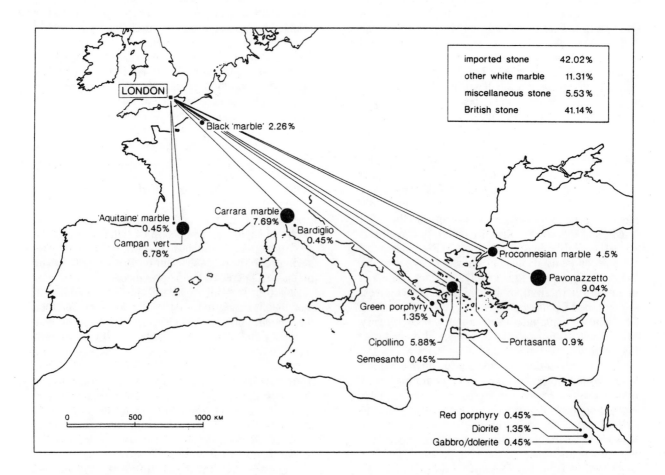

Figure 5.5   Sources of imported Roman marble found in London. Numbers of fragments expressed as percentages (after Pritchard 1986, Fig. 2).

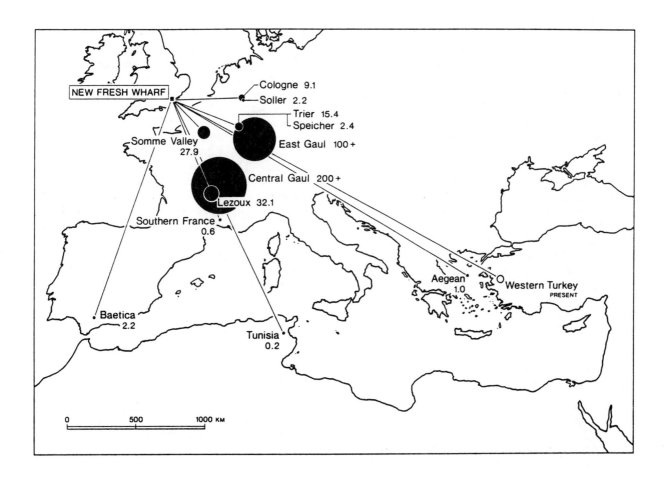

Figure 5.6   London: New Fresh Warf; early to mid third century pottery supply. All types of imported pottery expressed as EVE's (extracted from Richardson 1986).

The finds from the infill of the early 3rd (225 – 245) century quay at New Fresh Wharf, London serve as an example of the character of regional and long distance trade at this time (Miller *et al.* 1986) (Figure 5.6).   On the one hand there were large quantities of East Gaulish and Central Gaulish sigillata (the latter possibly residual) and other fine wares as well as other regional pottery imports from Picardy/Pas de Calais and the Eifel; on the other, there were small quantities of east Mediterranean and north African amphorae. Besides pottery, there were imported writing tablets of cedar, silver fir, larch and Norway spruce, fragments of Carrara marble, onyx veneer, etc. The large collection of fragments of leather clothing and shoes also undoubtedly contains some imported pieces. Altogether the finds represent an extraordinary concentration of material at a time when cross-Channel trade was much reduced in volume. Given the scarcity of 3rd century imports elsewhere in Britain, we should hesitate to

extrapolate the London finds to the province as a whole. Nevertheless the deposits are associated with a new and massive waterfront which could hardly have been constructed if the volume of traffic was absolutely negligible. This may serve to reinforce the view that the traffic of the 1st and 2nd centuries had been extraordinary in its scope and volume. However that may be, the demise of Central Gaulish sigillata and other fine ware production at the beginning of the 3rd century and the corresponding end of East Gaulish production by the middle of the 3rd century, combined with the end of the imports of Spanish and Gaulish amphorae, marks a turning point in the character and direction of regional and long distance traffic between Britain and the rest of the empire around the mid-3rd century.

Thereafter regional and long distance trade never return to the volume of the early Roman period, despite the undoubted prosperity of Britain in the 4th century. In any case the volume of long distance trade appears to have been falling from the end of the 1st century. The explanation of this decline has to be sought in the extraordinary character and circumstances of early Roman trade with Britain, where relatively low value goods travelled long distances overland in quantity. Whether similar patterns will emerge in other parts of the empire, such as along the Danube or in the East, between the Mediterranean and the frontier in question, we have yet to discover. Long distance, high volume traffic is otherwise limited to the sea, particularly the Mediterranean, with a rapid fall-off in the quantity of goods found inland. The situation in the northwestern provinces in the early Roman period represents a brief interruption of the pattern of limited distributions of low value artefacts in an essentially land-locked area. The decline in trade has been attributed to political conditions in the late empire which were considerably less stable than in the 1st and 2nd centuries. Nevertheless, and despite the rapid devaluation of the silver coinage, long distance traffic continued to flourish around the shores of the Mediterranean (as is reflected in the wide distribution and frequency of, for example,

African amphorae and table ware). The only indication that volume had been reduced is provided by the fall in the number of recorded shipwrecks (Hopkins 1980, Fig.1), but there are important biases in their reported distribution (such as an absence of wrecks on the Africa - Italy route), which severely distort the figures. In the case of Britain, it has already been argued that the character of regional and long distance traffic in the early empire is best explained by a high level of spending occasioned by the presence and activities of a large garrison, rather than by the productivity of the native economy. The beginning of the 3rd century (208 – 211) saw the last major Roman campaigns in the north of Britain and thereafter the island seems to have become a military backwater. The combination of a number of strands of circumstantial evidence points to a reduction in the military establishment to a level of about 10–20,000 thousand troops (James 1984). This, rather than political uncertainties and the rapid devaluation of currency, which affected the whole empire, may well account for the major decline in Britain's regional and long distance trade between the mid 2nd and mid 3rd centuries.

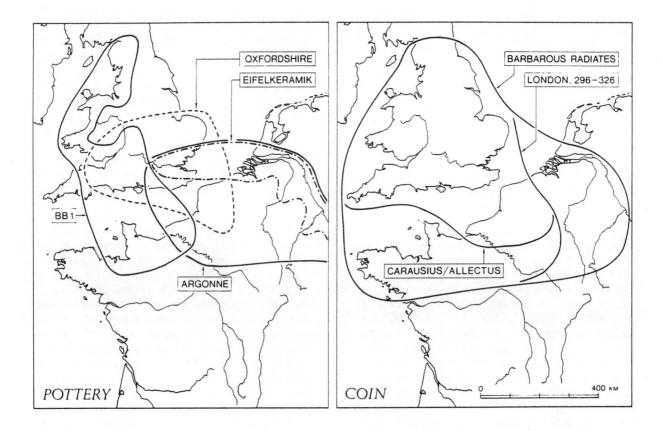

Figure 5.7   a) Main distribution areas of fourth century pottery: Argonne ware; Dorset BB1; Eifelkeramik; Oxfordshire ware.

b) Main circulation areas of barbarous radiates, Carausian coinage and issues of the London mint c. A.D. 296-326.

The cross-Channel trade from the mid-3rd to the end of the Roman period is distinguished by its regional character. Although exotic goods continued to filter through from the Mediterranean and the eastern empire, Britain's economic relations were linked most strongly with Gallia Belgica and Germania Inferior. Although these links may have been just as important earlier on, the evidence is swamped by the mass of material evidence relating to long distance traffic. These regional links are composed of a number of strands, of which coinage may be considered first (Figure 5.7). During the Gallic empire (259 – 275) Britain shared a common coinage with Gaul. In particular northern Gaul (Gallia Belgica) shared with Britain the phenomenon of the 'barbarous radiate' issues. Although there is an extraordinary variety of types and evidence for production on both sides of the Channel, die-links show that coins of this type did cross to Britain (Boon 1974, Fig.4; Davies, pers. comm.). In any case the lesser volume of regular Gallic and Central Empire coinage serves to underline the homogeneity of Britain and northern/northwestern Gaul. Although political factors determined the minting and issue of coinage in the first place, the area in which particular coinages circulated will be heavily influenced by patterns of trade and marketing. In fact barbarous issues circulated in small numbers widely within the empire, just as central empire issues reached Britain and northern Gaul (C. King 1981). However, the bulk of the barbarous radiate coinage is concentrated in northern Gaul and Britain. The regional circulation of coinage is again demonstrated by the coinage of Carausius which is also found in northwestern Gaul (Casey 1977). Once again political factors come into play as, for a time, Carausius held a small amount of territory, probably based at Boulogne. However his coinage circulated more widely than any possible area over which he might have exercised political control. This pattern is reiterated more clearly when London had an official mint from 296 (Fulford 1977, Fig.10). Considerable quantities of London coins have been found in northwestern Gaul; as far east as Trier numbers are by no means negligible and a trickle reached Spain and the Mediterranean. In the same way and over the same period large quantities of coin from the mint at Trier found their way to Britain; the numbers of coins from other, more remote mints is also impressive, though those from eastern mints are outnumbered by issues from other western mints. Once again part of the explanation may lie with the way the coin was distributed in the first place in order to discharge the debts of the state. London may not have produced enough coinage for the diocese's needs, though, if this were the case, it is puzzling to find so many examples of her coins across the Channel, even if not all reached their destination within a short period of their minting. As Callu (1980) has argued with late Roman coin finds from Mediterranean sites, it is difficult to account for the widespread diffusion of issues from certain mints unless trade and general economic interaction is responsible. As the number of operational mints declines in the 4th century, so it becomes increasingly difficult to identify particular areas of circulation, as provinces and dioceses come to draw from a shrinking pool of mints.

Other evidence (Figure 5.7) can now be introduced to complement that of the coinage to link Britain, particularly the southeast, with northern Gaul (north of the Loire). It may be appropriate to extend this zone eastwards to include the lower Rhine. If we take first the evidence of pottery (Fulford 1977; 1987b) we find that Argonne ware of the late 3rd to early 5th century date is found widely distributed in Gallia Belgica and along the Rhine. It is also found in southeastern Britain in appreciable amounts, focussing on the areas either side of the Thames estuary. Likewise Oxfordshire ware, which is the major fine ware of southern Britain, is found in some quantities in northwestern Gaul, probably traded out via the Thames and Kent. Other complementary and overlapping distributions include those of cooking wares, such as Mayen ware, which has a linear distribution along the Rhine (Redknap 1987) and across the Thames to Britain, where finds like Argonne ware concentrate either side of the estuary. Southern British black-burnished ware (Dorset BB 1) has a marked western emphasis in its distribution and is, correspondingly, found mostly in Normandy and Brittany (Martin and Dufournier 1983), suggesting a western Channel trade-axis to complement that of the Rhine - Thames (Fulford 1987b). The continuation of Atlantic traffic is evidenced by céramique à l'éponge, which originates in western Gaul and may best be considered as part of the continuing undercurrent of long distance traffic (see below, and Galliou *et al.* 1980). It is found in southern Britain. In addition to pottery, certain types of glass ware attributed to Rhenish or northern Gaulish glass-houses, such as engraved bowls and 'Frontinus' bottles, are reasonably common in Britain (Price 1978). The interlocking character of the distributions of this range of artefacts between northern Gaul, Germany and Britain recalls the patterns of coin circulation described above.

Clearly cross-Channel traffic in the later Roman period was not just confined to low-value artefacts and coin with a sprinkling of exotic, luxury goods. But what were the main cargoes (cf. Fulford 1977; 1978)? Written sources are of some help. Panegyrics dated to the late 3rd and beginning of the 4th century allude to the quality of British wool; woollen items listed in Diocletian's price edict, which was promulgated in the eastern empire, also hint at the importance of British woollens, if not the wool itself (Wild 1970; 1978). However we must recognise that there is no quantitative data to amplify these sources and that we may only be dealing with luxury items. The same holds true with the evidence of food exports. There is the tantalising story of Julian building a fleet in the late 350s to transport grain from Britain to supply the Rhineland, which had been devastated by Germanic raids. While Zosimus depicts this as an extraordinary measure, other sources imply that Julian was restoring the *status quo* (Frere 1967:349; Wightman 1985:267–68). There is no reason, on archaeological grounds, why we should not believe that there was a regular traffic of grain from Britain in the 4th century. On the other hand, if we interpret the volume of traffic in low-value goods as an index of the scale of that grain supply, the latter was not very large. Unless the barges were very small, we should not assume that they normally approached a figure of 600 (or 800!). Nevertheless this example serves to illustrate a degree of economic interdependence (at subsistence level) between Britain, north Gaul and the lower Rhineland, which is supported by the artefactual evidence described above. Finally, we should not overlook minerals. The wreck off the north coast of Britanny carrying inscribed lead ingots of British origin is probably of 3rd or 4th century date (L'Hour 1987). Also, as Bayard and Massy (1983:154) suggest, the late Roman lead coffins in northern and western Gaul were probably made of British lead. In return Britain received precious metal (such as the Mildenhall treasure), wine, textiles and a host of other goods.

While the pattern of Britain's trade in the early Roman period is consistent with its position as an active frontier of the empire, that of the later Roman period is quite different. Its volume and character in the archaeological record are not dissimilar to those of the medieval period (Fulford 1978), but are consistent with the regionalisation of the late empire. Otherwise there are no obvious 'imperial' characteristics. Now that we have begun to define the changing character of Britain's economic relations with the rest of the empire, it is important to acquire comparative material from other provinces to set it all in context.

Acknowledgements

I am grateful to Brian Williams for drawing all the figures.

December 1987.

References

Allen D.F. 1975 Cunobelin's gold. *Britannia* 6:1–19.

Bayard D. and Massy J.-L 1983. *Amiens Romain. Samarobriva Ambianorum. Revue Archéologique de Picardie*, Heilly.

Bogaers J.E. 1983 Foreign Affairs. In B. Hartley and J. Wacher (eds.), *Rome and her Northern Provinces*. Gloucester: Alan Sutton, 13–32.

Boon G.C. 1969 Belgic and Roman Silchester: the excavations of 1954–8 with an excursus on the early history of Calleva. *Archaeologia* 102:1–81.

Boon G.C. 1974 Counterfeit coins in Roman Britain. In J. Casey and R. Reece (eds.), *Coins and the Archaeologist*. BAR 4. Oxford, 95–171.

Callu J.P. 1980 The distribution and the role of the bronze coinage from 348–392. In C.E. King (ed.), *Imperial Revenue, Expenditure and Monetary Policy in the Fourth Century AD*. BAR S76. Oxford, 95–124.

Casey P.J. 1977 Carausius and Allectus - rulers in Gaul? *Britannia* 8: 283–301.

Cleere H. and Crossley D. 1985 *The Iron Industry of the Weald*. Leicester.

Cunliffe B.W. 1984a Iron Age Wessex: Continuity and Change. In B.W. Cunliffe and D. Miles (eds.), *Aspects of the Iron Age in Central Southern Britain*. University Committee for Archaeology Monograph 2. Oxford, 12–45.

Cunliffe B.W. 1984b Relations between Britain and Gaul in the first century BC and early first century AD. In S. Macready and F.H. Thompson (eds.), *Cross-Channel Trade between Gaul and Britain in the Pre-Roman Iron Age*. Society of Antiquaries Occasional Paper 4. London, 3–23.

Cunliffe B.W. 1987 *Hengistbury Head Dorset Vol.1. The Prehistoric and Roman Settlement, 3500 BC–AD 500*. University Committee for Archaeology Monograph 13. Oxford.

Drinkwater J.F. 1983 *Roman Gaul: the Three Provinces 58 BC–AD 260*. London.

Fitzpatrick A. 1985 The distribution of Dressel 1 amphorae in northwest Europe. *Oxford Journal of Archaeology* 4(3): 305–40.

Fulford M. 1977 Pottery and Britain's Foreign Trade in the later Roman Period. In D.P.S. Peacock (ed.), *Pottery and Early Commerce*. London, 35–84.

Fulford M. 1978 The interpretation of Britain's late Roman trade: the scope of medieval historical and archaeological analogy. In J. du Plat Taylor and H. Cleere (eds.), *Roman Shipping and Trade: Britain and the Rhine Provinces*. CBA Research Report 24. London, 59–69.

Fulford M. 1984a *Silchester Defences 1974–80*. Society for Promotion of Roman Studies Britannia Monograph 5. London.

Fulford M. 1984b Demonstrating Britannia's economic dependence in the first and second centuries. In T.F.C. Blagg and A. King (eds.), *Military and Civilian in Roman Britain*. BAR 136. Oxford, 129–142.

Fulford M. 1987a *Calleva Atrebatum*: an interim report on the excavation of the oppidum, 1980–6. *Proceedings of the Prehistoric Society* 53:271–8.

Fulford M. 1987b La céramique et les échanges commerciaux sur la Manche à l'époque romaine. In L. Rivet (ed.) *Societé Française d'Etude de la Céramique Antique en Gaule: Actes du Congrés de Caen 1987*. Marseille, 95–106.

Galliou P. 1984 Days of Wine and Roses? Early Armorica and the Atlantic Wine Trade. In S. Macready and F.H. Thompson (eds.), *Cross-Channel Trade between Gaul and Britain in the Pre-Roman Iron Age*. Society of Antiquaries Occasional Paper 4. London, 24–36.

Galliou P., Fulford M. and Clément M. 1980 La diffusion de la céramique 'à l'éponge 'dans le nord-ouest de l'empire romain. *Gallia* 38:265–278.

Going C.J. 1987 *The Mansio and other sites in the southeastern sector of Caesaromagus: the Roman pottery*. CBA Research Report 62. Chelmsford Archaeological Trust Report 3.2.

Gowland W. 1901 The early metallurgy of silver and lead. Part 1: Lead. *Archaeologia* 57(2):359–422.

Green C. 1980 Roman Pottery. In D.M. Jones (ed.), *Excavations at Billingsgate Buildings 'Triangle', Lower Thames Street, 1974*. London and Middlesex Archaeological Society Special Paper No. 4:39–81.

Haselgrove C.C. 1982 Wealth, prestige and power: the dynamics of political centralisation in southeast England. In C. Renfrew and S. Shennan (eds.), *Ranking, Resource and Exchange*. Cambridge, 79–88.

Haselgrove C.C. 1984 Romanisation before the Conquest: Gaulish precedents and British consequences. In T.F.C. Blagg and A.King (eds.), *Military and Civilian in Roman Britain*. BAR 136. Oxford, 5–63.

Hassall M. 1978 Britain and the Rhine Provinces: epigraphic evidence for Roman Trade. In J. du Plat Taylor and H. Cleere (eds.), *Roman Shipping and*

Trade: Britain and the Rhine provinces. CBA Research Report 24. London, 41–48.

Hawkes C.F.C. and Hull M.R. 1947 *Camulodunum: First Report on the Excavation at Colchester, 1930–1939*. Society of Antiquaries Research Report 14. Oxford.

Helbaek H. 1964 The Isca Grain. A Roman plant introduction in Britain, *The New Phytologist* 63:158–64.

Hingley R. 1982 Roman Britain: the structure of Roman Imperialism and the consequences of Imperialism on the Development of a peripheral province. In D. Miles (ed.), *The Romano-British Countryside*. BAR 103(1). Oxford, 17–52.

Hopkins K. 1980 Taxes and trade in the Roman Empire (200 BC–AD 400). *Journal of Roman Studies* 70:101–125.

Hurst H.R. 1985 *Kingsholm*. Gloucester Archaeological Reports 1. Cambridge.

James S. 1984 Britain and the late Roman Army. In T.F.C. Blagg and A. King (eds.), *Military and Civilian in Roman Britain*. BAR 136. Oxford, 161–86.

Kent J.P.C. 1981. The origins of coinage in Britain. In B.W. Cunliffe (ed.), *Coinage and Society in Britain and Gaul: some current problems*. CBA Research Report 38. London, 41–43.

King. A. 1981 The decline of samian ware manufacture in the northwest provinces: problems of chronology and interpretation. In A. King and M. Henig (eds.), *The Roman West in the Third Century*. BAR S109. Oxford, 55–78.

King C.E. 1981 The circulation of coins in the western provinces AD 260–295. In A. King and M. Henig (eds.), *The Roman West in the Third Century*. BAR S109. Oxford, 89–126.

L'Hour M. 1987 Un site sous-marin sur le côte de l'Amorique: l'épave de Ploumanac'h. *Revue Archéologique de l'Ouest* 4:113–131.

Marsh G. 1981 London's samian supply and its relationship to the development of the Gallic samian industry. In A.C. and A.S. Anderson (eds.), *Roman Pottery Research in Britain and Northwest Europe*. BAR S123. Oxford, 173–238.

Martin T. and Dufournier D. 1983 Recherches sur la diffusion de la black-burnished ware sur le littoral bas-normand au IV siècle. *Actes du 150 Congrès National des Sociétes Savantes, Caen, 1980. La Normandie Etudes Archéologiques*. Paris: 65–83.

Middleton P. 1979 Army supply in Roman Gaul: an hypothesis for Roman Britain, In B.C. Burnham and H.B. Johnson (eds.), *Invasion and Response: the case of Roman Britain*. BAR 73. Oxford, 81–97.

Miller L., Schofield J. and Rhodes M. (ed. T. Dyson) 1986 *The Roman Quay at St. Magnus House, London. Excavations at New Fresh Wharf, Lower Thames Street, London 1974–78*. London and Middlesex Archaeological Society Special Paper No. 8. London.

Millett M. 1980 Aspects of Romano-British Pottery in West Sussex. *Sussex Archaeological Collections* 118:57–68.

Milne G. 1985 *The Port of Roman London*. London.

Partridge C. 1981 *Skeleton Green*. Society for the Promotion of Roman Studies Britannia Monograph No. 2. London.

Peacock D.P.S. and Williams D.F. 1986 *Amphorae and the Roman Economy*. London.

Price J. 1978 Trade in glass. In J. du Plat Taylor and H. Cleere (eds.), *Roman shipping and trade: Britain and the Rhine provinces*. CBA Research Report 24. London, 70–78.

Pritchard F.A. 1986 Ornamental stonework from Roman London. *Britannia* 17:169–89.

Redknap M. 1987 *Mayener Ware and Eifelkeramik: the Roman and medieval pottery industries of the West German Eifel*. University of London unpublished Ph.D.

Reece R. 1973 Roman Coinage in Britain and the Western Empire. *Britannia* 4:227–51.

Richardson B. 1986 Pottery. In Miller *et al*. 1986, 96–138.

Sealey P.R. 1985 *Amphoras from the 1970 Excavation at Colchester Sheepen*. BAR 142. Oxford.

Smith C.R. 1907 *Proceedings of the Society of Antiquaries of London*. 2nd Series 21 (1906–7): 268–92.

Smith C.R. 1909 *Proceedings of the Society of Antiquaries of London*. 2nd Series 22 (1907–9): 395–414.

Straker V. 1987 Carbonised cereal grain from first century London: a summary of the evidence for importation and crop processing. In P. Marsden (ed.), *The Roman Forum Site in London: discoveries before 1985*. London, 151–155.

Todd M. 1981 *Roman Britain 55 BC–AD 400*. London.

Todd M. 1987 *The South West to AD 1000*. London.

Tylecote R.F. 1986 *The Prehistory of Metallurgy in the British Isles*. London.

Wheeler R.E.M. and Wheeler T.V. 1936 *Verulamium. A Belgic and Two Roman Cities*. Society of Antiquaries London Research Report 11. Oxford.

Wightman E.M. 1985 *Gallia Belgica*. London.

Wild J.P. 1965 A Roman silk damask from Kent. *Archaeologia Cantiana* 80:246–50.

Wild J.P. 1970 *Textile Manufacture in the northern Roman provinces*. Cambridge.

Wild J.P. 1978 Cross-Channel trade and the textile industry. In J. du Plat Taylor and H. Cleere (eds.) *Roman Shipping and trade: Britain and the Rhine Provinces*. CBA Research Report 24. London, 79–81.

Willems W.J.H. 1984 Romans and Batavians: a regional study in the Dutch Eastern River Area, II. *Ber. Rijksdienst Oudheidkund. Bodemonderz.* 34:39–331.

Wilmott T. 1982 Excavations at Queen Street, City of London 1953 and 1960, and Roman timber-lined wells in London. *Transactions of the London and Middlesex Archaeol. Soc.* 33:1–78.

6.   Pottery in the Later Roman North: a case study

Jeremy Evans

Much of the pioneering work in Romano-British pottery studies originally took place in the Roman north, the first real breakthrough being made before the First World War by F.G. Simpson and Philip Newbold (Gibson and Simpson 1909 and 1911; Newbold 1913a and 1913b) on small scale excavations at Haltwhistle Burn, Limestone Bank, Poltross Burn and High House. The careful study of the pottery from these sites helped to refine the chronology of northern material and it also provided the first quantitative data on the forms (and to some extent the fabrics) present. After the First World War much further work took place on pottery from the frontier which considerably refined the chronology of northern material, both by E.B. Birley and principally by the late J.P. Gillam (Birley 1930; Hodgson and Richmond 1938; Richmond and Gillam 1951; Gillam 1957) but quantification was left to M.R. Hull who continued Simpson's and Newbold's methodology first on the northern Signal Stations (Hull 1932) and finally on the Camulodunum material (Hawkes and Hull 1947).

The lack of known kiln sites and the main interest in chronology at the time when efforts in quantification took place in the north led to little attempt being made at studying trade patterns through pottery and when these were taken up (Gillam 1939, 1951a) quantification had been abandoned (only occasionally being used (Gillam 1957) on late 4th century material, probably because Hull's Signal Stations report (1932) was available for comparison).

The study of trade patterns in the north from pottery without the use of quantification has led to some useful, but in some ways rather misleading studies. To the student in southern Britain who examines the literature but not the material in the north, Dales ware (Gillam 1951a; Loughlin 1977), Derbyshire ware (Gillam 1939), Black Burnished ware category 1 and Black Burnished ware category 2 (henceforth BB1 and BB2, Gillam 1976; Gillam and Greene 1981; Williams 1977) would appear to be the main fabric types in the north in the 3rd-earlier 4th centuries A.D. But the former two fabrics do not appear to exceed 1% of any northern assemblages of the period north of York. Similarly it is well known that Crambeck and Huntcliff type calcite gritted fabrics were major elements in northern supply in the late 4th century, but the shape of that distribution is only just becoming clear (Evans 1989a) and explanations for it have been rarely advanced.

Quantified and semi-quantified reports are now slowly beginning to appear (Perrin 1981; Rigby 1980; Bidwell 1985) though there appears to be a danger that they will quantify fabrics without quantifying forms. Analytical work on northern pottery was pioneered by Richards (1960), Williams (1977) and Loughlin (1977) and has advanced our knowledge of fabric distribution from particular sources, but, because it was not framed within quantitative studies, by itself it has contributed little to our knowledge of the relative importance of these fabrics in supply within the region, or to the presence of competition or otherwise between them.

To turn from studies of fabric supply to supply itself in the area from the Humber-Mersey line to the frontier in the 3rd and 4th centuries; one of the most persistent features throughout this period is the great divide between supply in east Yorkshire and supply over the rest of the region, as Rigby has noted (1980:94). Within east Yorkshire the vast bulk of pottery in use comes from within the region, with some material from north Lincolnshire, but little from without the region except such specialist items as mortaria and colour-coated wares which were not manufactured locally. Throughout the rest of the north and especially in the north-west most pottery was imported into the region, and even in the north-east large quantities of material were imported, especially BB2, though there is growing indirect evidence of some local production in the Catterick region (Hartley K. forthcoming; Bell and Evans forthcoming) and probably in County Durham (Evans 1985).

The source of the bulk of ceramic supply, locally or from distant sources, seems to reflect other deep differences between these two areas. In east Yorkshire and also in the Vale of York pottery is supplied in quantity across the whole spectrum of the settlement hierarchy, to forts, towns, villas and rural sites. In County Durham some rural sites do consume reasonable amounts of pottery e.g. Catcote in the lowlands (Long 1988), but sites in the Pennines and the north-west appear to consume very little indeed, little if any more than sites in Northumberland, beyond the frontier. Pottery arrives in quantity at forts, vici and the military towns of Carlisle, Kirkby Thore and Corbridge, but there are no villas, and rural sites are almost aceramic.

In these circumstances the contrasts in supply become easier to explain, because, though little excavated, rural sites must have accounted for the vast majority of the population, as in any agrarian society. If towns and vici were not operating as nodes in a distribution network, but, like the forts, as isolated pools of 'Romanised' consumers, then the lack of an indigenous pottery industry continuing on from the 2nd century military associated kilns (Swan 1984, Map 4) may be more explicable. A local industry which did not have a concentration of consumers, but only isolated pools of them, would have to sustain high transport costs to succeed, whereas a large scale producer like BB1 might plug into supply routes in other commodities, where the pre-existence of bulk movements reduced transport costs (King 1981).

On this model the *vici* and the towns of the north-west did not serve as markets for their rural hinterland, for ceramics at least, but only served the Roman military market, directly subsidised by the flow of military pay and supplies out of taxation. Whether or not this was the case, the lack of a pottery industry in the north-west after the 2nd century certainly deserves an explanation.

The other side of the ceramic divide is also rather curious, ie. the ceramic isolation of east Yorkshire. This breaks down in the early 4th century with the rise of the Crambeck industry and the export of reasonable quantities of the early to mid fourth century calcite gritted ware forms into the north-east, but is very marked still in the 3rd century. Knapton type jars are ubiquitous throughout the region in the period and, whilst it is not certain, it seems probable that many of them originate from a single source. More surely, Holme-on-Spalding Moor products are widely and commonly found in the southern part of the region, apparently being a major item in assemblages of later 3rd and especially early 4th century date over much of the area south of the Vale of Pickering. Both of these industries supply across the predicted market areas of several towns in east Yorkshire, but they do not seem to reach in any quantity at all into the predicted market area of York, a lesser distance than areas supplied in quantity within the region. The key to explaining this phenomenon would seem to be that York is in a different *civitas* and that some form of social constraint was still operating on trade across the tribal boundary (Evans 1988).

This is not to suggest that the economy of east Yorkshire was embedded (there would seem to be some cause to suggest that this was nearer the case for much of the economy in the northwest where the full package of 'Romanisation' seems barely to have penetrated), but it does seem possible that the area remained socially and culturally isolated, preferring its own symbols to those of more distant areas.

Outside the fort at Malton, where traditional oxidised northern 'military type' ceramics were in use, the 1st to 2nd century groups from such sites as Langton (Corder and Kirk 1932), Crossgates (Corder 1958), Rudston (Rigby 1980) and Beadlam (Evans and Rigby in prep) were all dominated by ceramics in 'native' tradition and the 'Romanized' types at these sites seem more related to grey ware north Lincolnshire types, a region with which the east Yorkshire area seems to have had continuing ceramic contacts (Swan 1984). In contrast, the site at Lingcroft Farm near York, though it may be exceptional, converted to the use of 'Romanised' style material in quantity far quicker (Jones 1988). Though somewhat outside the brief of this paper, there also seems to be a rather sharp ceramic boundary down to the early 4th century between the south Yorkshire area and the southern Vale of York, with south Yorkshire and Dales ware products apparently being common at Doncaster in the 3rd century (Loughlin 1977, note 35) yet fifteen miles further north at Castleford in the late 3rd century they are absent and over 60% of the assemblages is supplied by BB1 (Evans 1985).

In the northern region excluding east Yorkshire,

BB1 and BB2 are major fabric types in the 3rd century, together with a series of sandy grey wares generally reflecting the forms of these, though there would seem to be greater conservatism in typological change amongst these grey wares. The most important paper on BB1 and BB2 in the north came from the late John Gillam (Gillam and Greene 1981) who, through a formula of predicted transport costs and relative numbers of the two types from sites, has attempted to show evidence of competition between BB1 and BB2 across the frontier. In terms of his relative quantification he found good evidence that transport costs constrained the distribution of the two fabric types and that BB1 was far less circumscribed than BB2, which he accounted for by its quality in terms of its function as a cooking ware. However, there was a clear assumption made in this paper of economic competition between the two fabrics, rather than just transport cost forming a constraint and it was implicit that no other fabric type was involved in this competition. If the latter two points were the case then it might be expected that the combined percentage of BB ware would be a comparatively stable element in assemblages travelling across the frontier, as it appears to be in the case of competition between Oxfordshire and New Forest fine wares (Hodder and Orton 1976, Fig. 5.77). The figures available from published sources and recent examination of 3rd century groups *per lineam valli* (Evans 1985; Evans 1989b) suggest otherwise, with high levels at both coasts dropping in the central sector, which must cast considerable doubt on there being actual competition between the two fabric types rather than merely the constraint of transport costs; though the data are not good enough to demonstrate the point it may be that BB2 was suffering from competition from the grey wares.

The origin of the bulk of the grey wares is difficult to demonstrate. They could originate from somewhere in the Midlands, but there is a lack of such items as Dalesware and south Yorkshire products which might be expected to accompany the grey wares if they arrived from such a source. The grey wares also appear to be concentrated in the north-east. Visual attempts at their classification seem to have been less than wholly successful, but large scale sampling by neutron activation analysis may provide a clue (Evans 1985). This has tended to divide the samples into three basic groups but membership of these is not divided equally at different sites as might be expected if each site was taking a supply from a general flow from beyond this region. Instead individual sites seem to provide a greater proportion of one particular group which would tend to suggest local production in north-east England.

Finally, to turn to the situation in the late 4th century in the north, it is generally known that two major centres one at Crambeck in east Yorkshire, the other somewhere else, probably in the Vale of Pickering, provided much of the ceramics used in the area north of the Humber-Mersey line. However, applying quantitative techniques to assemblages of this period demonstrates that this distribution cannot be easily explained as an economic phenomenon resulting from free market forces. The distribution of Crambeck and Huntcliff types flies in the face of any distribution model constrained by transport costs. Indeed in part there are negative fall-offs with more Crambeck material being found further from the kiln site. Doncaster, south of the Humber, is only *c.* 67km from the kiln site, but it was beyond the core of the Crambeck distribution whilst Lincoln, with a very large late 4th century group (Darling 1977), lacks any trace of Crambeck products and is *c.* 100km from the kiln site. Yet, in the north-west, over the Pennines, Crambeck products are common at Birdoswald (*c.* 147km), Ravenglass (*c.* 165km) and throughout the region up to *c.* 180km from the kiln site. The only obvious explanation of the Crambeck and Huntcliff type distribution, in the north-west at least, is the operation of some form of administrative action, the proverbial 'military contract' (Evans 1989a).

The other striking thing about the Crambeck distribution, in the late 4th century especially, is how dissimilar it is to the other major regional suppliers with which it is usually compared, the Oxfordshire, New Forest, Nene Valley and Alice Holt industries. Unlike the first three of these it is not primarily a fine ware producer; the bulk of Crambeck products are grey wares. There is no major evidence that the fine wares were distributed over a greater area than the grey wares. Unlike Alice Holt the grey ware types are principally tablewares and must have been distributed for that purpose and not as containers for some other commodity.

Fulford (1975) has suggested that the New Forest industry, at least, was producing less material in the late 4th century. This would certainly not seem to be the case for the late 4th century northern industries. As John Gillam has pointed out, 'how abundant they (late 4th century types) are may be gauged from the fact that at South Shields in 1966 and 1967 there were more vessels of defined Crambeck types (Corder and Birley 1937), or of developed Huntcliff types, than there were of all other types from all other levels of the site taken together, and this in spite of the fact that developed Crambeck and Huntcliff types were on the market for less than one sixth of the total period of occupation' (Gillam 1973, 62).

The end of the Crambeck industry would seem to come early in the 5th century. There is no evidence of the types continuing in production after coin-use had ceased, which Reece (1974) suggests should be in the second or third decades of the century. A few pieces are found on two early Saxon sites in east Yorkshire at Wykeham (Moore 1965) and Crossgates Seamer (Rutter and Duke 1958) but there do not seem to be any good grounds for believing in extended production in the 5th century. The end of Roman Britain in the north in ceramic, and indeed other material terms, came with a bang not a whimper, probably within the lifespan of a single generation. The cause of this, perhaps quixotic as it may appear, being the end of taxation in cash (Evans 1983). There is no trace of a sub-Roman ceramic industry. Some trends develop in the 4th to early 5th centuries which might be regarded as representing

some 'de-Romanization' of northern ceramics (such as the re-appearance of Iron Age forms and the rising quantities of handmade fabrics in use), but they belong to the history of 'might have beens' for the 5th century. There is as yet no evidence of any later 5th century northern British ceramic tradition, and this author doubts if there ever will be.

References

Birley E.B. 1930 The pottery. In Richmond I.A. and Birley E.B. Excavations on Hadrian's Wall in the Birdoswald-Pike Hill Sector 1929. *Transactions of the Cumberland and Westmorland Antiquarian and Archaeological Society* 30:169–205.

Corder P. 1958 The pottery. In Rutter J.G. and Duke G. *Excavations at Crossgates near Scarborough, 1947–56.* Scarborough and District Archaeological Society Research Report No.1.

Corder P. and Kirk J.L. 1932 *A Roman villa at Langton, near Malton.* Roman Malton and District Research Report No.4.

Darling M. 1977 *A group of late Roman pottery from Lincoln.* The Archaeology of Lincoln. Vol. 16–1.

Evans J. 1983 Towns and the end of Roman Britain in northern England. *Scottish Archaeological Review* 2 (2):144–149.

Evans J. 1985 *Aspects of later Roman pottery assemblages in northern England.* Unpublished Ph.D thesis, University of Bradford.

Evans, J. 1988 All Yorkshire is divided into three parts: social aspects of later Roman pottery distribution in Yorkshire. In Price, J., Wilson, P.R. and Briggs. S. (eds.) *Recent Research in Roman Yorkshire* BAR 193. Oxford, 323–337.

Evans, J. 1989a Crambeck: the development of a major northern pottery industry. In Wilson, P.R. (ed.) *The Crambeck Roman Pottery Industry.* Leeds.

Evans, J. 1989b Neutron activation analysis and Romano-British pottery studies. In Henderson, J. (ed.), *Scientific Analysis in Archaeology.* Oxford and Los Angeles, 136–162.

Evans J. and Rigby V. in prep. The coarse pottery from Beadlam villa.

Fulford M.G. 1975 *New Forest Roman Pottery.* BAR 17. Oxford.

Gibson J.P. and Simpson F.G. 1909 The Roman fort on the Stanegate at Haltwhistle Burn. *Archaeologia Aeliana* 3rd Series 5:213–285.

Gibson J.P. and Simpson F.G. 1911 The milecastle on the wall of Hadrian at Poltross Burn. *Transactions of the Cumberland and Westmorland Antiquarian and Archaeological Society* 11:390–461.

Gillam J.P. 1939 Romano-British Derbyshire ware. *Antiquaries Journal* 19:429–437.

Gillam J.P. 1951 Dalesware: a distinctive Romano-British cooking pot. *Antiquaries Journal* 31:154–164.

Gillam J.P. 1957 Types of Roman coarse pottery in northern Britain. *Archaeologia Aeliana*, 4th series 35:180–251.

Gillam J.P. 1973 Sources of pottery found on northern military sites. In Detsicas A. (ed.) *Current Research in Romano-British Coarse Pottery.* CBA Research Report 10:53–62.

Gillam J.P. 1976 Coarse fumed ware in north Britain and beyond. *Glasgow Archaeological Journal* 4:57–80.

Gillam J.P. and Greene K. 1981 Roman pottery and the economy. In Anderson A.C. and Anderson A.S. (eds.) *Roman Pottery Research in Northwest Europe.* BAR S123. Oxford.

Hawkes C.F.C. and Hull M.R. 1947 *Camulodunum. First Report on Excavations at Colchester 1930–1939.* Society of Antiquaries of London Research Report 14. Oxford.

Hodder I. and Orton C. 1976 *Spatial Analysis in Archaeology.*

Hodgson K.S. and Richmond, I.A. 1938 The coarse pottery from Bewcastle. In Richmond I.A., Hodgson K.S. and St. Joseph J.K. The Roman fort at Bewcastle. *Transactions of the Cumberland and Westmorland Antiquarian and Archaeological Society* 28:195–237.

Hull M.R. 1932 The pottery from the Roman signal stations on the Yorkshire coast. *Archaeological Journal* 89.

Jones, R.F.J. 1988 The hinterland of Roman York. In Price, J., Wilson, P.R. and Briggs, S. (eds.) *Recent Research in Roman Yorkshire* BAR 193. Oxford:161–170.

King A. 1981 The decline of samian ware manufacture in the northwest provinces: problems of chronology and interpretation. In King, A. and Henig, M. (eds.) *The Roman West in the Third Century.* BAR S109. Oxford, 55–78.

Long C.D., 1988 The Iron Age and Romano-British Settlement at Catcote, Hartlepool. *Durham Archaeological Journal* 4:13–36.

Loughlin N. 1977 Dalesware; a contribution to the study of Roman coarse pottery. In Peacock D.P.S. (ed). *Pottery and Early Commerce: characterisation and trade in Roman and later ceramics.* London, 85–146.

Mitchelson N. 1950 A late fourth century occupation site at Seamer, near Scarborough. *Yorkshire Archaeological Journal* 37:420–429.

Moore J.W. 1965 An Anglo-Saxon settlement at Wykeham. *Yorkshire Archaeological Journal* 41:403–444.

Newbold P. 1913a The pottery and the periods of occupation. In Simpson, F.G. Excavations on the line of the Roman wall in Cumberland during the years 1909–1912. *Transactions of the Cumberland and Westmorland Antiquarian and Archaeological Society* 12:297–397.

Newbold P. 1913b Excavations on the Roman Wall at Limestone Bank. *Archaeologia Aeliana* 3rd Series, 9:54–74.

Perrin J.R. 1981 *Roman pottery from the Colonia: Skeldergate and Bishophill.* The Archaeology of York 16/2.

Reece R. 1974 Numerical aspects of Roman coin hoards in Britain. In Casey, P.J. and Reece R. (eds.), *Coins and the Archaeologist.* BAR 4. Oxford, 78–94.

Richards E.E. 1960 Report on Black Burnished ware from Mumrills. In Steer, K.A. (ed.), Excavations at Mumrills Roman fort, 1958–60. *Proceedings of the Society of Antiquaries of Scotland* 94:129–30.

Richmond I.A. and Gillam, J.P. 1951 The temple of Mithras at Carrawburgh. *Archaeologia Aeliana* 4th Series, 19:1–92.

Rigby V. 1980 The coarse pottery. In I.M. Stead *Rudston Roman Villa.*

Rutter J.G. and Duke, G. 1958 *Excavations at Crossgates near Scarborough, 1947–56.* Scarborough and District Archaeological Society Research Report No.1.

Swan V.G. 1984 *The Pottery Kilns of Roman Britain.* R.C.H.M. Supplementary Series No.5.

Williams D.F. 1977 The Romano-British Black-Burnished industry: an essay on characterisation by heavy mineral analysis. In Peacock, D.P.S. (ed.), *Pottery and Early Commerce: characterisation and trade in Roman and later ceramics.* London.

7. The Urbanisation of Roman Britain

R.F.J. Jones

The towns of Roman Britain were the apex of the settlement hierarchy. Our view of their role and the dynamics of their development lies at the heart of any attempt to understand what was going on in Roman Britain. Was Britain successfully urbanised, suggesting profound changes in social and economic structure? Or were the towns no more than superficial cosmetic changes imposed on a continuing Iron Age system by a combination of a romanised élite and the Roman provincial government?

We know a lot about the towns of Roman Britain, their plans, buildings and historical development, especially when compared with what is known in reliable detail in other provinces of the Roman Empire. In recent decades there have been some very large and expensive excavations carried out in them. Yet attention has too often concentrated on the accumulation of details of topography. The processes of urbanisation are sometimes debated, but less often considered systematically (cf. Frere 1975a; 1979; Jones 1987). The state of information on the larger towns was summarised in the mid-1970s by John Wacher in a book which typifies a common approach (Wacher 1975). The book was able to include the results of a surge of then recent excavations which were unpublished in detail. It still provides an impressive corpus of descriptions and a source of valuable references. What it lacks is any serious attempt to tackle the question of the forces behind the growth and development of towns. In this it has been followed by more recent collections of papers (Grew and Hobley 1985; Schofield and Leech 1987). An important departure has been the rapid growth in new studies of the smaller urbanised settlements, providing a much sounder base on which to discuss them (Rodwell and Rowley 1975; Sommer 1984; Crickmore 1984; Esmonde-Cleary 1987; Smith 1987). We certainly still lack basic information about many aspects of many towns, so that substantial opportunities to discover new evidence from the ground cannot be missed. Nevertheless, we must not shirk the responsibility to try to make sense of what we have, in order to inform the next stages of research.

The most widely accepted models for the pattern of urban development in Roman Britain have derived from work at two towns in the southeast, Silchester and Verulamium, reinforced by observations from slightly further afield at Cirencester and Wroxeter. There have been large scale excavations at these sites, particularly those before the First World War at Silchester, now followed by current work by Michael Fulford, and at Verulamium in the 1930s under Mortimer Wheeler and in the 1950s under Sheppard Frere. It has been into the framework of the results of these excavations that modern city centre digging has been largely fitted. Of modern urban rescue excavations, only those in London have brought about a significant rethink in ideas on urbanisation – and London was outside the common pattern of Romano-British towns (cf. Roskams, this vol.).

It is clear that all urban settlements in Roman Britain did not follow the same path to development. London was distinctive in apparently arising neither as a new foundation of a colonia for Roman legionary veterans, like Colchester, Lincoln and Gloucester, nor as a planned centre for a tribal unit based on native social arrangements, like Verulamium, Cirencester, Caerwent, Leicester and others. Although the constitutional background to the foundation of a town obviously was influential, especially in its early history, in archaeological terms the most useful classification is between the planned and the unplanned towns. The coloniae and tribal centres were the planned towns, with street grids, and a variety of large public buildings and amenities. The unplanned towns were a heterogenous group of substantial nucleated settlements which seem to have grown up without these features. These groupings provide the framework within which the process of urbanisation can be considered. It will be discussed here in terms of its origins, development and end.

Origins

It is now well established that there were large nucleated settlements in pre-Roman Britain, particularly in the southeast (Collis 1984; Cunliffe 1985). It is probable that they had some central place functions, at least in terms of being centres of tribal authority, of some craft specialisation, and of a role in trade and exchange. How far they grew beyond being royal or aristocratic strongholds is uncertain. They can be accepted however as important steps towards urbanisation, revealing the kind of social complexity needed for the successful adaptation to Roman civil life (cf. Groenman-van Waateringe 1980). It is equally clear that there were very substantial differences beween the pre-Roman settlements and their Roman successors, at least in terms of urban form, even where a direct continuation from native oppidum to Roman town can be shown as at Verulamium (Frere 1983).

The planned Roman towns appeared astonishingly quickly. Certain places were chosen for rapid building programmes, characterised by the provision of a regular street grid and Roman types of public building, such as the forum-basilica complex as an administrative and political centre, the bath-house and the amphitheatre. It seems that one centre was chosen for this treatment in each area that became a Roman civitas and that broadly the definition of civitates followed native socio-political groupings. These programmes gave an obvious boost to the chosen sites compared with local centres which grew into the unplanned towns. Their earlier stages are much less known from excavation than their planned neighbours. It seems that their growth was organic and piecemeal, following the expansion of their predominantly economic functions in craft production and exchange. However, the processes by which the planned towns were established should illuminate how far there was a conscious adoption of the Roman model of urban life.

It is now clear that new architectural styles in substantial public buildings and Roman-style shops and workshops of timber were widespread by the later years of the first century AD at tribal centres like Verulamium (Frere 1983), Cirencester (Wacher and McWhirr 1982; McWhirr 1986), Silchester (Fulford 1985), and Exeter (Bidwell 1979). By the mid-second century the towns' main monumental public buildings had been erected in what was to remain their basic form. Fulford's discovery of large-scale buildings in timber at Silchester and his demonstration that the stone phases of public buildings may not have been completed until the second quarter of the second century do not weaken the essential point (Fulford 1985). Whether in timber or stone, buildings were constructed on a monumental scale and with public functions, and the fundamentals of the town plans were laid out in the first century. Such developments are all the more significant because they happened at the tribal centres. Within Britain itself only the colonia at Colchester, founded in 49, can have been seen as a formal model for these new towns, since the coloniae at Lincoln and Gloucester were not set up until around the end of the century. Furthermore, recent excavations at both Colchester and Gloucester have shown that their earliest civilian buildings were of very much the same kind as contemporary ones at Verulamium (Crummy 1984; Hurst 1976; Frere 1972).

The speed of urban development in the tribal centres demands explanation. There can be little question that they were rapidly provided with the characteristic features of the classical Roman town, in its northern provincial version. What is debated is whether the impetus for this growth came from the Roman administration or from the native aristocracy. The case for Roman government action rests on three points: the fact that some kind of Roman military base preceded many towns, the design of the forum-basilica complex at many sites, and a sentence in Tacitus' life of Agricola.

The idea that Romano-British urban settlements, large and small, derived from the civil settlements adjacent to early forts was first fully set out by Webster (1966). He argued that settlements developed alongside the conquest forts to supply the needs of the troops, but that when the army moved on some at least of the civilians stayed on to create the civil town. The case was based on the observation that early military finds had been made at many places which had later become towns. It was reinforced by the example of the early years of Cirencester, tribal centre of the Dobunni. The Roman town of Cirencester was built on the site of

the Roman army's fort and attendant civil settlement, rather than at the pre-Roman centre of Bagendon 5 km away (Wacher 1975:30–2).

At many towns in Britain, but not all, the plan of the forum seems to resemble more a military principia (headquarters building) than civilian fora in continental Europe, especially because the plan often did not include a temple on the side opposite to the basilica (Atkinson 1942:345–62; cf. Todd 1985).

The argument for military and government involvement in building the towns of Roman Britain is sparked by a short passage by Tacitus in his life of his father-in-law Agricola, governor of Britain from 78 to 84. Describing the year 79, Tacitus wrote:

> Hortari privatim, adiuvare publice, ut templa, fora, domos extruerent, laudando promptos, castigando segnes
>
> (Agricola:21)

The basic sense is straight forward – 'he encouraged privately and helped publicly (the Britons) to build temples, fora and houses, praising the speedy and criticising the slow'. This is commonly interpreted as meaning that soldiers were seconded to build towns, although it is not usually stated in what capacity they might have worked.

There are many weaknesses in all three of these arguments. Tacitus' sentence has received many glosses, some verging on the fanciful. It is hard to recall how few the actual words are when reading some of the elaborate confections built upon them in some standard texts on Roman Britain (cf. Blagg 1984:249–50). Agricola's aims are clear enough. The crucial issue is how he carried them out and whether his policies were continued for the next half century, the period over which the construction of public buildings went on. On that Tacitus says nothing; all the interpretations are of our own manufacture.

The link between Romano-British fora and military principia has long been disputed on grounds of a common root for both types of plan in late Republican and early Imperial architecture in northern Italy (Goodchild 1946; Ward-Perkins 1970). Recently more detailed studies have rejected significant connections between military and civilian architecture and craftsmen (Blagg 1980; 1984; this vol.).

Webster's case has firmer support in that there were undoubtedly military bases of some sort at many of the sites on which towns were established. However to have a key influence on urban origins the military presence must be assumed to have been a full-scale fort, even though the pattern of military dispositions in the conquest period is still poorly understood. In some cases there may only have been small detachments present for short spells, hardly enough to generate a significant attached settlement. Still there were places with sustained garrisons, as at Cirencester where there was military occupation for nearly thirty years. In that time the place became an important route centre for Roman roads. When the army moved out, the fort site provided an open area set into the newly created road system. It was therefore a logical choice for the construction of a new town suited to the new conditions of the Roman province.

The issue of a positive choice is crucial. By definition the planned towns were deliberate; they resulted from a decision made to build them in a certain way in a certain place. Who took the decision? That question leads to the most fundamental weakness in the arguments for the towns being Roman government initiatives. They fail to take proper account of the social and economic structures of the native British population (cf. Jones 1987). Firstly, the forts of the conquest period very likely were located reflecting the distribution of existing native settlements, since concentrations of potentially hostile people were at least as important strategic considerations as river-crossings (cf. Breeze 1985). =Webster's case then required a group of left-over camp followers to have achieved sufficient power within the native tribal structures to have been able to determine where the centre of tribal administration should be located. This seems implausible, given the standard Roman policy of setting up local government in a new province by minimal modifications to existing arrangements. The sudden growth of the tribal centres was much more probably the result of decisions taken by the aristocracies of the tribes themselves. Without strong evidence to the contrary we should not reject the common pattern of urban development throughout the Roman Empire, where the local élites paid for the town buildings and amenities in one way or another (Duncan-Jones 1985). The passage in *Agricola* is hardly explicit enough to support an alternative view. The people leading the surge of building in the late first and early second centuries were then the tribal élites, the very group supposed to have been encouraged by Agricola to do so. They were not however the same individuals who had been in charge at the time of the conquest in 43. A new generation had taken over by the Flavian period who had grown up in a Roman province. The decision to build towns in Roman style was a measure of their commitment to new ways of the Roman Empire.

The origins of the unplanned towns are naturally more hazy, since by definition they did not appear as the result of deliberate acts of foundation. Many seem to show occupation from the later first century. Frere (1975b) argued strongly for military antecedents for the smaller towns, on the grounds that many more of them showed evidence of some kind of early military activity than of any iron age phase. The kind of process typically advanced by those who favour the theory of military origins fits the smaller towns much better than the tribal centres, since they raise none of the broader issues of political power within tribal society. Nevertheless more recent studies have argued that the military case is at best unproven, that the creation of posting stations along the major roads may have acted as a more significant stimulus to the growth of nucleated settlements (Smith 1987:7–9), that the main force behind the successful development of small towns was their incorporation into the new communications system (Burnham 1986). Both these lines of argument reinforce the idea that the unplanned towns were organic growths spawned by economic forces.

Development

What was built so rapidly in the late first and early second centuries was the most visible part of the large towns, the public buildings and the streets. They were the framework of their towns: the details were filled in more gradually. Shops and workshops came almost immediately, as at Verulamium (Frere 1972). Large private houses for the élites themselves seem not to have been built for another generation or more (cf. Walthew 1975). The mobilisation of will and resources seen in the initial setting up of the towns did not however provide the criteria on which to judge the overall success or failure of urbanisation in Roman Britain. Those criteria are to be found in measuring the vitality of continuing urban life through the succeeding decades and centuries, the maintenance of public amenities and the development of economic life. In economic terms the planned and unplanned towns come together, since the unplanned towns appear to have been predominantly economic entities, lacking the broader range of central place functions revealed by the wider variety of building types found in the planned towns.

Size

There is one apparently simple measure of urban success – how big did towns become? Although estimating ancient populations is notoriously difficult, it cannot be ducked here. Establishing some order of magnitude for urban populations is essential for understanding what kind of places the towns were. The only explicit contemporary statistic comes from Tacitus, recording the Roman losses in the Boudican revolt at Colchester, Verulamium and London. He gives a figure of seventy thousand dead (Tacitus, *Annals* XIV:33). This seems a very high figure for a time less than twenty years after the first conquest of Britain, especially as it apparently refers to deaths, not just casualties. There is no particular reason why Tacitus should have inflated the total of Roman losses by a significant factor. Nevertheless, there has been a reluctance to accept the implications of these figures, that there were populations in the order of twenty thousand at each of the three towns. Most have concluded that there must have been large numbers of people taking temporary refuge in the towns, or that Tacitus simply got the figures wrong. That view tends to be supported by the archaeological evidence for the towns at this time, which shows that they were well provided with timber workshops and shops, but hardly on a scale commensurate with Tacitus' figures.

Frere's examination of a variety of approaches and analogies concluded with figures in the order of five thousand for a substantial tribal centre, up to a maximum of perhaps twenty thousand for the biggest places (1987:252–3). This seems consistent with other sources of information such as cemetery populations (cf. Jones 1977, 20; 1984a, 41), and with estimates for comparable towns in other parts of the Roman Empire (Duncan-Jones 1974:259–77). It is also possible to fix some scale from the civilian settlements outside the auxiliary forts. If the garrison was five hundred men, and half of them were married (legally or not), with two surviving children to each union, the total population of the settlement would have been one thousand two hundred and fifty, plus any other traders, veterans and so forth. This estimate seems modest for the size of a fort and vicus population and seems consistent with the figures proposed for the civilian towns, when their respective layouts are considered.

Figures of the order of magnitude of five to ten thousand people in most tribal centres, and one to two thousand in the smaller towns, suggest settlements big enough for the larger ones to have generated substantial service needs for their own populations. Such approximations do not of course allow for any estimate of demographic changes within the Roman period. Equally they do not suggest that any more than a very small proportion of the total population of Roman Britain lived in towns.

The size of area occupied gives a more direct way of assessing the size of towns. It is at least open to direct archaeological measurement, even though difficulties remain over comparing varying intensities of settlement and deciding exactly where a town stops (cf. Esmonde-Cleary 1987). Estimates of population based on the buildings in a town are of limited use. Inevitably, the critical factor of how many people to assign to a house is more or less informed guesswork, but it is only at Silchester and to a lesser extent at Caerwent and Verulamium that we can even begin to reconstruct the Roman townscape. In the later period at least, occupation at these towns seems to have been thinly spread, with plenty of open space, not at all like the labyrinthine congestion of the centre of Pompeii.

The area defended provides some basis for comparison. The lines of the earthwork defences of the British towns were apparently mostly constructed in the later second century (Frere 1984a), and in most cases were broadly followed by later stone circuits. The areas enclosed by the stone defences form a continuum, but the main tribal centres can be rather arbitrarily arranged into three groups. The largest were Cirencester (*c*. 96ha), Verulamium (*c*. 80ha), and Wroxeter (*c*. 72ha), the middle group consisted of Winchester (*c*. 58ha), Canterbury (*c*. 48ha), Leicester, Silchester, Chichester and Exeter (all *c*. 40ha), and the smallest were Dorchester (*c*. 32ha), Aldborough (*c*. 30ha), Caerwent (*c*. 18ha), and Caistor-by-Norwich (*c*. 14ha) (Figure 7.1). Although it is clear that the larger tribal centres, with London and the coloniae, were the biggest and most important towns in the province, there was some overlap in terms of simple size of area between the smaller tribal centres and the bigger unplanned towns. For example, a typical size for an unplanned town would be that of Neatham, of

something between 8 and 14ha (Millett and Graham 1986:154). The extreme case for an unplanned town is Durobrivae (Water Newton), where the most recent estimate suggests that the defended enclosure of *c*. 17ha was only a part of a total area occupied of perhaps 120ha (Esmonde-Cleary 1987:142). Although our knowledge of the internal buildings of the unplanned towns is poor, there is little indication that they were ever provided with the variety of structures which public planning gave to the planned ones: public baths, amphitheatres, or macella.

At Silchester and Caistor-by-Norwich the original layout of the street grid exceeded the area eventually defended (Wacher 1975). At Wroxeter the later defences seem to have enclosed a rather bigger town than was first intended (Barker 1985). These appear to be indicators of how successfully the town developed from the original scheme. The idea can be developed further, following a hint from Frere (1987:254). The size of the forum complex, usually thought to be laid out in the initial plan of the town, can be directly compared with the area enclosed by the defences, where the lines were usually set no earlier than the late second century. Reasonable estimates can be made for both figures in eight cases (Figure 7.2). The proportion of the later defended area occupied by the forum complex is remarkably consistent: Caistor-by-Norwich 3.2%, Caerwent 2.4%, Exeter 2%, Silchester 1.9%, Leicester 1.9%, Wroxeter 1.4%, Verulamium 2.3%, Cirencester 1.8%. Although too much precision cannot be claimed for these calculations, the trend is clear. The hierarchy of the sizes of early forum complexes remained much the same for the hierarchy of later defended areas. It suggests that the initial scheme of town layout was determined by local factors of available wealth, which remained powerful through the Roman period.

Public amenities

After the initial layout of the towns, the greatest change in their topography was the construction of defences. The British towns seem to have been exceptional in the west in having earthwork defences by the end of the second century. It seems that these were built around both major and minor centres at approximately the same time. Only in London was a stone circuit built then (Maloney 1983). Frere (1984a) has argued strongly for a date towards the end of the second century, and for the explanation of the defences that they were a response to an emergency. It is hard to find a convincing alternative, since there is a close consistency in the archaeological dating evidence found at many sites, and the widespread building of defences at this time was clearly anomalous in the Roman west, particularly around small centres. Before then defences were exceptional, and generally indicated high or special status. Earlier defences are known at the coloniae of Colchester, Lincoln and Gloucester, at Verulamium (which also may have had the enhanced legal status of municipium), and at Exeter (where the defences of the earlier legionary fortress were retained). At Silchester, Winchester and

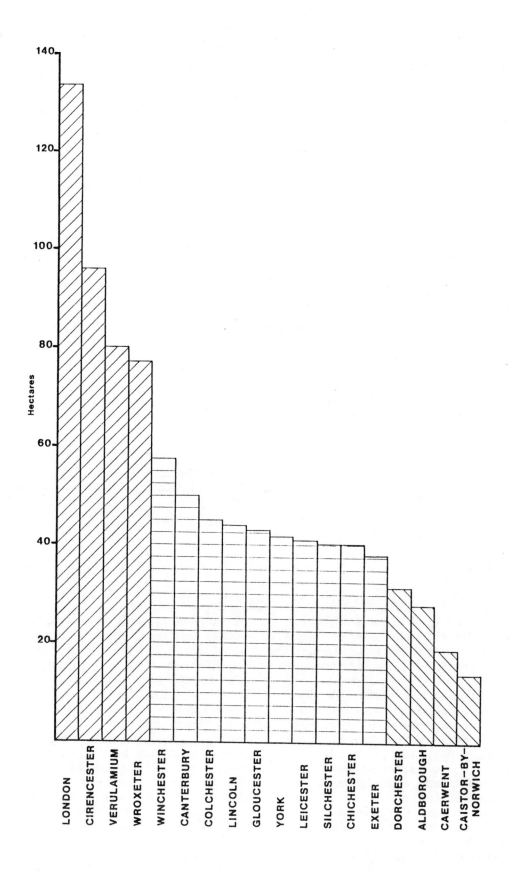

Figure 7.1   The enclosed areas of the larger towns of Roman Britain. These are defined as walled areas except for Gloucester, which includes an estimate of the extra-mural settlement area. Shading defines three size groupings.

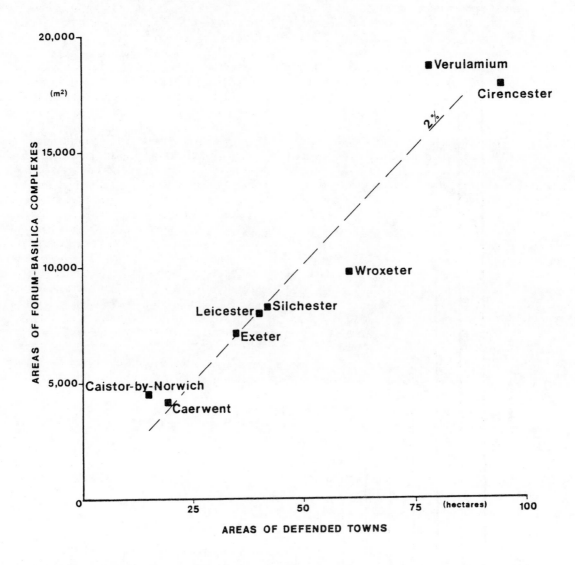

Figure 7.2   The relationship of the areas of forum-basilica complexes to defended areas in Romano-British towns.

Chichester there were earth defences in the first century, but they had exceptional histories as they are presumed then to have lain within the client kingdom of Cogidubnus, and so to have been strictly outside the Roman province (Frere 1984a:66).

Whatever lay behind the surge of rampart building, the defences were clearly deemed worthwhile, since through the third century stone walls were added at most major sites, usually set into the front of the existing earth bank. This process must have been the responsibility of the towns themselves and represents a strong commitment to enhancing public facilities through the third century, and into the fourth when external towers were often added. It is unclear whether the third century building was inspired by ambitions to improve status and appearances or by practical defensive motives. In either case urban defences became a major preoccupation and cost for the towns.

By the later third century the creation of new public buildings had become a rarity. In most places

the perceived essentials of civilised urban life had already been provided; a new forum was hardly necessary. However there has been a growing body of evidence to suggest that important public facilities were abandoned in several places by the end of the third century or early in the fourth. At Wroxeter the forum was burnt down late in the third century and not rebuilt (Atkinson 1942). At Silchester the basilica was used for metal-working from about the same time through the fourth century (Fulford 1985:53–4). At Canterbury and Exeter public baths were abandoned as bath-houses (Blockley 1980; Bidwell 1979:122). Combined with discoveries of general occupation in London being on a much reduced scale from perhaps the middle of the second century (cf. Roskams, this vol.), such discoveries have led to radical reassessments of the whole process of urbanisation in Roman Britain. Reece (1980) argued for a substantial decline in the towns from as early as the mid-third century, and concluded that the experiment had therefore effectively failed.

More thorough assessments of the evidence throughout the province have now shown this picture to be only part of the story (Brooks 1986; Frere 1987:235–56). Modifications or expansion of public facilities can be found through the third and into the fourth centuries: the theatres at Canterbury and Verulamium, the basilicas at Verulamium and Cirencester, the market-hall at Verulamium, the forum at Caistor. The list is at least as convincing as that for the abandonment of public amenities, especially as in excavation changes of use are easier to document than simple maintenance and continuity. Brooks has also shown that the mundane but essential matter of road-mending was kept up at least at Winchester, Cirencester, Lincoln, Gloucester, Colchester and Verulamium (Brooks 1986:82–3).

The best conclusion at present seems to be that the towns retained the necessary facilities and amenities to function as towns through the Roman period at least to the middle of the fourth century. There was change, the trend of which was away from the public grandeur of the first and second centuries. This occurred in different towns at different paces. It was demonstrated more passively than actively. If the forum burnt down as at Wroxeter, the decision taken was the passive one of not rebuilding it, rather than of actively demolishing it.

Economic base

How far did an urban economic base develop? What did the thousands of people in the towns do? Some performed tasks on behalf of the rest of the towns' inhabitants, like street and sewer cleaning. Yet it has been hard to make a convincing picture of the economic activities pursued in the towns; traces of bronze and iron working do not make a metal industry. Most production in the ancient world was organised at no higher than a craft or workshop level. Therefore, even where such activities might have been dominant in a town's economy, the archaeological evidence would tend to consist of a series of separate small or medium-scale workshops. Given the limitations on survival of organic materials like wood, textiles and food, it is hardly surprising that only glimpses of the urban economic base have been documented (cf. Richmond 1966). The explanation for the absence of clear evidence for extensive specialised production inside towns has to be either that such evidence has survived poorly in the archaeological record, or that it was never there at all. If town dwellers were not involved in secondary production or service work, they must have been working in primary production, most probably horticulture, agriculture or animal husbandry. Yet there is even less evidence for any significant commitment to these activities inside Romano-British towns. The occasional building inside a town which may have been used for agricultural purposes, as perhaps in fourth century Cirencester (McWhirr 1986), only serves to underline its peculiarity because of the scarcity of parallels.

Typical urban buildings were the succession of structures in Insula XIV at Verulamium (Frere 1972). What were they for? Our best interpretation available is that those buildings which seem to have been shops and workshops were indeed shops and workshops – and that they were the characteristic workplaces of the majority of town-dwellers. At the centre of any discussion on exchange is the question of the use of money (cf. Reece, this vol.). It is at least clear that coins were being used in towns throughout the period, and up to the fourth century much more in towns than in any other settlements. The role of towns as distribution centres has received some attention, suggesting that they did perform the function to some extent, but it is an area in need of more systematic research (Hodder 1974; Fulford 1982). What is more evident is the place of towns as consumers. The predominance of towns for coin finds in the earlier centuries seems to be matched for almost every other class of artefact. Again there has been very little systematic study of regional distributions of manufactured goods other than pottery, but the quantities of finds from towns appear to be overwhelmingly dominant (e.g. Crummy 1983 from Colchester; Frere 1984b from Verulamium). The distinctive nature of consumption in towns is also shown in the choices of meat eaten (King 1984; this vol.).

Such consumption had to be paid for in some way. If townspeople did not produce their own needs in food, clothing and shelter, they had to obtain them through exchanging what services and goods they did produce. That is the essence of specialisation in an urban economy (cf. Braudel 1981:481). It appears to have applied in Roman Britain to both planned and unplanned towns. There is little to suggest at present that specialised craft production in the countryside on villa estates was developed on a large scale, although some was clearly taking place (e.g. at Langton, Goodall 1972). This does not mean that urban craftsmen and shopkeepers became politically strong or organised enough to take any real power. What evidence there is suggests that real wealth and power remained with the descendants of the tribal aristocracy. It does appear however that there was a distinctive urban economic pattern in Roman Britain, which has important implications for understanding the Romano-British economy as a whole. It means that the towns acted as hubs of specialised production and distribution in a system which embraced the whole of society.

Settlement hierarchies

The extent to which there was real change in settlement pattern in Roman Britain can be best appreciated by examining the overall network of settlements, rather than regarding towns as unique places (cf. Rubertone and Thorbahn 1985; Blanton 1976; Rollwagen 1975). The very simplest classification of nucleated settlements is straightforward and has already been used, planned towns with extensive public buildings and unplanned towns without any. However the picture can be refined by techniques of ranking settlements by their size. Johnson (1981) has argued that size-frequency distribution of settlement is a useful measure of the relative integration of that settlement system. Based upon long-standing geographical approaches, the rank-size measure provides a practical way of describing and comparing settlement systems. Many settlement systems were observed to conform to the rule that there was a linear relationship between rank and size: the second largest settlement in a given system would have half the population size of the largest one, the third largest would have a third the the size of the largest, and so on. Plotted graphically, this arrangement gives a log normal distribution (Figure 7.3). Deviations from this rank-size rule occur when either there is a greater difference between the sizes of the largest and smaller settlements than the rule would suggest ('primate' or 'concave' deviations), or when there is less difference between them ('convex' deviations). Johnson (1981) used a range of examples to argue that convex distributions characterise low levels of integration in the settlement system. He suggests that primate distributions occur when a single large settlement in a region enjoys specially favoured conditions, as in the case of a colonial capital, or where middle sized settlements are missing from the analysis either because they were located outside the region being considered or because they did not exist for some reason. This raises one of the crucial issues determining the validity of this test; do the archaeological data being studied correspond to a meaningful settlement system? Are the boundaries sensibly set? This problem is recognised both by Johnson himself and by Voorrips (1981). There is also considerable debate about the appropriate interpretation of systems that conform to log-normal distributions and those that do not. Nevertheless the approach commends itself as a clear way of studying settlements as inter-related systems; it at least provides a first outline of the relationships in the group of settlements. It has already been used to effect by Willems (1983) for the Dutch Eastern River Area based on postulated population sizes. Our detailed knowledge of Roman Britain allows it to be applied to settlements based upon broadly reliable estimates of the area occupied.

The first set of data considered consists of the defended areas of all the major planned towns of Roman Britain. The pattern is a clearly convex distribution. A simple histogram of the same information suggests that the urban sites may be grouped into three sets (cf. Figure 7.1). The large towns of more than 70ha (London, Cirencester, Verulamium, and Wroxeter), the middle group of 70–40ha (Winchester, Leicester, Colchester, Lincoln, Gloucester, York, Canterbury, Silchester, Chichester and Exeter), and the small group of less than 40ha (Dorchester, Aldborough, Caerwent and Caistor-by-Norwich). There is a weak ranking structure over the province as a whole, suggesting that there was little interaction between individual sites due to a lack of integration into a province-wide system. The size of each town seems from this perspective to have been most effectively defined by local factors, rather than

broader influences. This applies equally when only the presumed tribal capitals are considered.

The next question to pose is whether any greater integration is discernible at a regional level. Urbanised settlements in the territory of the Trinovantes (Rodwell 1975) behave oddly in this analysis. There appear to be two patterns grafted together. Colchester is by far the biggest centre and creates something of a primate effect. Yet at the same time the smaller settlements considered separately from Colchester show a convex pattern and little overall ranking, suggesting that these sites again relied predominantly upon their own positions within their local settlement systems.

Some interpretations of the urban systems of Roman Britain can therefore be put forward. The individual major towns did not articulate well into a province-wide system. They existed much more as centres to their regions. Within those regions they were dominant compared to smaller urban centres. Yet then the same pattern was repeated, with the smaller towns showing little integration into an overall rank system; again they must be presumed to have related most to their local communities. These patterns suggest that urbanisation in Roman Britain drew on local social and economic structures, rather than being an imposed superficial system. Such interpretations can only be preliminary statements about Romano-British urban systems. The crude spatial and chronological measures used here can be substantially refined, and comparisons can be made with other data such as exchange patterns. Nevertheless the approach offers new insights into the process of urbanisation.

The increased attention paid to the unplanned towns in recent years has consolidated the view that they did originate without deliberate pre-planning, although some may have succeeded some military installation (Rodwell and Rowley 1975; Crickmore 1984; Smith 1987; Burnham 1986; Stead and Rigby 1986; Millett and Graham 1986). They continued effectively throughout the Roman period and were defended with earth ramparts in much the same way as the planned towns (Frere 1984a). The clear conclusion to draw is that they performed necessary functions within local social and economic systems, since there is no indication that they were sustained artificially by subsidies for public amenities, as might be claimed for the planned towns. The same conditions of needing to earn a living outside basic food production applied to the inhabitants of the unplanned towns just as much as to those of the large planned town. In most cases the archaeological evidence suggests that their answer lay in the same kinds of economic activities as could be found in the planned towns; those that were carried out in the common workshop-type building, presumably craft production and buying and selling. Exceptional cases drew prosperity from being centres of religious cults, such as Springhead in Kent or most dramatically Bath. Since they were not created by the conscious stimulus of planning, the success of the unplanned towns provides some of the best evidence that urbanisation genuinely occurred.

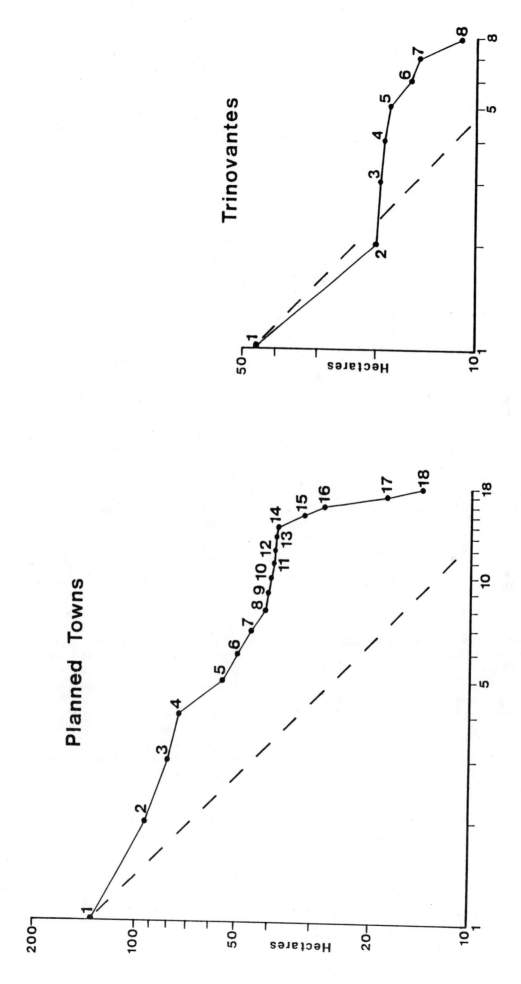

Figure 7.3   Rank size curves for the planned towns of Roman Britain and for the urbanised centres of the Trinovantes (logarithmic scales). The broken line shows the log normal distribution. The planned towns are: 1. London 2. Cirencester 3. Verulamium 4. Wroxeter 5. Winchester 6. Canterbury 7. Colchester 8. Lincoln 9. Gloucester 10. York 11. Leicester 12. Silchester 13. Chichester 14. Exeter 15. Dorchester 16. Aldborough 17. Caerwent 18. Caistor-by-Norwich. The Trinovantes towns are: 1. Colchester 2. Coddenham 3. Hacheston 4. Heybridge 5. Great Chesterford 6. Long Melford 7. Chelmsford 8. Braintree.

Planning was also a characteristic of the early Roman period. Most of the unplanned towns of southern Britain began at that time, broadly contemporary with their planned neighbours. The pattern in the north was different. The growth of nucleated settlement was often demonstrably associated with the army and with continuing military activity. However by the third century there are strong indications of distinct urban settlements with increasing autonomy from the military. By that time the idea of laying out a town with the public amenities expected around AD 100 had waned. It is therefore unreasonable to judge northern urbanisation by the criterion of planned public amenities. The problems of defining civilian and military developments in the north in the later Roman period were recognised by Wacher (1971). It has been generally accepted that Corbridge and Carlisle must be regarded as towns, though usually qualified as 'garrison' or 'frontier towns' (cf. Salway 1965; McCarthy 1984). However the recognition that there was a civilian authority the *civitas Carvetiorum* in Cumbria at least from the mid-third century has wider implications (cf. Higham 1986). Legally therefore this set Cumbria on much the same footing as areas in the south. Also, it must now be counted as likely that a similar organisation was set up in the northeast of England, perhaps with a centre at Corbridge. At the same time fieldwork at a number of sites has demonstrated that the civilian settlements alongside forts were often much larger than is usually appreciated. This is true for example at Binchester, Piercebridge and Chester-le-Street, all in County Durham (cf. Sommer 1984). Where the fort at Binchester covered just under 4ha, there is an area of at least another 8ha covered by the civil settlement, much of it shown by nineteenth century excavation to be intensely occupied with a sequence of stone buildings, in a depth of deposit surviving to 3 metres (cf. Ferris and Jones, this volume). Such civilian activity cannot sensibly be seen as a mere adjunct of the fort. It seems much more probable that it was acting as some kind of central place for the surrounding region. There is thus some difficulty in knowing whether to classify fourth century Binchester as a fort or a town. A similar pattern may be discerned for a number of other sites in the north, suggesting that the urbanisation process was still at work in the north of Roman Britain. The apparent growth of economic activity in the north from the middle to later Roman period provided a pattern of settlement that lacked the planned towns of the early Roman period in the south, but did have parallels with the unplanned towns throughout the province (cf. Jones 1984b). The differences between urbanisation in the north and south may therefore be seen as more in chronology than in substance.

End

The details of excavations and structures related to the end of towns in Roman Britain have been well summarised by Brooks (1986) and Frere (1987). There is now little question that Britain stopped being urbanised and that Anglo-Saxon urban growth did not follow closely upon Roman antecedents. What is in question is how soon the process of Roman urban decline set in, and therefore how substantive the earlier changes had been. Crucial to this argument is the technical archaeological dating of structures and deposits in the fourth and fifth centuries.

The kind of problem is exemplified by the sequence of structures found at Verulamium in Insula XXVII (Frere 1983:220). A Roman town house was dated by a coin of Valens as no earlier than *c*. 380. The subsequent statigraphic sequence of repairs and modifications to that house, a large buttressed building and a water-pipe, are effectively undated. The end of abundant dating materials in the form of coins and pottery dated closely from the coins leaves only a very coarse chronology for any structures that actually were in use at any time after about 380. The possibility of residuality in the coins makes uncertainty the only prudent approach. Even if the coins issued in the late fourth century did not remain in use for the period of up to two centuries recently suggested for Carthage (Reece 1984:172–3), a few coins remaining in people's possession for a few decades would easily distort the neat dating schemes ending in 410 that are sometimes favoured. Our interpretations must therefore always take account of the fact that the latest coin finds on a site provide no more than a strict *terminus post quem*. Therefore when Brooks (1986:83) notes that changes in public buildings at Exeter, Leicester, York and Verulamium took place *in* the late fourth century, it would be more properly put as 'no earlier than the late fourth century'. She also seems to accept the argument from Wacher (1964:14) that the lack of small coins on the floor of the forum piazza in Cirencester suggested that the forum remained in use into the fifth century 'when coinage was no longer in circulation'. This can be no more than speculation based on speculation, since we can only confidently know the date of issue of the coins, not their period of circulation or date of loss.

This argument of course plays havoc with any attempt to make a tidy synthesis based upon the hard evidence of explicit dating material. The ends of this argument are loose, however much we might wish they were not. Yet they lie loose in the first half of the fifth century. The detailed evidence cited by Brooks (1986) and Frere (1987) has demonstrated that urban settlement continued in Roman Britain at least to the late fourth century, effectively refuting Reece's arguments for a much earlier decline (Reece 1980).

Reece's paper did however perform the essential task of focusing attention on the process of urban decline. What in archaeological terms was decline? The most popular criteria are a reduction in the area of a town occupied (seen as equivalent to a reduction in population), lack of maintenance or abandonment of public amenities, and reduction in economic activity. The first two can clearly be shown to have occurred in Romano-British towns (Brooks 1986); the third criterion is elusive throughout, as we have already seen. Since production and distribution centred on towns have not been easy to define, their absence is even more difficult to investigate. We are left with the absence of new coinage in the fifth century and the apparent disintegration of specialist production, or at least specialist pottery production (Fulford 1979). If towns did indeed play a specialised role in the overall economic system, and it is hard to see how they did not, the decline of towns is set inevitably into the context of general economic decline in the Roman West. The towns provided markets for buying and selling. Their disappearance suggests a reduction in scale of such activities, with serious consequences for any farm or estate dependent on those markets.

Yet the economic role of towns provides only part of the picture. Just as the planned towns may have owed their origins to the political agenda of the ruling élites, as argued above, so towns may still have been centres of political authority amid their economic decline. It may be that the water pipe in fifth century Verulamium (Frere 1983) is better explained as a sign of a continuing social authority, rather than of continuing public amenities. The water may have more likely served the residence of some powerful individual or family, rather than a public fountain. Similarly the timber complex discovered at Wroxeter suggests a private residence, not a public monument. Such tantalising evidence points to Roman town sites becoming in the fifth century magnates' residences, in the middle of large areas that were defended, but scarcely populated, rather reminiscent of pre-Roman territorial oppida. If such images are corroborated elsewhere, the continuity of some occupation and of some importance cannot be equated with the continuity of urbanisation.

Conclusions

This essay has attempted to outline the interplay of political and economic factors in the process of urbanisation in Roman Britain. It is my view that the burden of archaeological evidence from the towns points to a continued vitality in both planned and unplanned towns. Large nucleated settlements seem to have served their regions as central places, even if we can often still only guess at what exactly those services were. Documentary and literary evidence from the Mediterranean parts of the Roman Empire show towns filled with specialised craftsmen and providers of services, bakers, barbers and sewer cleaners (e.g. Hopkins 1978; Millar 1981). The archaeological versions of this type of evidence are hard to find. Too much of our discussion of the economic base of Romano-British towns rests on assumptions rather than evidence. We need new and rigorous assessments of what the people who lived in towns actually *did*. The internal evidence from the towns themselves can provide part of the answer. Another perspective can come from systematic studies of the distributional role of towns within their regions (cf. Fulford 1982). Fundamental work is still needed too on the topography of many towns, especially the smaller unplanned ones.

As our information expands in these areas, our understanding of the economic functions of urban settlements will improve. However it seems unlikely that future research will undermine the evidence for rapid and vigorous growth of urban centres in the late first and early second centuries and for the continuation throughout the Roman period of the settlement system then created. These essential points show that change was real. Building upon pre-Roman experiences, but transforming them, urbanisation in the Roman period reveals substantive change in social organisation. Its decline in the late fourth and fifth centuries was equally substantial, with equal implications for change in society. The explanation of that decline which was shared in many parts of the Empire requires more space than can be given here.

References

Atkinson D. 1942 *Report on Excavations at Wroxeter (the Roman City of Viroconium), in the County of Salop 1923–27*. Oxford.

Barker P.A. 1985 Aspects of the topography of Wroxeter (Viroconium Cornoviorum). In *Roman Urban Topography in Britain and the Western Empire*, F.O. Grew and B. Hobley (eds.), pp.109–17. CBA Res Rep 56.

Bidwell P. 1979 *The Legionary Bath-house and Basilica and Forum at Exeter*. Exeter Archaeol Rep 1.

Blagg T.F.C. 1980 Roman civil and military architecture in the province of Britain: aspects of patronage, influence and craft organisation. *World Archaeol* 12(1):27–42.

Blagg T.F.C. 1984 An examination of the connexions between military and civilian architecture. In *Military and Civilian in Roman Britain*, T.F.C. Blagg and A.C. King (eds.), pp.249–64. Oxford: Brit Archaeol Rep, Brit Ser 136.

Blanton R.E. 1976 Anthropological studies of cities. *Annu Rev Anthropol* 5:249–64.

Blockley K. 1980 The Marlowe car park excavations. *Archaeol Cantiana* 96:402–5.

Braudel F. 1981 *The Structures of Everyday Life: the Limits of the Possible*, Transl. S. Reynolds. Collins.

Breeze D.J. 1985 Roman forces and native populations. *Proc Soc Antiq Scot* 115:223–8.

Brooks D.A. 1986 A review of the evidence for continuity in British towns in the 5th and 6th centuries. *Oxford J Archaeol* 5(1):77–102.

Burnham B.C. 1986 The origins of Romano-British small towns. *Oxford J Archaeol* 5(2):185–203.

Collis J.R. 1984 *Oppida. Earliest Towns North of the Alps*. Sheffield: Dept. of Archaeology, Sheffield University.

Crickmore J. 1984 *Romano-British Urban Settlements in the West Midlands*. Oxford: Brit Archaeol Rep, Brit Ser 126.

Crummy N. 1983 *The Roman Small-finds from Excavations in Colchester 1971–79*. Colchester: Colchester Archaeological Report 2.

Crummy P. 1984 *Excavations at Lion Walk, Balkerne Lane and Middleborough, Colchester, Essex*. Colchester: Colchester Archaeological Report 3.

Cunliffe B. 1985 Aspects of urbanisation in northern Europe. In *Roman Urban Topography in Britain and the Western Empire*, F.O. Grew and B. Hobley (eds.), pp.1–5. CBA Res Rep 56.

Duncan-Jones R.P. 1974 *The Economy of the Roman*

Empire. Cambridge: Cambridge University Press.

Duncan-Jones R.P. 1985 Who paid for the public buildings in Roman cities? In *Roman Urban Topography in Britain and the Western Empire*. F.O. Grew and B. Hobley (eds.), pp.28–33. CBA Res Rep 56.

Esmonde-Cleary A.S. 1987 *Extra-Mural Areas of Romano-British Towns*. Oxford: Brit Archaeol Rep, Brit Ser 169.

Frere S.S. 1972 *Verulamium Excavations I*.

Frere, S.S., 1975a. Verulamium and the towns of Britannia. In *Aufstieg und Niedergang der römischen Welt*, H. Temporini (ed.), II,3:290–327.

Frere S.S. 1975b The origin of small towns. In *The Small Towns of Roman Britain*, W. Rodwell and T. Rowley (eds.), pp.4–7. Oxford: Brit Archaeol Rep, Brit Ser 15.

Frere S.S. 1979 Town planning in the western provinces. In *Festschrift zum 75 jährigen Bestehen Römisch-Germanischen Kommission*. Mainz am Rhein: Beiheft zum Bericht der Römisch-Germanischen Kommission 58 :87–103

Frere S.S. 1983 *Verulamium Excavations II*.

Frere S.S. 1984a British urban defences in earthwork. *Britannia* 15:63–74.

Frere S.S. 1984b *Verulamium Excavations III*. Oxford Univ Comm Archaeol Mono 1.

Frere S.S. 1987 *Britannia*, 3rd edn. Routledge.

Fulford M.G. 1979 Pottery production and trade at the end of Roman Britain: the case against continuity. In *The End of Roman Britain*, P.J. Casey (ed.), pp.120–32. Oxford: Brit Archaeol Rep, Brit Ser 71.

Fulford M.G. 1982 Town and country in Roman Britain – a parasitical relationship? In *The Romano-British Countryside*, D. Miles (ed.), pp.403–19. Oxford: Brit Archaeol Rep, Brit Ser 103.

Fulford M.G. 1985 Excavations on the sites of the amphitheatre and forum-basilica at Silchester, Hampshire: an interim report. *Antiquaries J* 65(1):39–81.

Goodall I.H. 1972 Industrial evidence from the villa at Langton, East Yorkshire. *Yorkshire Archaeol J* 44:32–7.

Goodchild R.G. 1946 The origins of the Romano-British forum. *Antiquity* 20:70–7.

Grew F.O. and Hobley B. (eds.) 1985 *Roman Urban Topography in Britain and the Western Empire*. CBA Res Rep 59.

Groenman-van Waateringe W. 1980 Urbanisation and the north-west frontier of the Roman Empire. In *Roman Frontier Studies 1979*, W.S. Hanson and L.J.F. Keppie (eds.), pp.1037–44. Oxford: Brit Archaeol Rep, Inter Ser 71.

Higham N.J. 1986 *The Northern Counties to AD 1000*. Longmans.

Hodder I. 1974 Some marketing models for Romano-British coarse pottery. *Britannia* 5:340–59.

Hopkins K. 1978 Economic growth and towns in classical Antiquity. In *Towns in Societies*, P. Abrams and E.A. Wrigley (eds.), pp.35–77.

Hurst H. 1976 Gloucester (Glevum): a colonia in the West Country. In *The Roman West Country*, K. Branigan and P.J. Fowler (eds.), pp.63–80. David and Charles.

Johnson G.A. 1981 Monitoring complex system integration and boundary phenomena with settlement size data. In *Archaeological Approaches to the Study of Complexity*, S.E. van der Leeuw (ed.), pp.143–88. Cingula 6, Universiteit van Amsterdam.

Jones R. 1977 A quantitative approach to Roman burial. In *Burial in the Roman World*, R. Reece (ed.), pp.20–5. CBA Res Rep 22.

Jones R.F.J. 1984a The cemeteries of Roman York. In *Archaeological Papers from York presented to M.W. Barley*, P.V. Addyman and V.E. Black (eds.), pp.34–42. Yorks Archaeological Trust.

Jones R.F.J. 1984b Urbanisation in the Roman north. *In Settlement and Society in the Roman North*, P.R. Wilson, R.F.J. Jones and D.M. Evans (eds.), pp.87–8. Univ Bradford, Yorks Archaeol Soc.

Jones R.F.J. 1987 A false start? The Roman urbanisation of western Europe. *World Archaeol* 19(1):48–57.

King A.C. 1984 Animal bones and the dietary identity of military and civilian groups in Roman Britain, Germany and Gaul. In *Military and Civilian in Roman Britain*, T.F.C. Blagg and A.C. King (eds.), pp.187–218. Oxford: Brit Archaeol Rep, Brit Ser 136.

McCarthy M.R. 1984 Roman Carlisle. In *Settlement and Society in the Roman North*, P.R. Wilson, R.F.J. Jones and D.M. Evans (eds.), pp.65–74. Univ. Bradford, York Archaeol Soc.

McWhirr A. 1986 *Houses in Roman Cirencester*. Cirencester Excavations 3

Maloney, J. 1983 Recent work on London's defences. In *Roman Urban Defences in the West*, J. Maloney and B. Hobley (eds.), pp.96–117. CBA Res Rep 51.

Millar F.G.B. 1981 The world of the *Golden Ass*. *J Roman Stud* 71:63–75.

Millett M. and Graham D. 1986 *Excavations in the Romano-British Small Town at Neatham, Hants., 1969–79*. Hampshire Fld Club Archaeol Soc Mono 3.

Reece R. 1980 Town and country: the end of Roman Britain. *World Archaeol* 12:77–92.

Reece R. 1984 Coins. In *Excavations at Carthage: the British Mission, vol. I,1: The Avenue du Président Habib Bourguiba*, by H.R. Hurst and S.P. Roskams, pp.171–81. Sheffield: Dept. Archaeology Sheffield University/British Academy.

Richmond I.A. 1966 Industry in Roman Britain. In *The Civitas Capitals of Roman Britain*, J. Wacher (ed.), pp.76–86. Leicester: Leicester University Press.

Rodwell W. 1975 Trinovantian towns and their setting: a case study. In *The Small Towns of Roman Britain*, W. Rodwell and T. Rowley (eds.), pp.85–101. Oxford: Brit Archaeol Rep, Brit Ser 15.

Rodwell W. and Rowley T. (eds.) 1975 *The Small Towns of Roman Britain*. Oxford: Brit Archaeol Rep, Brit Ser 15.

Rollwagen J. 1975 Introduction: the city as context: a symposium. *Urban Anthrop* 4(1):1–4.

Rubertone P.E. and Thorbahn, P.F. 1985 Urban hinterlands as frontiers of colonisation. In *The Archaeology of Frontiers and Boundaries*, S.W. Green and S.M. Perlman (eds.), pp.231–49. Academic Press.

Salway P. 1965 *The Frontier People of Roman Britain*. Cambridge: Cambridge University Press.

Schofield J. and Leech R.H. (eds.) 1987 *Urban Archaeology in Britain*. CBA Res Rep 61

Smith, R.F. 1987 *Roadside Settlements in Lowland Roman Britain*. Oxford: Brit Archaeol Rep, Brit Ser 157.

Sommer C.S. 1984 *The Military Vici of Roman Britain*. Oxford: Brit Archaeol Rep, Brit Ser 129.

Stead I.M. and Rigby, V. 1986 *Baldock: the Excavation of a Roman and Pre-Roman Settlement 1968–72*. *Britannia* Mono 7.

Todd M. 1985 Forum and Capitolium in the early Empire. In *Roman Urban Topography in Britain and the Western Empire*, F.O. Grew and B. Hobley (eds.), pp.56–66. CBA Res Rep 59.

Voorrips A. 1981 To tailor the inflected tail: reflections on rank-size relationships. In *Archaeological Approaches to the Study of Complexity*, S.E. van der Leeuw (ed.), pp.189–96. Cingula 6, Universiteit van Amsterdam.

Wacher J. 1964 Cirencester 1963: fourth interim report. *Antiq J* 44:9–19.

Wacher J. 1971 Yorkshire towns in the fourth century. In *Soldier and Civilian in Roman Yorkshire*, R.M. Butler (ed.), pp.165–77. Leicester: Leicester University Press.

Wacher J. 1975 *The Towns of Roman Britain*. Batsford.

Wacher J. and McWhirr, A. 1982 *Early Roman Occupation at Cirencester*. Cirencester Excavations 1.

Walthew C.V. 1975 The town house and the villa house in Roman Britain. *Britannia* 6:189–205.

Ward-Perkins J.B. 1970 From Republic to Empire: reflections on the early provincial architecture of the Roman West. *J Roman Stud* 60:1–19.

Webster G. 1966 Fort and town in early Roman Britain. In *The Civitas Capitals of Roman Britain*, J. Wacher (ed.), pp.31–45. Leicester: Leicester University Press.

Willems W.J.H. 1983 Romans and Batavians: regional developments at the imperial frontier. In *Roman and Native in the Low Countries*, R. Brandt and J. Slofstra (eds.), pp.105–28. Oxford: Brit Archaeol Rep, Inter Ser 184.

8. London - New Understanding of the Roman City

S. Roskams

Summary

Investigation has meant that much more can be said about Roman London than even a decade ago. Although it apparently lacks the military or pre-Roman origins usually seen as essential for success, the early Roman town expanded quickly to become the major administrative and trading settlement of Britain. A full interpretation of its role depends on whether one characterises the contemporary system as a 'free market' or 'administered' economy.

Late Roman London was very different, some evidence suggesting demise, other prosperity. Testing hypotheses on the causes of such change will be the work of the next decade.

Introduction

In the last two decades considerable resources have been put into the archaeological investigation of London. This work has been directed for the Museum of London by the Department of Urban Archaeology, with responsibility for the core of the Roman and medieval city, and by a variety of other units covering areas outside this. The latter groups have recently been brought under the umbrella of the Department for Greater London Archaeology. They are funded by central and local government and, to an increasing extent, by grants from developers of threatened sites.

A large number of archaeologists have been employed in London, and a vast increase in information about Roman London has resulted from their efforts. Hence previous works of synthesis (RCHM 1928; Merrifield 1965; Biddle and Hudson 1973) have been quickly superceded. What follows can only be a brief summary of recent discoveries and some of their implications. The interested reader is therefore referred to Marsden 1980, Morris 1982, Merrifield 1983 and Milne 1985 for general reading, and to particular works and archival reports held at the Museum of London for detailed studies.

Early Roman London

Despite previous suggestions of a pre-Roman forerunner or of a military origin for London, recent work gives no support for a major Iron Age settlement on the site. Equally, any fort established during the conquest would have been situated at a ford at Westminster, to the west of the Roman town (Hobley 1979:311ff). The initial roads through Southwark led towards this ford and were only diverted a decade later to the new bridging point.

This diversion, allowing the gravel islands on the south bank to be connected with two low brickearth hills on the north bank, determined the position of what was to become the provincial capital of Britain. Previous circumstantial evidence for the position of this bridge, based on street alignments, has been reinforced recently by the discovery of some of its physical remains (Milne 1985:44ff), together with massive timber-faced terraces constructed on either side of the bridgehead before AD 100. These features are testimony to the importance of London's trading links, whilst environmental evidence gives information on the river levels and tidal regime which shipping using the port would have encountered. Warehouses behind the quays show that the provision of storage facilities was part of an integrated development of the waterfront area involving terracing the hillside and laying out streets connecting it with the area to the north. Here lay the 'civic centre' of London (Marsden 1978). Together with the proposed Governor's Palace further west (Marsden 1975), such monumental buildings testify to the administrative importance of London. Commercial and good quality domestic buildings (Hammer 1985; Williams 1985 and references) show that other elements in the settlement were expanding at a corresponding pace. Thus the destruction of the area in the Boudiccan rebellion, though widespread, only resulted in a short disruption of the overall trend.

Rapid development in the late 1st century is also evident on the southern bridgehead (e.g. Sheldon 1974) and to the west of the town centre. In the latter area, recent work suggests that the settlement was intended to be large from the start and grew rapidly in the first ten years (Perring and Roskams forthcoming). But the planning proposals evident in its initial layout came to full fruition in the Flavian period when commercial, domestic and industrial zones can be distinguished, each with differing degrees of topographical organisation.

The picture thus emerges of a large, successful planned town based around administration and trade with related domestic, commercial and industrial activities. The traditional view of Roman towns (e.g. Wacher 1975:30ff) sees them as products of pre-Roman or military centres which develop into towns due to the entrepreneurial activity of individual citizens. London's success is difficult to explain in this way given its apparent lack of such origins.

An alternative view sees the Roman economy as socially embedded, rather than a free market, with the exchange of Roman imports within the province reinforcing social relationships. Polanyi (1963) has suggested that a 'port of trade' – a controlled entry point for such goods – is an expected feature of such a system. The characteristics of London – its political and geographical setting, the signs of internal organisation, the presence of the procurator and public buildings, its nodal role in trade routes, together with evidence of trading facilities and foreign traders – all support it being such a place and thus implies an early Roman administered economy. Even if the case is unproven, the important point is that, with archaeological evidence on a sufficient scale, we can test competing hypotheses on the nature of the ancient economy and thus make a significant contribution to such fundamental issues.

Late Roman London

From the late 2nd century, many parts of London show significant changes. Major buildings such as the 'Governor's Palace', several bathhouses and possibly even Cripplegate Fort seem to have gone out of use. On the waterfront the 3rd century quay became derelict and the warehouses behind it were modified. Domestic and commercial structures on both sides of the river were dismantled and covered by a horizon of dark earth, possibly a cultivated soil. All of this suggests the relative demise of London as a major nucleated settlement.

But there are also some signs of prosperity. The settlement was enclosed in *c.* AD 200 (Maloney 1983), with the riverside wall added later in the 3rd century (Sheldon and Tyres 1983). Monumental structures were built in the previously undeveloped southwest part of the city (Williams 1982) and a temple of Mithras in the Walbrook valley (Merrifield 1983:183ff for dating). Finally some town houses with good quality floors and walls were constructed at this time. But these buildings were much less concentrated than their early Roman counterparts and all of these features were set in a very different landscape from before.

In order to understand fully the character of late Roman London we need more excavation of its structures and more artefactual studies and environmental analyses. But equally, if we are to move from a descriptive account of its character to an understanding of why it changed, we must formulate hypotheses for the role of towns in late Roman Britain along the lines adopted for the early Roman town. Creating models from such hypotheses and testing them by interpreting and re-interpreting excavation data will be the task of those studying Roman London in the coming decade.

References

Biddle M. & Hudson D. 1973 with Heighway C. *The Future of London's Past.* Worcester.
Hammer F. 1985 Early Roman buildings in Fenchurch Street. *Popular Archaeology* 6, No.12:7–13.
Hobley B. 1979 Military considerations in the Lower Thames valley during the AD 43 campaign and their relevance to the origins of Londinium. In Hanson W.S. and Keppie J.F. (eds.), *Roman Frontier Studies, 1979. Papers presented to the 12th International Congress of Roman Frontier Studies.* BAR S71. Oxford, 311–315.
Maloney J. 1983 Recent work on London's defences. In Maloney J. and Hobley B. (eds.), *Roman Urban Defences in the West.* CBA Research Report 51. London, 97–117.
Marsden P. 1975 The excavation of a Roman palace site in London, 1961–1972. *Transactions of the London and Middlesex Archaeological Society* 26:1–102.
Marsden P. 1978 The discovery of the civic centre of Roman London. In Bird J., Chapman, H. and Clark J. *Collectania Londiniensia.* London and Middlesex Archaeological Society, Special Paper No.2: 89–103.
Marsden P. 1980 *Roman London.* London.
Merrifield R. 1965 *The Roman City of London.* London.
Merrifield R. 1983 *London: City of the Romans.* London.
Milne G. 1985 *The Port of Roman London.* London.
Morris J. 1982 *Londinium.* London.
Perring D. and Roskams S. forthcoming. The Development of Roman London West of the Walbrook.
Polanyi K. 1963 Ports of trade in early societies. *Journal of Economic History* 23:30–45.
R.C.H.M. (England) 1928 *An Inventory of the Historical Monuments in London. III: Roman London.* London.
Sheldon H. 1974 Excavations at Toppings and Sun Wharves, Southwark. *Transactions of the London and Middlesex Archaeological Society* 25:1–116.
Sheldon H. and Tyres I. 1983 Recent dendrochronological work in Southwark and its implications. *London Archaeologist* 4, No.13:355–261.
Wacher J. 1975 *The Towns of Roman Britain.* London.
Williams T. 1982 St Peter's Hill. *Popular Archaeology* 4, No.1:24–30.
Williams T. 1985 Redevelopment in the City – what is new? *Popular Archaeology* 6, No.14:31–36.

9. Lincoln

M. J. Jones

Lincoln was chosen as a site for a legionary fortress by the Ninth legion *Hispana* as its principal base in the conquest and occupation of the lands of the Corieltauvi, the modern East Midlands. It lay at a gap in the Jurassic limestone ridge where Ermine Street crossed the river Witham (Whitwell 1970). The army was here for about 30 years, *Legio* IX being replaced by *Legio* II *Adiutrix* in AD 71, before this legion too moved on. By the end of Domitian's reign, the site of the former fortress had been given the status of *colonia*. As well as many time-served legionaries, the population probably contained natives and traders from the start. The hillside to the south of the fortress/*colonia*, which has already produced hints of settlement associated with the legionary occupation, was densely occupied by the early 2nd century. It was also subsequently provided with a street grid, and later surrounded with fortifications which reached almost to the river. The settlement grew on all sides, but especially to the south along the route of Ermine Street and the Fosse Way (Figure 9.1). Its continuing commercial prosperity may have helped its candidacy to be capital of the 4th century province of *Flavia Caesariensis*.

History of Investigation

The first twenty-five years of systematic excavation in the city, from the founding of the Lincoln Archaeological Research Committee in 1945, followed guidelines laid down by Sir Ian Richmond. Richmond was at the time producing his classic essay, 'The Roman City of Lincoln', still the basic account (Richmond 1946). Increasingly during the 1960s, however, the selection of sites for investigation was being affected by redevelopment schemes, and during the following decade the pace of excavation struggled to keep up with that of urban renewal. The primary achievement of the ARC's lifetime was the location and elucidation of the defensive sequence of the upper enclosure.

Even this had to take place against a background of the needs of the modern city, and in such circumstances the pursuit of single-period research objectives can be a frustrating activity. A large proportion of the fortress and upper *Colonia* is covered by listed buildings within an important conservation area, and most open spaces are scheduled as ancient monuments. The justifiable emphasis on preservation limits opportunities for excavation. Moreover, some of the settlement areas outside the walls and immediate hinterland of the Roman city lie beneath the sprawl of the modern conurbation, often in areas developed in the last two centuries and unlikely to be accessible again for some time.

While the need to preserve by record will continue, the emphasis in future years will be on survey,

evaluation of deposits, and post-excavation work. It is only in the late 1980s that we have begin to study in detail the vast amount of material recovered during and since the 1970s, to take stock of the present state of knowledge, and to determine priorities for further work in the context of current research problems. It should go without saying that a primary consideration is the publication of all previous work of significance. A formal and comprehensive Sites and Monuments Record – preparation of which is now in progress – is also an essential basis for planning future projects.

It is perhaps to be expected that the work of the past fifteen years or so has added new dimensions to our knowledge as well as deepening it, and in some ways we are wiser in assuming less. The latter is best illustrated by the history of the study of the street pattern (Jones 1985). Fifty years ago a grid similar to that of the new, roughly contemporary *colonia* of Timgad was presumed (Baker 1938). The discovery of the underlying fortress had implications for the origin and development of the *colonia* layout (an idea developed by Crummy 1982). Similarly, an attempt to discern the Roman pattern on the assumption that most modern streets were of Roman origin – as in many Italian towns – was shown to be misguided. The study of the medieval street systems on Roman sites in Britain showed clearly that the Roman grid had invariably been lost and a new plan imposed before the Norman Conquest (Biddle 1976). Nevertheless, some progress has been made more recently on this problem, and it continues as a priority.

Origins

Many questions still remain about the basic chronological framework. The discovery of a Late Iron Age settlement in the valley (Darling and Jones *et al* 1988) was, in retrospect, no great surprise (May 1984), but we do not yet understand its relationship to the earliest military occupation or to the associated civil settlement. The position of the fortress at the gap in the Jurassic ridge is a strategically significant one; its proximity to an existing settlement owed more to geographic determinants than to a political decision. The nature of the first fortress itself remains problematical, with the possibility of a Claudian base south of the river in the area of the known cemeteries (Jones 1985). More precise dating for these early levels is desirable, but not easily obtainable.

The legionary occupation obviously covered a much larger area than the 15 hectare fortress site, and further investigation is needed to understand the general layout (Jones 1988). Although the defences have been examined at several points, of the internal buildings only the *principia* has been identified (Jones 1980; Jones and Gilmour 1980). This con-

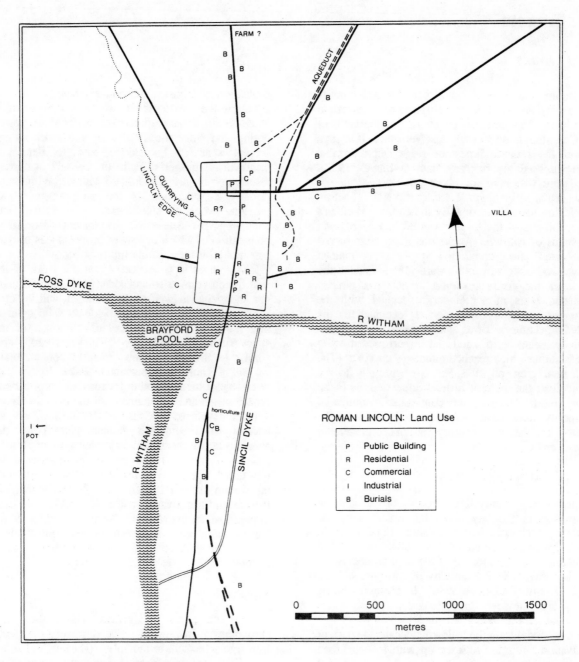

FARM ?

AQUEDUCT

LINCOLN EDGE

QUARRYING

VILLA

FOSS DYKE

BRAYFORD
POOL

R WITHAM

R WITHAM

horticulture

SINCIL DYKE

I ←
POT

ROMAN LINCOLN: Land Use

P	Public Building
R	Residential
C	Commercial
I	Industrial
B	Burials

0   500   1000   1500

metres

Figure 9.1   Roman Lincoln: land use.

firmed that the fortress faced east.

Questions about the size of the garrison and its accommodation, and about the extent to which buildings and streets were reused in the early *colonia* are still to be answered (cf. Colchester, Crummy 1984). Beyond the *enceinte*, hints of contemporary occupation have come to light to the west and east of the fortress and to the south, both on the hillside and in the valley, which are potentially of great interest. There are possibilities for work in these areas in the future. No systematic work has yet been done to the north. It would be interesting to learn the size of the extra-mural settlement at the time of the *colonia's* foundation.

The Colonia

Lindum Colonia has furnished architectural, artefactual, and epigraphic evidence of metropolitan cultural influences, more than many Romano-British towns (Richmond 1946:68). This impression is corroborated by the suggested plan of the forum (Jones and Gilmour 1980), which had a plan turned through 90 degrees from that of the underlying *principia*. The north wall of the basilica still survives (though relatively unknown) to a height of 8 metres. A report on the public baths, excavated 1956–8, is still awaited, but promised soon. As Richmond suggested, an intensive examination of the sewer system may well be the key to the street pattern, but in a modern built-up area there are great difficulties

Lincoln

involved in its exploration. Although principal
buildings of the fortress and colonia are of
international significance, it is unlikely that many
opportunities will arise in the foreseeable future for
examination, since they lie beneath protected historic
buildings in a Conservation Area. Even those
features of which Lincoln is best known, e.g. its
aqueduct, need much more attention if the system is
to be understood (Lewis 1984). The defences have
been as thoroughly examined as those of any
Romano-British town; they show a complex
sequence found also at Gloucester and Cirencester.

Large-scale redevelopment of the lower hillside
since c. 1960 has been accompanied by extensive –
though far from comprehensive – excavation.
Survival on the steeper part is uneven; the stepped
construction of Ermine Street was located at a depth
of 5m, the floor of a house to the southeast of this site
immediately beneath the modern ground surface.
The fortifications of the lower city have also been
subject to close study, as a result of which certain
aspects are better understood, but in the nature of
things new problems have arisen. There is for
instance no apparent solution to the discrepancy – of
over a century – between the dating of the defences
on the west to c. 200 and those on the east to the
early 4th century (Jones and Gilmour forthcoming;
Wacher forthcoming). Much rubbish was apparently
dumped on the later rampart; its contents might
suggest that it was derived from earlier dumps.
Inside the walls, fragments of several town houses
and other buildings have been uncovered, some of
them interestingly of 4th century date and on a grand
scale.

Recent work at Lincoln has made a relatively
significant contribution to study of suburbs, a topic
which has attracted too little attention in general
(Jones 1981; Esmonde Cleary 1987). We now know
that at Lincoln the commercial areas continued to
grow well into the 3rd century (Figure 9.1), with at
least one area of former cemetery given over to this
development, but we need to discover something of
the actual trades carried out (partly by investigating
the 'backyards') and to look for clues to tenurial
arrangements. Did this growth reflect the city's
increasing prosperity, or were commercial activities
being displaced from within the walls? Some large
modern excavations of cemeteries are a pressing
need, both to enable some analysis of the anatomical
evidence, and to look for traces of any early Anglo-
Saxon churches.

The cemeteries – which contained barrows,
'loculi', and mausolea – appear to have been most
extensive in the 3rd and 4th centuries, a period which
saw some change in the town, but little which could
certainly be interpreted as 'decay 'until well after c.
350. The designation of provincial capital status and
the establishment of organized Christianity in the
early part of the century may have provided a fillip in
terms of civic pride, if not necessarily to the
economy. Were the large new establishments in the
lower town connected at all with the presence of the
new administration or a continuation of an existing
trend? The defences of the city were being

strengthened after 350. A preliminary sample of the
pattern of coin loss, compared to other towns, may
reflect a floruit up to c. 375–80 (Reece and Mann
1983). This is relatively late in the provincial
context, and could be interpreted as indicating the
city's 'peripheral 'location in the decentralization of
the economy (Hingley 1982). Coins also form a
significant part of the evidence for the continuation
of organized life into the early 5th century, if not
beyond, but again, as at other sites, we do not yet
know how late pottery was being manufactured in the
local kilns (Darling 1977).

Prospects

These economic questions represent some of the
problems to which we should be turning out
attention, utilizing 'modern 'methods of analysis and
testing hypotheses wherever possible (Cunliffe
1984). Large assemblages of artefacts, especially if
well stratified and with low residuality, have much to
tell us, and there is much yet to be done on traditional
tasks such as the pottery sequence, and on building
materials (Darling 1977, 1984; Fenton in Jones
1980). Investigation of some wet deposits, prolific in
environmental remains, is essential to provide a more
balanced picture; and these will include waterfront
sites to provide data on the course of the rivers,
bridges, canals and dykes, tidal flow, etc (Gilmour
and Guy forthcoming). Scientific analysis to date has
indicated something of the extent which the Witham
and associated canals and drains were recut in the
Roman period (op. cit.). The emphasis of urban
renewal is likely to fall in the extramural areas,
containing the waterfront, and affecting sites of
cemeteries and of commercial activity.

The study of the town in its agricultural
environment does of course involve intensive
fieldwork outside the walls, but controlled and large
samples of animal bones and environmental remains
from urban contexts have a part to play, and a start
has been made (Scott forthcoming). It may be
possible eventually to test hypotheses about the
relative and changing importance of Lincoln and the
surrounding minor towns as market and production
centres (see most recently Hingley 1982, Burnham
1986). Britain has furnished no definite evidence to
date for the cultivation of land by centuriation around
the coloniae, something which might be expected –
but was the land already intensively farmed? The
relationship of the existing native farmsteads to
succeeding villas and their estates is one avenue of
enquiry. The use of local or 'imported' raw materials
can be studied with regard to both pottery and
buildings. Again, little has so far been achieved.

The breakdown of the urbanized imperial system
has to be examined in terms of both political and
socio-economic changes. Lincoln grew to be very
successful commercially and, perhaps for this reason,
was rewarded with special political status in the 4th
century. Its subsequent decline physically and
economically was, even if belatedly, inevitable in
view of the changing system which had maintained
it. Study of the relationship of the 'dark earth' layer
to remains of Roman buildings and property

71

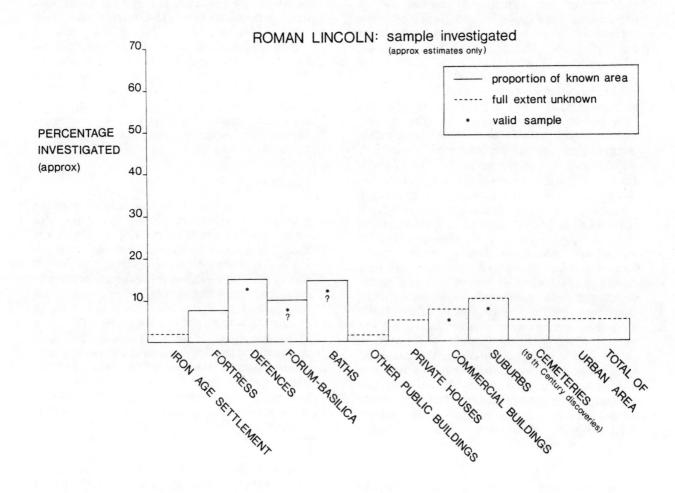

Figure 9.2   Roman Lincoln: the sample of the archaeology investigated.

boundaries is one key to what happened to the city. It appears that certain areas were given over to agriculture or horticulture during or after the 5th century. Although there is some evidence, as in London, for open spaces and agricultural activity in the 2nd to 4th centuries, this had happened only on a limited scale. The evidence of the use of the forum courtyard for burial in the 5th/6th centuries suggests that an ecclesiastical centre survived within the walled area, perhaps associated later with an aristocratic element; investigation of adjacent sites should look for further traces, however slight, of any contemporary residential establishment.

In summary, the town and all it spawned, all upon which it depended, is still known only in the barest outline (Figure 9.2). What is striking in view of its peripheral location in an imperial province is the extent of its Romanization (first noted by Richmond 1946). Much of the evidence so far won from the ground is in need of careful processing and synthesis. What we possess is only the smallest sample, and a larger database is essential for understanding the settlement and how it developed. While all aspects of the city are of interest, of immediate concern are the plan and accommodation of the fortress and its

relationship to the *colonia* (Jones 1988), the major public buildings, and the topography and development of the later town. Threatened sites with well-preserved deposits should therefore be excavated, especially if they are large, or comprise elements of a composite objective. They will provide much data on which to study economic and cultural aspects. This does not mean that we should not try to make sense of what we have, using all the methods at our disposal: every new hypothesis should stimulate further interest and lead to a refinement of our knowledge.

References

Baker F.T. 1938 *Roman Lincoln*. Hist. Assoc. Lincoln.

Biddle M. 1976 Towns. In D.M. Wilson (ed.), *The Archaeology of Anglo-Saxon England*, 99–150.

Burnham B. 1986 The origins of Romano-British small towns. *Oxford J. Archaeol.* 5.2:185.

Crummy P. 1982 The origins of some major Romano-British towns. *Britannia* 13:125–34.

Crummy P. 1984 *Excavations at Lion Walk, Balkerne Lane, Middleborough, Colchester, Essex*. Colchester Archaeological Report No.3. Colchester.

Cunliffe B.W. 1984 Images of Britannia. *Antiquity* 58:175–8.

Darling M.J. 1977 A late Roman group of pottery from Lincoln. *Archaeol. Lincoln* 16.1. London.

Darling M.J. 1984 Roman pottery from the upper defences. *Archaeol. Lincoln* 16.2.

Darling M.J. and Jones M.J. 1988 Early Settlement at Lincoln. *Britannia* 19:1–56.

Esmonde Cleary A.S. 1987 *Extra-Mural Areas of Romano-British Towns*, BAR 169.

Gilmour B.J.J. and Guy C.G. forthcoming Excavations at Brayford Pool 1972–86. *Archaeol. Lincoln* 8.1.

Hingley R. 1982 Roman Britain: the structure of Roman imperialism... In Miles D. (ed.), *The Romano-British Countryside*. BAR 103:17–52.

Jones M.J. 1980 The Defences of the Upper Roman Enclosure. *Archaeol. Lincoln* 8.1.

Jones M.J. (ed.) 1981 Excavations at Lincoln: third interim report. *Antiq. J.* 61:83–114.

Jones M.J. 1985 New streets for old: the topography of Roman Lincoln. In F. Grew and B. Hobley (eds.), *Roman Urban Topography in Britain and the Western Empire*. CBA Research Report 59. London, 86–93.

Jones M.J. 1988 Lincoln. In G. Webster (ed.), *Fortress Into City* London.

Jones M.J. and Gilmour B.J.J. 1980 Lincoln: *principia* and forum: a preliminary report. *Britannia* 11:61–72.

Jones M.J. and Gilmour B.J.J. forthcoming The Defences of the Lower Roman City. *Archaeol. Lincoln* 7.2.

Jones M.J. and Wacher J.S. 1987 Period Survey: Roman (towns). In J.A. Schofield and R.H. Leech, *Urban Archaeology in Britain*. CBA Research Report, 61.

Lewis M.J.T. 1984 Our debt to Roman engineering: the water-supply of Lincoln to the present day. *Industr. Archaeol. Rev.* 7.1:57–73.

May J. 1984 Major settlements of the later Iron Age in Lincolnshire. In F.N. Field and A.J. White (eds.), *A Prospect of Lincolnshire*. Lincoln, 18–22.

Reece R. and Mann J.E. 1983 Roman Coins from Lincoln 1970–79. *Archaeol. Lincoln* VI.2.

Richmond I.A. The Roman city of Lincoln, and the four *coloniae* of Roman Britain. *Archaeol. J.* 103:26–84.

Scott S. forthcoming Animal Bones from Lincoln. *Archaeol. Lincoln* 18.2.

Wacher J. S. (ed.) 1985 *Priorities for the Preservation and Excavation of Romano-British Sites*. Society for the Promotion of Roman Studies. London.

Wacher J.S. forthcoming *Excavations at Silver Street, Lincoln*.

Whitwell J.B. 1970 *Roman Lincolnshire*. Lincoln. New edition in preparation.

Future publication of excavations carried out in the city will appear in the series *The Archaeology of Lincoln*, published by the Council for British Archaeology.

10. The Romano-British Countryside: the Significance of Rural Settlement Forms

Richard Hingley

'A thorough investigation is needed of the ways in which agricultural production was organised in the various parts of the Graeco-Roman world. ... the main desideratum is a concentration upon the precise conditions in each individual area at different periods: only upon the basis of a whole series of regional analyses can any secure general conclusions be arrived at.' (Ste. Croix 1981:218–9).

Introduction

The intention in this paper is to consider certain concepts and themes that are of relevance to the study of Romano-British rural settlement. No attempt will be made to review the wealth of settlement evidence for the province; rather the intention is to consider a range of models which examine the meaning of the evidence (see Hingley 1989 for a fuller review).

The ideal of the author would be to write a social history of rural settlement (Ste. Croix 1981:218). This social history would involve a discussion of broad aspects of social organisation, land tenure and economic organisation set within the context of the influence of the Roman administration on the development of the province. Owing to the nature of the archaeological and historical evidence, it is at present impossible to write a comprehensive social history of Roman Britain (Todd 1978:197).

As a consequence a range of models that provide some insight into the social and economic organisation of Romano-British communities will be discussed in this paper. The approaches advocated are spatial in nature and direct attention towards the study of the social significance of settlement form and settlement distribution.

Terminology

There is a great wealth of evidence for Roman rural settlement which indicates that lowland Britain was covered by a dense distribution of settlements of a variety of forms. Taylor has quoted a density of one settlement per 0.4 or 0.5 square kilometres in east Northamptonshire and areas of Bedfordshire and comparable densities have been recorded elsewhere (Taylor 1985:83; C. Smith 1977; Hallam 1970; Williamson 1985).

Romano-British settlement sites vary in size, form, wealth, function and location. The largest sites in the countryside are 'small towns', many of which are of urban rather than rural character. At the other end of the scale are small farmsteads, probably the homes of single nuclear or extended families. Between small towns and farmsteads are a range of sites of varying size, sometimes called 'villages' and 'hamlets' (e.g. Hallam 1970).

Wealth is considered to be of importance in distinguishing settlement types. Villa houses were substantial buildings constructed using surplus wealth and can be distinguished from other non-villa farming settlements. Function is also of importance; the majority of rural settlements were primarily agricultural (Applebaum 1972), but small towns had a trading and perhaps in some cases an important industrial function.

Villa

The term 'villa' is derived from classical texts and has been applied to the British settlement evidence by analogy (only one reference to a villa occurs in contemporary writings on Britain; Rivet 1969:174). Classical authors were not consistent in the way they used the term. Rivet's model is derived from Varro and Columella and suggests that the villa was the means by which a rich town-dweller exploited the countryside; villas were the countryside estates of the town-dweller, often run by bailiffs and only occasionally visited by the owner (Rivet 1969:178–182). Other Roman authors, however, use the term in a variety of different ways (Percival 1976:13) and it is impossible to derive a consistent model of the meaning of 'villa' from the classical literature.

When the term is used by archaeologists it is usually reserved for a building that occurs in comparative isolation (ie. not in an urban location) and is 'romanised' in form (Collingwood 1930:113). The range of physical manifestations that define romanisation in this context include the use of stone and tile/slate, as opposed to the use of timber, daub and thatch in many non-villa dwellings, and often the occurrence of tessellated floors/mosaic pavements, painted plaster, heated rooms and bath suites. However, it is not possible to define a clear demarcation of villas from non-villa settlements using archaeological evidence (Percival 1976:15).

To many archaeologists the existence of a villa building indicates the location of a private estate belonging to the villa owner. In fact the link between the villa and the private estate is an assumption (Slofstra 1983). A villa, as defined from archaeological evidence, is a status indicating building form and no more. The construction of a villa building was clearly a fashionable way of investing surplus wealth.

This is why villa type buildings occur in large towns (see Wacher 1974 on Cirencester) and in villages/small towns (see below). The surplus accumulated to construct a villa building may have been derived from industry, or trade, and need not always relate to the ownership and exploitation of an agricultural estate. That agriculture and land-ownership appear to have been the main forms of wealth in the Roman Empire (Duncan-Jones 1974:33) indicates that many villas will have been related to ownership, or at least control, of an estate. If the term is to be of any more value than a description of the form of a building, however, it will be necessary to discover more about the nature and context of the settlements on which these buildings occur.

Non-villa Settlements

Non-villa settlements as a class of sites are poorly understood. The sites are rarely studied and there is a tendency to consider non-villa settlements in negative terms, that they are the homes of the poor and lowly, of those who failed to become romanised. Non-villa settlements tend to be defined by absence: both of buildings that show any high degree of wealth investment and romanisation and also the actual or implied absence of material items of wealth, such as imported pottery, fewer coins and wealthy metalwork. Literary texts mention slaves and tenants, often linked to agricultural estates, and evidence also exists for peasant landowners in some areas of the Empire (MacMullen 1974; Ste. Croix 1981); non-villa settlements are assumed to have been the homes of members of these social groups.

In fact it is wrong to consider these sites in purely negative terms as they do not form an undifferentiated class. A range of settlement sizes occur and differences in size may be related to variations in the social and economic organisation of communities (see below). In addition it is probable that the wealth of those who lived in non-villa settlements varied from site to site. It will even be suggested below that the villa building was not necessarily the aim of all wealthy Romano-British farmers.

Small Towns

Fairly large villages occur in southern Britain and small towns are also very common (see Todd 1970; Rodwell and Rowley (eds.) 1975; and R. Smith 1987 for small towns). It is not altogether clear where the demarcation between villages and small towns occurs. Size appears to have some significance; sites classed as small towns are usually at least ten hectares in size and can be as large as 50 or more hectares (introduction to Rodwell and Rowley (eds.) 1975). Some villages, however, appear to be as large as the less extensive small towns. The division is presumably one between villages which had a primarily agricultural function and small towns which were involved, at least in part, in trade and industry. The twelve farms which make up the non-villa settlement at Catsgore (Somerset) appear to have had an agricultural function (Leech 1982); the contrast with small towns such as those at Water Newton (Cambridgeshire; Wilson 1975:9), or Alcester (Warwickshire; Booth 1980) is immediately apparent. At Water Newton, Alcester, and a range of other small towns, the settlements are very extensive and considerable evidence has been found for trade and industry. Water Newton and Alcester, however, appear to have prospered more than the average small town and other small towns often have a less obviously urban character. In fact it can take

extensive excavation to establish whether a site is a small town or a village (e.g. Stonea; Potter and Jackson 1985). As small towns had a range of non-agricultural functions and are considered by Jones elsewhere in this volume they will not be discussed in detail in this paper.

The Organisation of the Settlement

Building Form

It is not possible to review in detail the vast quantity of evidence for the form of buildings on rural sites in southern Britain. Instead the intention is to discuss a number of models for the significance of particular building forms that occur on these sites.

Non-villa buildings are not usually particularly elaborate. On some sites timber round houses, little different from Iron Age houses, occur in Roman contexts (see Williams 1976; Leech 1982). For example at Odell (Bedfordshire) timber round houses occur throughout the life of the Roman farm, although one rectangular timber house was also constructed (Simco 1984). At Catsgore (Somerset) round timber houses were replaced by rectangular buildings after the 2nd century and a similar trend is apparent on many rural settlement sites (Leech 1982).

Rectangular timber, or stone and timber, dwellings are common on non-villa settlements and also on settlements that were to become villas. At Catsgore a number of timber huts with stone footings have been excavated on the village site and the 4th century houses appear to have been constructed largely in stone (Leech 1982). At Bradley Hill (Somerset) two similar buildings are known (Leech 1981). Leech has discussed this type of dwelling house; they have two or three rooms, one of which is larger than the others and contains a hearth (1982).

The poverty and simplicity of the simple oval and rectangular dwelling probably indicates the low social and economic standing and the absence of social differentiation amongst those who lived in non-villa settlements. It does appear, however, that individual dwelling houses were often integrated into farm compounds on these sites and this will be discussed below.

The use of stone in construction is often thought to represent the influence of Roman culture. Thus Richmond, Wilson and Drinkwater consider any rectangular stone-built dwelling that occurs in rural isolation to be a villa (Richmond 1969; Wilson 1974; Drinkwater 1983). In fact stone is often no more than a locally available building material and need not indicate any high degree of surplus investment. Richmond's class of 'cottage house' villas (Richmond 1969:52) are very little different in form and significance from the rectangular timber and stone dwellings at Catsgore. In this paper it is considered that in order to classify a simple rectangular dwelling as a cottage villa it is necessary to identify additional indicators of surplus investment such as mosaics or a bath-house.

Richmond also distinguishes 'winged corridor

houses', 'hall houses', 'aisled houses' and 'courtyard houses' (1969). Hall villas have one large room and a number of smaller rooms. These buildings are actually very similar to the simple rectangular dwellings discussed by Leech, although with the addition of a winged corridor façade. It has been suggested that hall villas relate to a particular type of social structure involving a headman and a lineage (e.g. J.T. Smith 1978b). In addition it has recently been argued that at Barnsley Park (Gloucestershire) a kin group of three families, who held land in some form of joint proprietorship, were converted into a modified kin group resident within a single hall villa (J.T. Smith 1985). It has also been argued that aisled houses had a similar significance to hall villas and housed a headman and associated lineage (J.T. Smith 1963).

The addition of wings and corridor was a way of constructing a fashionable façade for a dwelling; such façades were added to simple rectangular houses, cottage houses, hall houses and aisled houses. The significance of the rooms behind the façade probably varies, but winged corridor buildings as a group form the most common type of villa in Roman Britain (D.J. Smith 1978). Courtyard villas were extensive and wealthy establishments and represent a level of wealth above that of the winged corridor house (Richmond 1969:59). J.T. Smith has recently argued that a 'unit system' occurs in many courtyard and some winged corridor houses (J.T. Smith 1978a; 1982); he suggests that some form of joint occupancy or proprietorship occurred and that the individual villa can be divided into a number of units, each representing a single family. The villas discussed by Smith commonly appear to consist of two or three units, but examples with more than three elements are rare. Utilising the arguments of D. Clarke on Glastonbury Lake Village (see Clarke 1972), J.T. Smith has suggested that the comparatively small elements of hierarchy observable in the Iron Age village are expressed in more obvious and durable form in the courtyard villa (J.T. Smith 1978a:328).

J.T. Smith's ideas of villa form are of great interest as they suggest the indigenous contribution to Romano-British culture. The Roman conquest provided a situation in which villa construction became possible; however, it is necessary to study the context of the adoption of Roman norms. Romanisation was not merely a passive acceptance of Roman culture and law, but a manipulation to create a unique Romano-British civilization.

Farm Compound Organisation

In contrast to the information for building form, the evidence for farm compound organisation is scarce. Excavations on a number of sites have, however, produced evidence for compounds. At Bradley Hill (Somerset) two houses and a barn probably belonged to an extended family (Leech 1981). At Catsgore six individual farm compounds out of an original total of about twelve have been excavated, and development can be seen in many of the individual Catsgore compounds: Complex One began in Phase One with a single dwelling house, but by Phase Two consisted

of a pair of dwellings, perhaps representing the dwelling of an extended family (Leech 1982).

Compounds appear to exist on other non-villa settlements in both upland and lowland Britain (Hingley 1989), although excavation is commonly on too small a scale to identify these units clearly. The farm compound is a similar phenomenon to the occurrence of two or more dwelling houses on villa sites; individual farm compounds can also be related to the Glastonbury compound. In other words, multiple buildings with a range of functions which form distinct family units occur at Glastonbury, in the Catsgore/Bradley Hill farm compound, and in the unit system villa.

The Form of the Settlement

Few sites have been excavated on a large scale and as a consequence little evidence exists for the organisation of the rural settlement at a scale above that of the individual farm compound.

At Claydon Pike (Gloucestershire) the Iron Age settlement was reorganised in the late 1st/early 2nd century, possibly with occupants of differing status on either side of a track. The excavator has tentatively proposed a military presence on the site and Claydon Pike may have acted as a local centre for the collection of taxes in kind. Soldiers may perhaps have resided in the 'wealthy' area of the site and slaves in the compound to the west (Miles 1984).

In addition areas of differing wealth have been found on other settlement sites. At Catsgore one farm compound appears to be wealthier than the others and has been called a villa (Leech 1982). Winged corridor buildings exist within villages/small towns at Tiddington (Warwickshire; Palmer 1982), Hibaldstow (Humberside; R. Smith 1987) and Camerton (Avon; Todd 1976). At Gatcombe (Somerset) a cluster of buildings, probably associated with a large villa, lie within a walled enclosure (Branigan 1977). Todd has argued that in cases like these the village may have been the home of the farm workers on an estate belonging to a villa owner (Todd 1978:207). At Gatcombe this explanation seems quite plausible; however, at Catsgore, Hibaldstow, Tiddington and Camerton, the 'villas' are only marginally larger or more ornate than the standard dwellings and at these sites the villa owner may have been the village elder or chief rather than the village owner (see Bloemers and Willems on the Dutch site of Rijswijk; Bloemers 1983; Willems 1984).

The Size of the Settlement

Roman rural settlements vary a great deal in size. The best researched area is the Fenland (Cambridgeshire, Norfolk and Lincolnshire) where Hallam, from the results of an extensive field survey project, has been able to distinguish 'single farms', 'small hamlets' (two to three farm clusters), 'large hamlets' (four to six) and 'small villages' (seven or more; Hallam 1970). Evidence for variation in settlement size occurs elsewhere in southern Britain; for example Bradley Hill (Somerset) is a single farm, Chisenbury Warren (Wiltshire) appears to represent a cluster of at least four farms and Catsgore had about twelve separate farms (Leech 1982).

In the Fenland the evidence appears to indicate a progressive nucleation of settlement through time, until some form of calamity, perhaps caused by flooding, in the late 2nd/early 3rd century (Hallam 1970, Table A). In areas outside the Fenland comparable evidence is scarce, although at Catsgore only four out of the six excavated farm compounds dated from the first phase of settlement (Leech 1982).

What is the relevance of variation in the size of individual settlements? In some areas nucleation may be related to the growing consolidation of holdings by individuals in the later Empire (MacMullen 1974; Percival 1976:174–7). Nucleated settlements may in some cases represent 'bond hamlets' (Wightman 1975). Developing nucleation in the Fenland appears, however, to be occurring rather too early and may alternatively represent the divided inheritance of an area of land. Single families may have settled, or have been settled, in the area during the 1st century AD and then have grown into multiple households through the sharing of land between children of each generation. Clarke's suggestions concerning Glastonbury, that the extended nature of the family and the large size of the settlement related to the need for communal activities in a marshland environment (Clarke 1972), could also be of relevance for the Roman Fens, where co-operation over enterprises such as drainage will have been necessary.

It is clear that variation of settlement size also occurs in Iron Age Britain. For example the Tollard Royal site (Wiltshire) can hardly represent more than a single family (Wainwright 1968), while Glastonbury Lake Village at its maximum extent may have contained six extended families, or 120 people (Clarke 1972). Settlements of varying size occur throughout the Iron Age and Roman periods. Nucleation of settlement may in fact relate to communal farming (see Stevens 1966; J.T. Smith 1978a). Even if this was so, however, variation in settlement size need have no tenurial connotation. Literary evidence indicates a range of modes of land tenure, and descent of land between generations might follow a similar pattern whether the property was owned, or rented on a long-term lease.

It has been suggested that villas also vary in size and that some villas contain at least three households. It is possible that the process of villa development is similar in some cases to the process of non-villa settlement nucleation, with multiple households developing due to divided inheritance. If this is correct courtyard houses need be little different from non-villa hamlets in anything but their wealth.

The Organisation of the Landscape

How do sites relate together in the landscape? In this section a number of studies of systems of settlement will be reviewed. These models are tentative, as it is impossible to excavate whole systems of settlement and the evidence for making statements about regional settlement patterning is never adequate.

Economic Models for Settlement Development

If villas represent the investment of surplus in symbols of status then it would seem probable from the number of villas in Britain that a 'new élite' of wealthy individuals developed through the expansion of agriculture and the marketing of surplus produce (Rivet 1969; Wightman 1975:623).

Hodder and Millet have attempted to model the relationship of villas to towns (1980). This analysis is, however, based on an inadequate data base and detailed intensive studies of local regions are required before realistic conclusions can be obtained (Hingely 1989).

A thorough study is required of the relationship of villa and non-villa settlements to communication networks, to markets in major and minor towns, and to raw materials and industry. Presumably settlements in easy contact with a market prospered more than those distant from a market. In fact the absence of civilian markets may be one of the main reasons for the absence of villas from the military uplands of Britain (Jones and Walker 1983). In the lowlands industrial production and marketing will have provided a means for obtaining the surplus necessary to adopt 'Roman' standards.

Settlement Hierarchy and Estates

An alternative way in which a surplus may have been accumulated was in the hands of an estate owner with tenants; this was probably the economic basis of the largest villas (Todd 1978). There is very little direct evidence for villa estates in Britain (see Applebaum 1972; also see Wightman 1975 and Percival 1976 for the more complete evidence for estates in Gaul). The development of a villa through exploitation of an estate, however, was perhaps the cause of the evolution of an indigenous élite on several sites in southern England.

A number of 'early' villas and also several courtyard villas have been argued to represent the homes of an indigenous élite. 'Early' villas are those that developed at an earlier date than would have been expected for the areas in which they are located. Of particular interest is a group of villas in the Cotswolds of Gloucestershire and Oxfordshire. At Ditches (Gloucestershire) a villa has recently been located and partly excavated about three miles northwest of the possible Late Iron Age tribal centre at Bagendon. This villa lies within a 'hillfort', the defences of which were flattened around AD 50–70 when the villa was constructed. The excavators have suggested the possibility of continuity of landholding on this site (Trow and James 1985).

In Oxfordshire two 'early' villas at Ditchley and Shakenoak are within the North Oxfordshire Grim's Ditch which, like Bagendon, is a 'territorial oppidum' of Late Iron Age date. A number of other villas (including Northleigh) also occur within the Grim's Ditch and it has been argued that the occurrence of early villas and courtyard villas indicates the survival of a Late Iron Age estate and its subsequent division in the Roman period (Hingley 1988). Elsewhere the early courtyard villa at Fishbourne (West Sussex) is inside the Selsey territorial oppidum (Cunliffe 1971), while the courtyard villa at Woodchester (Gloucestershire) is close to a possible territorial oppidum at Minchinhampton (Clarke 1982). Both of these villas have been linked with the possible survival of a pre-conquest élite into the Roman period.

If settlement hierarchy is to be comprehended in greater detail it will be necessary to conduct intensive studies of individual areas, which would provide a more detailed understanding of the spatial form and temporal dynamics of the Romano-British estate.

Possible Social Constraints on Villa Development

Two models have developed that attempt to explain villa distribution in terms of the social organisation of communities. Stevens used Welsh law tracts to interpret the archaeological evidence. Two systems were identified; the first system involved the free kin holdings (*gwely*). These groups owed dues and rent to the lord of an administrative district, but land was owned by the *gwely*. In contrast to this *tir cyfrif* involved groups of bondmen tied to land which was not their own. Stevens argued, from a superficial review of the settlement evidence, that farmsteads in southern and eastern Britain were derived from multiple *gwely* units. To the north and west the supposed pattern of nucleated hamlets and isolated farms represented the homes of bond communities and the lords of the district respectively. Stevens suggested that 'rich' villas occur in areas with *tyr cyfrif* tenure, while *gwely* tenure produced many small villas (Stevens 1966).

The second model was developed by Collingwood to explain settlement organisation on Cranborne Chase and this model has recently been used to analyse Iron Age and Romano-British communities in the Upper Thames Valley (Collingwood and Myres 1937; Hingley 1988). In the Oxford Clay Vale large-scale groups with a communal division of territory occur in the Iron Age and Roman periods and in this lowland area villas appear to be absent. In contrast, social groups in the limestone Oxford Uplands appear to have been small-scale and economically independent of one another, villas are common in the Roman period. The villa, as a material symbol of wealth, may indicate the dissolution of traditional community ties. An individual might have been discouraged from constructing a symbol of his individual success over others (Hingley 1988).

With these comments in mind the Fenland information is of interest. The existence of nucleated settlement and the absence of overt display of wealth has resulted in the interpretation of the Fenland as an area inhabited by poor tenants and slaves, probably an Imperial estate (see Frere 1967:275–7 for discussion). It is clear, however, that considerable wealth existed in the hands of some individuals within Fenland society by the 4th century AD (Salway 1970:16; Potter 1981:129). Some of this wealth, rather than being invested in status indicated by building forms, appears to have been spent on portable items of material value, such as bronze, pewter and silver vessels. Potter has suggested that these wealthy individuals may have been non-tied tenants on an Imperial estate (1981).

The existence of wealth in the hands of some individuals within the 4th century Fenland indicates the falsity of the idea that villas were the only symbol of wealth and status available to rural farmers. Salway has suggested that the investment of wealth in portable metalwork expresses peasant mentality and the desire to hide wealth to avoid higher taxation (1970:16). Is it possible that the evidence actually indicates an alternative method of surplus investment? Status could have been created and maintained through feasting – hence the finds of metalwork. Feasting was a traditional Celtic act of communal generosity, rather than one which symbolised the success of an individual or a single family over others within the community.

The idea that the villa building need not have been the ideal of all free and wealthy Roman farmers may seem controversial to Romanists with a classical education. It is necessary to remember, however, that contemporary views on Roman Britain are constrained by the available literary sources available and that the indigenous background of social groups in Roman Britain will have had an important influence on the adoption of Roman culture.

Prospect

In this paper attention has been directed towards aspects of social organisation by studying the spatial organisation of rural settlements. Information for the organisation of the household at the scale of the building, the farm compound and the villa compound has been discussed. In addition the organisation of households within individual settlements has been considered. Finally, an attempt has been made to consider the distribution of social groups across the landscape.

Information on all of these aspects of study is limited. This is partly because Romanists tend to label rural settlements and consider that no further analysis is necessary. Investigation is directed towards establishing whether a settlement is a villa, a 'native settlement', or a small town, but little attempt is made to understand sites in their contexts. As a consequence few studies have been made of whole settlements and even fewer of whole landscapes. The complex systems of social organisation that once existed cannot be reconstructed from the scraps of evidence that are the results of piecemeal research and this is partly why a provincial social history is not possible. Regional surveys aimed at recovering whole settlement landscapes (e.g. Hallam's Fenland survey), combined with extensive excavation of selected sites will improve the data base. In addition a more flexible terminological and conceptual framework will enable a detailed understanding of variation in settlement within and between regions.

References

Applebaum S. 1972 Roman Britain. In H.P.R. Finberg (ed.), *The Agrarian History of England and Wales, Volume 1:2 (AD 43–1042)*. Cambridge: 3–277.

Bloemers J.H.F. 1983 Acculturation in the Rhine/Meuse Basin in the Roman period: a preliminary survey. In R. Brandt and J. Slofstra (eds.), *Roman and Native in the Low Countries*. BAR S184. Oxford: 159–210.

Booth P.M. 1980 *Roman Alcester*. Warwick Museum.

Branigan K. 1977 *Gatcombe Roman Villa*. BAR 44. Oxford.

Clarke D. 1972 A provisional model for an Iron Age society and its settlement system. In D. Clarke (ed.), *Models in Archaeology*. Oxford: 801–869.

Clarke G. 1982 The Roman Villa at Woodchester. *Britannia* 13:197–228.

Collingwood R.G. 1930 *The Archaeology of Roman Britain*. London.

Collingwood R.G. and Myres J.N.L. 1937 *Roman Britain and the English Settlement*. London.

Crawford D.J. 1976 Imperial Estates. In M.I. Finley (ed.), *Studies in Roman Property*. London: 35–70.

Cunliffe B.W. 1971 *Excavations at Fishbourne, 1961–69*. London.

Drinkwater J.F. 1983 *Roman Gaul*. London.

Duncan-Jones R. 1974 *The Economy of the Roman Empire*. Cambridge.

Frere S.S. 1967 *Britannia*. London.

Hallam S.J. 1970 Settlement round the Wash. In C.W. Phillips (ed.), *The Fenland in Roman Times*. London, 22–113.

Hingley R. 1988 The Influence of Rome on Indigenous Social Groups in the Upper Thames Valley. In R.F.J. Jones et al. (eds.), *First Millennium Papers*. BAR S401; Oxford.

Hingley R. 1989 *Rural Settlement in Roman Britain*. London.

Hodder I. and Millett M. 1980 Romano-British villas and towns. *World Archaeology*. 12:69–76.

Jones G.D.B. and Walker J. 1983 Either side of the Solway: towards a minimalist view of Romano-British agricultural systems in the northwest. In J. Chapman and H. Mytum (eds.), *Settlement in Northern Britain 100 BC–AD 1000*. BAR 118. Oxford.

Leech R. 1981 The excavation of a Romano-British farmstead and cemetery on Bradley Hill, Somertown, Somerset. *Britannia* 12:177–252.

Leech R. 1982 *Excavations at Catsgore, 1970–3*. Bristol.

MacMullen R. 1974 *Roman Social Relations*. London.

Miles D. 1984 Romano-British settlement in the Gloucestershire Thames Valley. In A. Saville (ed.), *Archaeology in Gloucestershire*. Cheltenham, 191–211.

Morris P. 1979 *Agricultural Buildings in Roman Britain*. BAR 70. Oxford.

Palmer N. 1982 *Roman Stratford*. Warwick Museum.

Percival J. 1976 *The Roman Villa*. London.

Potter T.W. 1981 The Roman occupation of the central Fenlands. *Britannia* 12:79–133.

Potter T.W. and Jackson R. 1985 British Museum excavations at Stonea, 1983, *Fenland Research* 1:27–31.

Richmond I.A. 1969 The plans of Roman villas in Britain. In A.L.F. Rivet (ed.), *The Roman Villa in Britain*. London: 49–70.

Rivet A.L.F. 1969 Social and economic aspects. In A.L.F. Rivet (ed.), *The Roman Villa in Britain*. London: 173–216.

Rodwell W. and Rowley T. (eds.) 1975 *Small Towns of Roman Britain*. BAR 15. Oxford.

Royal Commission on Historical Monuments 1976 *Iron Age and Romano-British Monuments in the Gloucestershire Cotswolds*. London.

Salway P. 1970 The Roman Fenlands. In C.W. Phillips (ed.), *The Fenlands in Roman Times*. London: 1–21.

Simco A. 1984 *Survey of Bedfordshire: the Roman period*. London.

Slofstra J. 1983 An anthropological approach to the study of the Romanisation process. In R. Brandt and J. Slofstra (eds.), *Roman and Native in the Low Countries*. BAR S184. Oxford.

Smith C. 1977 The valleys of the Tame and the middle Trent – their population and ecology during the late first millennium BC. In J. Collis (ed.), *The Iron Age in Britain: a review*. Sheffield, 51–61.

Smith D.J. 1978 Regional aspects of the winged corridor villa in Britain. In M. Todd (ed.), *Studies in the Romano-British Villa*. Leicester: 117–48.

Smith J.T. 1963 Romano-British aisled houses. *Archaeological Journal* 120:1–30.

Smith J.T. 1978a Villas as a key to social structure. In M. Todd (ed.), *Studies in the Romano-British Villa*. Leicester: 149–86.

Smith J.T. 1978b Halls or yards? A problem with villa interpretation. *Britannia* 9:349–356.

Smith J.T. 1982 Villa plans and social structure in Britain and Gaul. *Caesarodunum* 17:321–51.

Smith J.T. 1985 Barnsley Park Villa: its interpretation and implication. *Oxford Journal of Archaeology* 4:241–51.

Smith R.F. 1987 *Roadside settlements in lowland Roman Britain*. BAR 157, Oxford.

Stevens C.E. 1966 The social and economic aspects of Roman settlement. In C. Thomas (ed.), *Rural Settlement in Roman Britain*. CBA Research Report 7, London, 108–28.

Ste. Croix G.E.M. de 1981 *The Class Struggle in the Ancient Greek World*. London.

Taylor C.C. 1983 *Village and Farmstead*. London.

Todd M. 1970 The small towns of Roman Britain. *Britannia* 1:114–30.

Todd M. 1976 The vici of western England. In K. Branigan and P.J. Fowler (eds.) *Roman West Country*. Newton Abbott, 99–119.

Todd M. 1978 Villas and Romano-British society. In M. Todd (ed.), *Studies in the Romano-British Villa*. Leicester, 197–208.

Trow S. and James S. 1985 *Ditches Villa 1985*. Privately circulated.

Wacher J. 1974 Villae in urbibus? *Britannia* 5:251–61.

Wainwright G. 1968 The excavation of a Durotrigian farmstead near Tollard Royal. *Proceedings of the Prehistoric Society* 34:102–47.

Wightman E.M. 1975 The pattern of rural settlement in Roman Gaul. In H. Temporini and W. Haase (eds.) *Aufsteig und Niedergang der ro^dmischen Welt* 24:584–657.

Willems W.J.H. 1984 Romans and Batavians: a regional study in the Dutch eastern river area. *Berichten Rijksdienst Oudheidkundig Bodemonderzoek* 34:39–331.

Williams J. 1976 Excavations on a Roman site at Overstone, near Northampton. *Northamptonshire Archaeology* 11:100–33.

Williamson T.M. 1984 The Roman countryside: settlement and agriculture in northwest Essex. *Britannia* 15:225–130.

Wilson D. 1974 Roman villas from the air. *Britannia* 5:241–61.

Wilson D. 1975 The 'small towns' of Roman Britain from the air. In W. Rodwell and T. Rowley (eds.), *The Small Towns of Roman Britain*. BAR 15. Oxford, 9–50.

11. Field Survey in Roman Britain: the Experience of Maddle Farm

V Gaffney and M Tingle

This paper discusses the potential for application of field survey within Romano-British archaeology. It argues that previous work has been hindered by a rigid site specific methodology and that extensive field survey may be able to correct this imbalance and open new avenues of research into villa economies, rural land-use and demography.

Perhaps one of the greatest handicaps to the development of Romano-British archaeology has been its material richness and apparent durability. The existence of an historical record and archaeological remains often of a spectacular nature has encouraged a complacency towards some aspects of the discipline which has in turn limited its development.

Romano-British field survey provides a case in point. A glance at most site reports invariably reveals a figure purporting to show a regional site distribution. Consideration of such maps generally intimates that the data base is an ad hoc growth, accepted by many Romano-British archaeologists without full concern for operating biases and exhibiting a touching belief in the invulnerability and total visibility of Romano-British sites. This naïvety, further expressed in the predilection for the exploration of the most obvious of sites, villas, towns and military works, has undoubtedly been eroded over the last 15 years. The generally sterile debate on the nature of villas current in the seventies at least forced recognition that life existed beyond the confines of a prestigious villa building (Todd 1978). But if the scale of study has increased, with notable exceptions it has rarely exceeded adjacent buildings with unequivocal links to the principal villa structure. Problems beyond the walls were considered unapproachable. The nature of land tenure and extramural land-use were beyond the reach of a data base that consisted largely of the most obvious landscape features and excavations of the most prolific sites. Beyond basic locational analysis Romano-British research strategies have largely evaded the action of the inhabitants of 'sites' within a landscape. Attempts to provide such information within the traditional framework eg. Branigan 1977, have been notably unsuccessful. Yet the potential of work both in an urban setting (Corney, in Fulford 1985) and in rural areas (Williamson 1984) is becoming apparent as research proceeds. Work carried out by the authors for the Maddle Farm project exemplifies the nature of some of the substantive problems now being faced by field survey in one aspect of Romano-British archaeology.

The Maddle Farm Project was a multi-stage survey centred on a small Romano-British villa complex near Upper Lambourn in Berkshire. Coupled with limited excavation designed to complement survey, the first phase of the project comprised a core survey in which all available land within a 2km circle around the villa was fieldwalked to provide an immediate context to the settlement. This was followed by an extensive transect sample survey designed to investigate the major topographic trends of the chalk scarp and linking the Maddle complex to the nearest substantial Roman buildings east and west known at the start of the survey (Figure 11.1). The field methodology described elsewhere (Gaffney *et al.* 1985) provided a firm quantitative basis for research. In the context of other work carried out on the prehistoric landscape of the area (Ellison and Bradley 1975; Richards 1978), linear ditches (Ford 1982a, 1982b) and the Celtic fields systems (Bowden *et al.* 1985), the extant data base and research potential of the area is impressive (c.f. Gaffney and Tingle 1989).

In the Roman context the Maddle Farm survey results have been enough to undermine the site specific nature of Romano-British rural studies. Pottery discard was extensive and although centred on the villa complex could be shown to be intermittent over an area of c. 500ha. rather than being restricted to obvious settlement areas, (Figure 11.2). This 'off-site' evidence has been related to Romano-British manuring practice based from within the settlement complex (Gaffney *et al.* 1985). Manuring as an archaeological phenomenon is not a new observation in prehistoric or Roman studies (Fowler 1983; Richards 1978). However in a field of research where it has been noted that 'there is almost no evidence of the systems operating on villa estates' (Percival 1976:20), the patterning in the Maddle survey allows behavioural analysis of the data at a number of novel levels. The pottery discard probably relates to distance dependent land-use parameters similar to site catchment analysis. The behavioural system related to the villa complex and evidenced through the pottery, displays regularities which have been related to the need to maximise land-use beyond the areas easily managed directly from the central settlement (Gaffney *et al.* 1985). This information has been used to estimate the behavioural territory of the villa. On the basis that if we can equate off-site discard with human activity and can expect a decrease in discard away from the principal site and toward the boundary we may produce a minimum catchment for a settlement by drawing lines of least resistance through the negative areas of surface data (Gaffney and Gaffney forthcoming).

Although this paper is far too short to cover a full discussion of such a method, several points can be made. The technique is based upon primary archaeological evidence and avoids the subjective pitfalls of boundary parameterisation dependent upon 'natural features' (Branigan 1977), or the gross generalisations of traditional site catchments or Thiessen polygons. The results can be used to model aspects of the contemporary Roman economy in conjunction with evidence for probable area of manured land, whilst estimates of the manpower

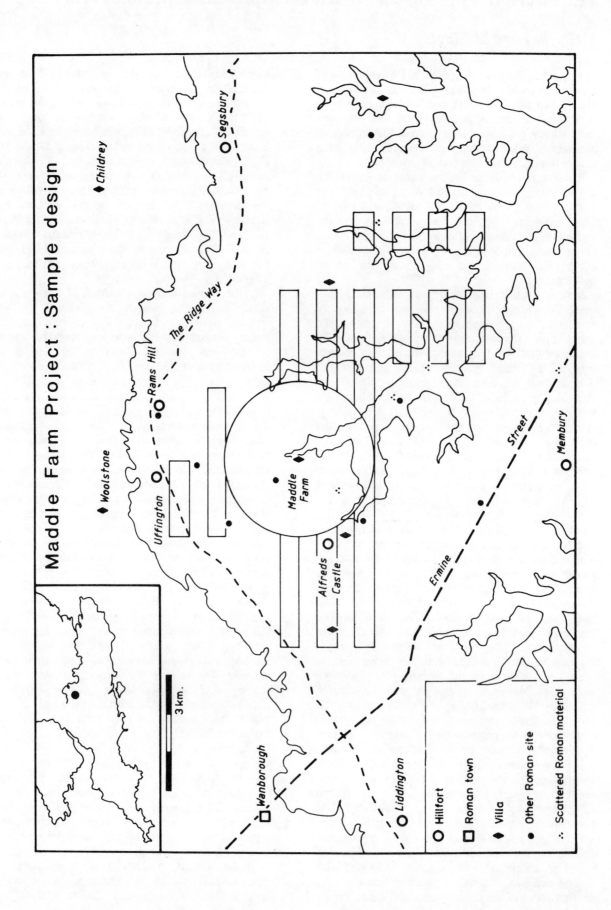

Figure 11.1   Maddle farm project: sample design.

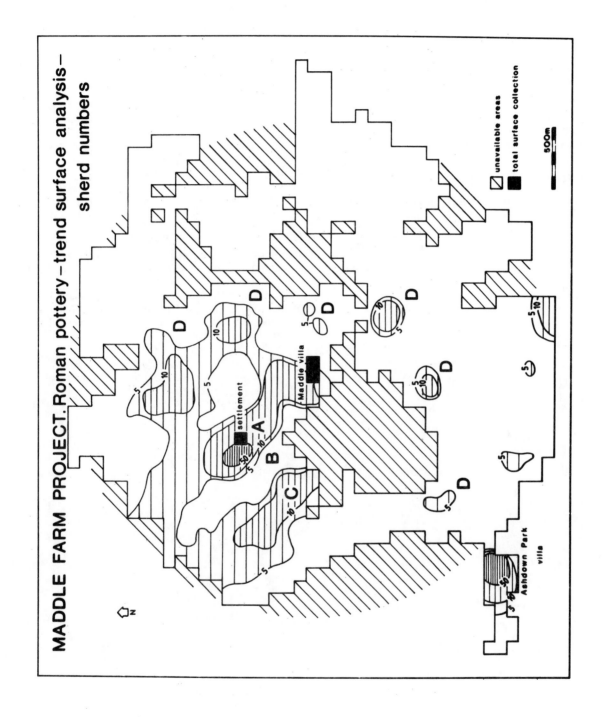

Figure 11.2   Maddle Farm Project: Roman pottery distributions.

demands of such economies will open new avenues of demographic research.

Undoubtedly such work carries inherent problems. The mobility of boundaries caused by a land market, the existence of extended territories, or common land, all of these factors could prove problematic. However if Romano-British archaeology is to grapple with the more substantive problems of the archaeological record, it has to attempt and test analysis of this nature. As Percival commented: 'There is clearly a long way to go before we can speak with any assurance on social and tenurial patterns as far as Britain and the British villas are concerned. But even such an unproductive discussion can help in a number of ways: by revealing the uncertainties and outlining the possibilities, it can give us a better idea of the kind of evidence we need' (Percival 1976:144).

Acknowledgments

The authors would like to thank Chris Gaffney for reading the article and commenting upon the contents in a number of ways. Mark Bowden drew the illustrations whilst Helen Weston typed the manuscript.

References

Bowden M., Ford, S. and Meese, G. 1985. The Celtic Fields Project, interim report. Berkshire Archaeological Field Research Group.

Branigan K. 1977. *Gatcombe Park Villa*. BAR 44. Oxford.

Ellison A. and R. Bradley 1975. *Rams Hill*. BAR 19. Oxford.

Ford S. 1982a. Linear earthworks on the Berkshire Downs. *Berkshire Archaeological Journal* 71:1–21.

Ford S. 1982b. Fieldwork and excavation on the Berkshire Grimms Ditch. *Oxoniensia* 47:13–36.

Fowler P. 1983. *The Farming of Prehistoric Britain*. Cambridge University Press.

Fulford M. 1984. *Silchester: Excavations on the defences 1974–80*. Britannia Monograph No.5.

Gaffney C., Gaffney, V. and Tingle, M. 1985. Settlement, economy or behaviour? Micro regional land use models and the interpreting of surface artefact patterns. In C. Haselgrove, M. Millett and I. Smith (eds.) *Archaeology from the Ploughsoil*. Sheffield, 95–109.

Gaffney C. and Gaffney, V. forthcoming.

Gaffney, V. and Tingle, M. 1989. *The Maddle Farm Project: An Integrated Survey of Prehistoric and Roman Landscapes on the Berkshire Downs* BAR 200. Oxford.

Percival J. 1976. *The Roman Villa*.

Richards J. 1978. *The archaeology of the Berkshire Downs: an introductory survey*. Reading. Berkshire Archaeological Committee.

Todd M. (ed.) 1978. *Studies in the Romano-British Villa*.

Williamson T.M. 1984. The Roman Countryside: settlement and agriculture in northwest Essex. *Britannia* 15:225–231.

12. Soldiers and Settlement in Wales and Scotland

W.S. Hanson and L. Macinnes

The impact of the Romans on the native population in Wales and Scotland is considered in terms of military, economic and social effects. Although the military campaigns are well attested, there is very little unequivocal archaeological evidence for direct conflict, nor much which will support ideas of major population displacement. Economic effects are not generally reflected in the development of a monetary economy, but rather in the form of Roman exploitation of resources and pressure on the existing agricultural regimes to meet the additional demands of the army, though the problem posed by the latter may have been overstated. In the early stages of occupation the Roman presence was felt mainly by the higher ranks of native society and may not have been as disruptive as is usually assumed. In contrast, the longer term occupation of Wales gradually brought about changes throughout native society and it is in this respect that Roman impact differed most between the two areas.

A consideration of the effects of the Roman imperial presence on the indigenous population of Britain is by no means a new theme. In the past, however, there has been a tendency to approach the subject in a rather one-sided and relatively simplistic manner. Some of the manifestations of the Roman civilisation, notably towns and villas, are so obviously new to Britain that there has been undue concentration upon them, the result being an over-emphasis on the Roman side of the equation – note the predominant use of the term Romanisation – and the reactions of the upper strata of native society. One advantage of considering this theme in the context of the military zone is that we can see the processes at an early stage of development and examine areas where the effects of the Roman presence appear to have been more limited. Consideration of both Wales and Scotland, regions broadly similar in topography and pre-Roman Iron Age cultural development, but different in their subsequent relationship with Rome, provide the potential for useful contrasts and comparisons to be drawn.

One major problem, and one reason for the usual concentration upon the Roman side of the equation, is the disparity between the sources of evidence available. Not only are Roman sites, both military and civilian, more readily identifiable from fieldwork and aerial photography, but in proportion to their numbers they have received an undue share of attention. Comparatively few native settlements of Late Iron Age or Romano-British date in these areas, with the exception of Jobey's work in Northumberland, have been systematically examined by excavation, and fewer still subjected to major investigation. By contrast there are relatively few Roman forts in either Wales or Scotland that have not been investigated at some time. Nor is the contrast simply between Roman and native sites, but rather

between military and civilian sites, for the location and excavation of *vici* have also been much neglected. Even where excavation has taken place, the level of information recovered from Roman and native sites is not easily comparable, particularly in terms of chronology. As well as the obvious advantage of producing coins, Roman sites usually provide large quantities of pottery, much of which is subject to quite precise dating, the result of many years of detailed study. This contrasts sharply with the situation on native sites where finds of all types are relatively uncommon and usually datable only in the broadest terms; even carbon-14 dating is too imprecise to provide much assistance. Indeed, the most useful dating evidence from native sites is often provided by Roman material, though this introduces its own bias. Bearing these problems in mind, an attempt is made below to consider the interaction between Roman and native in terms of three major themes: military confrontation, economic exploitation and social integration.

Obviously the primary impact of the Roman presence on the indigenous population was military. The process of conquest of both Wales and Scotland has been frequently rehearsed in print and need not delay us here. What is important for our present purpose is to emphasise the difference between campaigning and permanent occupation. The Romans campaigned in Wales for some 13 seasons, spread over 30 years, before complete conquest was achieved and the area permanently occupied. Thereafter the picture is one of the gradual withdrawal of Roman troops with only a limited presence beyond the 2nd century AD (Jarrett 1969:19–28; Davies 1980). Scotland, on the other hand, was never fully or permanently subjugated. Roman penetration into the Highlands was virtually non-existent, while the fluctuations of the northern frontier continue to provide much scope for academic study (e.g. Breeze 1982; Hanson and Maxwell 1983).

One obvious concomitant of the period of campaigning is the death in battle of large numbers of men of fighting age. The difficulty of quantifying the effect on native society, however, is equally obvious. We are rarely provided with figures in the literary accounts and where estimates are given their accuracy cannot go unquestioned. Tacitus indicates that some 10,000 Caledonians lost their lives at Mons Graupius (*Agricola* 37), but he had good reason to exaggerate the total in order to maximise the apparent size of Agricola's victory. Even so, the death toll was only one third of those assembled for battle and we have no evidence of any other encounter of similar magnitude during Agricola's Scottish campaigns, so that the overall impact on the population may not have been as drastic as might at first be assumed. No similar figures are provided for the Welsh campaigns, not even for the final confrontation with Caratacus. In fact, the battles seem frequently to have been little more than skirmishes with minimal losses (Tacitus, Annals 12, 39), though the taking of hostages and selling of captives into slavery would have added to the effect.

Archaeological evidence for this aggressive phase of Roman and native interaction is surprisingly slight. We might well have expected to find evidence of destruction or demolition of native settlements in the face of Roman attacks, but the few examples which have been postulated are highly dubious. Ironically, both of the hillforts in Scotland at which there is archaeological evidence of a siege by the Roman army appear to have been practice works. The defences of the hillfort at Burnswark were already in decay when it was used as a target by Roman artillery (Jobey 1978:67 and 98). The incomplete nature of the investing works at Woden Law has led to the suggestion that they were not constructed in earnest (Richmond and St. Joseph 1982:282-4); in fact, even their Roman date and suggested military function remains merely a hypothesis which is not entirely convincing. The only Scottish site which has been seriously put forward as suffering at Roman hands is the broch at Leckie (MacKie 1982), but there is no direct evidence that the attested fire and demolition there had anything to do with the army (Macinnes 1984a:238). Similar problems are involved in the interpretation of the slighting of the defences at two Welsh sites, Castell Odo (Alcock 1960:98-9) and the Breiddin (O'Neil 1937:106). In the former case there is no direct evidence of Roman date let alone responsibility, while at the latter the apparent slighting has been reinterpreted as deliberate levelling as part of the late Roman re-occupation of the hillfort (Musson 1976:299).

Evidence of native attacks on established Roman forts is no less problematic, though this has frequently been suggested as a factor in determining the Roman attitude towards an area (e.g. Clarke 1958:58). It can be difficult enough on archaeological grounds to distinguish between destruction and demolition, let alone determine the agency responsible, but the evidence continues to grow that the Romans demolished their own forts on evacuation, a process which sometimes involved the burning of unwanted timbers (Hanson 1978:302-4; Breeze and Dobson 1972:200-206). Deliberate filling of the well in the headquarters building at Caerhun and Brecon Gaer is precisely what we would expect to happen during clearing up by the Romans on evacuation (*contra* Simpson 1964:112-3).

Once subjugation of an area was complete and the Roman presence established on a more permanent footing, then longer term effects can be expected. The imposition of Roman garrisons is likely to have precipitated a certain amount of settlement dislocation, for at least two of the criteria which dictated the location of Roman forts would have resulted in a potential overlap with native sites. As well as concern for policing centres of population, Roman forts also seem to have been sited with regard to the local availability of agricultural produce (Higham 1982:108-110). Quite what would have

happened to native sites located within the area assigned to the fort, its *territorium*, is uncertain. The occupants may well have been turned off their land in favour of the inhabitants of a civilian settlement outside the fort, the *vicus* (Manning 1975:114), though aerial survey in the immediate vicinity of the fort at Old Carlisle in Cumbria suggests that native style farmsteads continued to be occupied and were linked to the *vicus* by trackways (Jones 1984:80-84). In some cases potential settlement dislocation may be attested archaeologically when Roman installations are seen to overlie native settlements. In Scotland this has been recorded at, for example, Cappuck (Richmond 1951:142-3) and Eildon Hill North (Steer and Feachem 1952), while at Brandon camp in the Marches the Romans actually re-used a pre-Roman Iron Age hillfort as a military base (Frere 1986). In all these examples, however, it is difficult to be certain that the native sites were actually in use at the time of the Roman occupation and not already long abandoned.

More dramatic and far reaching is the depopulation which has been suggested was a direct result of the Roman arrival in north Wales, northeast England and eastern Scotland. Noting the paucity of Roman finds from native sites in mid and north Wales till the 3rd century AD or later, when they appear on stone-built settlements of rectilinear form, and linking this with Tacitus' brief statement that virtually the whole of the Ordovices were killed (*Agricola* 17), Hogg has argued that Agricola's campaign so devastated the area that it remained wholly uninhabited until reoccupied by new Romanised settlers in the 3rd century (1966:30 and 35). The hypothesis has little to commend it. On the one hand, such statements in Tacitus were for rhetorical effect and should not be taken too literally. On the other, the evidence for continuity of native occupation from the Iron Age is increasing as a result of further excavation, as for example at Cefn Graeanog (information from R. White). This particular hypothesis serves to highlight the dangers of basing interpretations almost solely upon the presence or absence of Roman material on native sites when the mechanisms by which it arrived are unknown. In the case of mid and north Wales the pre-Roman Iron Age seems to have been largely aceramic which makes the paucity of 1st and 2nd century Roman pottery on native sites more understandable in terms of local conservatism in the adoption of new ideas (Davies 1974:39).

It was a similar juxtaposition of disparate strands of evidence by Collingwood which led to the suggestion of mass deportation to Germany of peoples from northeastern England and lowland Scotland after the Roman re-conquest in the 2nd century AD (Collingwood and Myres 1936:146). There is no doubting the presence on the Odenwald *limes* in the mid-2nd century of small ethnic units (*numeri*) of Britons as attested by epigraphy, but the excavation of one of their forts makes clear that the unit there was already in residence by the end of the 1st century (Baatz 1973:71). Moreover, wide-ranging field survey on native sites in Northumberland does not support the view of extensive depopulation, and may even indicate a steady increase (Jobey 1974).

What the presence of British units in Germany does serve to illustrate, however, is the principle of recruitment into the army from recently conquered areas. Nor are these the earliest examples from Britain. British recruits are attested in the 1st century AD and some were actually involved in the fighting at Mons Graupius (Dobson and Mann 1973:198–9). Though we rarely have direct evidence of the precise source of the recruits, there is a strong possibility of recruitment from both Wales and Scotland, particularly into these ethnic units (*numeri*) (Gillam 1984:293).

Although the interpretation of enforced depopulation from either Scotland or Wales is now largely rejected, it is still widely accepted that the Roman presence had considerable impact on native settlement, bringing about major changes normally referred to as the benefits of the *pax Romana*. In particular the changeover from hillforts to enclosed but non-defensive settlements is usually seen as a response to the Roman arrival. Recognition that a distinctive form of stone-built enclosed settlement in north Northumberland was occupied during the Roman period and that a large number of examples succeeded hillforts (Jobey 1965:56–8) is not sufficient, however, to establish a causal relationship. Indeed, there is growing evidence that in Scotland the move to less defensive forms of settlement may have occurred before the Roman arrival. At Broxmouth, in Lothian Region, the carbon-14 dates linked to the sequence of defences indicate that the hillfort had reached its final form long before the Roman period and had probably ceased to be maintained as a defended site (Hill 1982:189), while we have already noted that the rampart of the large hillfort at Burnswark was in disrepair by the mid-2nd century AD at the latest. A similar pattern of change has been suggested for the Welsh Marches where the abandonment of the large hillforts which dominate the area and the move to lower lying settlements was seen as a direct result of the Roman conquest (Stanford 1974:50–4). Over the last decade, however, aerial reconnaissance has demonstrated (e.g. Musson 1981) that a wider range of enclosures than was previously thought are to be found on the lower ground some of which, such as Collfryn and Bromfield (*A.W.* 1982:17–18; 1979:25–6), were certainly occupied in the pre-Roman Iron Age. Thus the interpretation of enforced displacement from defended to non-defended settlements is no longer tenable (Davies 1984:95). This is not to deny that some hilltop sites were still occupied at the time of the Roman arrival, and in some cases continued to be thereafter (Jobey 1976:198–203; Savory 1976:284–6), but rather that caution should be exercised in assuming that undated changes in settlement form or location were necessarily of Roman origin. There is, for example, no direct evidence that the unfinished state of a well-known group of hillforts in northeast Scotland had any connection with the Roman advance (*contra* Feachem 1966:70). Nor can we be certain that the

placing of a Roman watch-tower in the centre of the large fort at Eildon Hill did involve the removal of its inhabitants.

Thus direct Roman effects on the nature and location of native settlements have probably been overestimated. Despite the words Tacitus places in the mouth of Calgacus prior to the battle of Mons Graupius (*Agricola* 30), the Romans did not set out to create desolation in the areas they conquered. On the contrary they were concerned to control them efficiently and tax them effectively. There can be little doubt that economic exploitation was, and always had been, an important motivating factor in Roman conquest. Cicero's immediate reaction to Caesar's expeditions of 55 and 54 BC is disappointment at the lack of silver and other booty which was only partly offset by the provision of tribute (*Ep* 4, 18, 5) while Strabo twice explains Augustus' lack of interest in occupying the island by reference to the greater revenue obtained from customs' duties (*Geog.* 2, 5, 8). The quickest way to obtain a return from a newly conquered area was by taxation and, accordingly, the rapid imposition of tribute would have been standard practice. Since the main sources of revenue were a tax on land productivity (*tributum soli*) and a poll tax (*tributum capitis*), one important prerequisite was a census (Jones 1974:164–5). Fortuitously one British census official T. Haterius Nepos, is recorded from the latter part of Trajan's region apparently operating in lower Annandale in Dumfries and Galloway Region (Rivet 1982).

In exactly what form these taxes were paid is not known, but tax in kind was not common until the later Empire (Jones 1974:108–9). Under normal circumstances, the Roman authorities would have expected to receive coin. Neither Wales nor Scotland, however, had a pre-existing monetary system to which Roman coinage could have been tied, so coin must have been obtained in exchange for the provision of goods or services to, in the first instance, the military. Thus the extent to which Roman coinage is found on native sites should provide some insight into the process of economic integration of the newly conquered areas. In fact, in the 1st and 2nd centuries AD in both Scotland (Robertson 1975:386–9) and Wales (Davies 1983:82–5) coinage reaches native sites only sporadically and differentially. In the former, at least, the fluctuations do, indeed, seem to be a direct reflection of the presence or absence of Roman troops. The general paucity of finds makes it difficult to justify any claim that the Romans rapidly introduced a monetary economy, which in turn makes any explanation of the presence of Roman coin on native sites couched solely in terms of market forces rather difficult to accept. Coin could certainly have been obtained from Roman sources in direct payment for requisitioned foodstuffs, a system whose abuse we hear about during Agricola's governorship (Tacitus, *Agricola* 15), and presumably then used to pay taxes. One interesting parallel between Scotland and north Wales, which perhaps provides a pointer to the method of tax collection, is the concentration of coinage at certain larger native settlements. The hillforts at Traprain Law in Lothian Region (Sekulla 1982) and Braich y Ddinas in Gwynedd (Davies 1983:83–4), have both produced relatively large quantities of 1st and 2nd century Roman coins. This suggests that the Roman authorities used the local social system already in existence and had direct contact only with the upper strata of society. Thus once a tax assessment had been reached, demand for payment could have been made to the tribal leaders. It would then have been up to them how this sum was recouped from the wider population, for whom coin would have had little meaning except as bullion, or as a means of facilitating occasional direct exchange with Roman troops.

By the 3rd century AD, however, most rural sites in southwest Wales produce a few coins, as they gradually became more integrated into the Romano-British economic infrastructure (Davies 1983:87; 1984:112). By contrast in mid and north Wales site finds are uncommon and in Scotland quite rare. Even the late coins from Traprain Law seem to reflect either bullion or the deliberate discard of base metal with neither exchange value nor intrinsic worth (Sekulla 1982:288–9). The significance of the distribution of Roman coin hoards of various dates throughout Wales and Scotland remains elusive. Though some from Scotland, such as the mid-3rd century AD hoard from Falkirk or the 4th century hoard from Fort Augustus, may confidently be attributed to native ownership because of their date of deposition and/or geographical location in relation to the known periods and extent or Roman occupation, the method by which the coin reached their hands remains obscure (Robertson 1978:196).

The economic demands of the Roman army were considerable. Whilst on campaign it was standard practice for ancient armies to live off the land, so that the effect on local resources of the presence of an army of up to 30,000 men, the figure based broadly upon the estimates provided by Tacitus (*Agricola* 35–37), could have been quite dramatic. With the establishment of a permanent garrison the overall requirements were probably no less, for though the number of troops may have been slightly reduced, to around 20,000 men for each of our areas, they would have been present throughout the year. Even so the effect of the demand for foodstuffs would have been less devastating since the troops were more widely scattered. Because of the high cost of overland transport, bulk supplies such as grain were obtained locally wherever possible (Manning 1975). As already noted, this requirement was probably an important factor in determining the location of forts in areas of arable land. On the other hand, some supplies were brought in from long distances, such as the wine and olive oil which once filled the amphorae frequently found on excavation. Meat too is usually assumed to have been an important element of the soldier's diet (Davies 1971:126–8), though recent analyses of the sewage deposits from the Antonine Wall fort at Bearsden indicated a predominantly vegetarian diet (Knights *et al* 1983). Large numbers of animals were also required for transport, both as

mounts and beasts of burden, while the demand for leather for clothing, shoes, horse gear and even tents was considerable (Breeze 1984:269–72). It remains uncertain, however, whether taxation and these various military demands did stimulate local agricultural production and bring about pressure for change because of the different food preferences of the Romans.

Structural, artefactual and environmental evidence combine to indicate that a mixed farming system was in operation in the pre-Roman Iron Age in both Wales and Scotland. Grain processing and storage is well attested. Four-post structures in Wales, notably within hillforts, such as Moel-y-Gaer and the Breiddin, and enclosures like Llawhaden, are usually interpreted as buildings for food storage. In Scotland similar structures have occasionally been identified, as at Dryburn, while souterrains, particularly those in Angus, had a large storage capacity (Watkins 1980:198). In addition large field systems, probably of contemporary date, are known around Iron Age and Roman settlements in southern Scotland (Halliday 1982). While these have not been paralleled in Wales, environmental evidence there clearly demonstrates that extensive pre-Roman cultivation was taking place (Jones 1981:104), even spreading on to poorer soils as, for example, at Cefn Graeanog (information from R. White).

Whether or not the Roman presence did stimulate an increase in arable cultivation is still not clearly demonstrable. Pollen evidence for such an increase in northeast England is not precisely dated (Turner 1979), while an expansion on to more marginal land noted both in Wales (Hogg 1966:35) and northern Britain (Gates 1982:36–8) could well be of pre-Roman origin (Smith 1980:152). Nor is it even certain that any increase in arable exploitation which is attested can be directly attributed to the Roman presence since there is increasing evidence for climatic improvement at about this time which is likely to have been just as important a factor in stimulating such a development (Lamb 1981:56–7). Moreover, it is interesting to note that the change in the main arable crop in Wales from emmer to spelt wheat, once seen as a result of the Roman occupation, occurred in the pre-Roman period (Jones 1981:104).

The structural evidence from both regions suggests that Iron Age production had probably developed well beyond a purely subsistence level, with storage of the surplus either for redistribution or as seed corn to allow increased production. The souterrain settlements in Scotland, for instance, with their large storage potential, point to a highly organised exploitation of the landscape, while the oppida also probably reflect a coherent social and economic organisation (Macinnes 1982:67). In Wales, too, the size and apparent internal planning of some hillforts attest their considerable importance within the settlement hierarchy (Savory 1976:255). The ability to produce a surplus may have meant that the additional demands of the Roman forces could have been met without unduly stressing the economic system at least in the short term. Any shortfall could have been made good by imports, as had to be done for more exotic items not locally available, but to what extent this was necessary for staple foods is a matter of debate. Tacitus implies that grain requisitioned in the province was sometimes sent to garrisons on the frontier (*Agricola* 9) and Fulford argues that the importation of pottery from the continent was only a minor trade tacked on to bulkier cargoes of perishables (1984:135). Unfortunately, the one recorded example of imported grain at Caerleon seems to have been intended for brewing beer rather than making porridge (Helbaek 1964).

Survival of faunal evidence is not good in the highland zone in general and little analysis has been undertaken in either Wales or Scotland. The keeping of stock is well attested in Iron Age and Romano-British settlements in both areas, but there is as yet no clear evidence of the introduction of new types in the Roman period. The appearance of larger animals has been noted elsewhere in the province and attributed to Roman interference (Maltby 1981:194), but not enough analytical work has been carried out in our two regions to support this or indicate any change in the nature of livestock farming, such as from dairy to meat production on a larger scale. It is possible, moreover, that the meat requirements of the military have been overemphasised if the sewage deposits from the Roman fort at Bearsden prove to be typical (Knights *et al* 1983). Before any further progress can be made on these questions, comparisons must be made between environmental assemblages from both Roman and native sites in both areas, which in turn demands that uniform sampling strategies are adopted during excavation.

There are aspects of the economy, however, in which the Romans did systematically and deliberately exploit local resources. The best documented is the organised extraction of mineral resources throughout Wales from an early date. There are a number of lead pigs from north Wales bearing stamps of the emperor Vespasian, dated to AD 74 and 76, and even one with the name of a private individual, C. Nipius Ascanius, known to have been operating in the Mendips as early as AD 60 (Webster 1953:8–9 and 22–4). Precisely how early this systematic extraction began is uncertain, but it was clearly well under way even before Frontinus' campaigns of conquest which are generally thought to have brought most of Wales formally under Roman control (Davies 1980:261–2). What must be emphasised for our present purposes is that this was exploitation for Roman benefit. There is no question of local native development of the industry. The ownership of all mineral resources was vested in the emperor and extraction was often organised or supervised by Roman troops (Hanson 1986). Wales was particularly rich in minerals for not only was lead mined, mainly for its silver content, but also copper and gold. Though lead ores are known in Scotland, there is no evidence of Roman exploitation. The extraction of metals does seem to have resulted in the early development of some more Romanised centres (Davies 1984:101–2), but any impact upon the local population is hard to detect.

The massive construction programmes needed in the initial stages of the Roman conquest and consolidation must have created considerable demand for building material. Davies has drawn attention to the systematic quarrying of stone in Wales on a scale not readily paralleled in the pre-Roman period (1984:102), but the main material employed for fort building was timber. A strong case has been made against the long-held belief in the importation of pre-fabricated timber by the Roman army and in favour of the exploitation of local resources (Hanson 1978). The volume of timber required for the construction of an average auxiliary fort is quite considerable and would have involved the stripping of between 90 and 170 acres (37–71ha) of woodland. Though the local impact of such action would have been considerable the overall effect on the landscape has perhaps been overemphasised. Broadly contemporary native settlements may each have required the clearance of only some 3 to 5 acres of woodland for their construction, but their vastly greater numbers serve to place the Roman requirements into perspective (Hanson and Macinnes 1980:109–9). Though the literary tradition suggests that timber was always fairly readily available in Scotland, this is not to suggest that the whole country was covered with dense forest. Indeed, recent pollen analyses from two Roman sites in central Scotland, one of Flavian and one of Antonine date, indicate little change from the late 1st to the mid-2nd century AD; Roman impact there seems to have been negligible on a landscape already divided up and extensively cleared of woodland before their arrival (Boyd 1984).

Overall, it seems likely that the natural resources and indigenous production systems of Wales and Scotland could have accommodated most Roman demands. It is difficult to estimate the degree to which individual farming settlements may have been affected by a need for increased production – but the general picture is one of continuity not disruption. The adoption of an alien economic system as attested in Wales by the appearance of Roman villas should be seen as a product of Romanisation; as much the result of social as of economic forces. The suggestion that some sections of native society were affected by the Roman occupation rather more than others, with the basic core of the social order largely untouched, is one which does find some considerable support in the archaeological evidence.

The presence of Roman artefacts on native sites has been much discussed, particularly in Scotland (Robertson 1970), but comparatively little attention has been paid to the varying factors which may have contributed to their distribution. One major problem in any such study has been the reliance on Roman artefacts for dating non-Roman sites and the consequent difficulty in recognizing contemporary settlements which did not acquire Roman goods. Yet unless real gaps in the distribution pattern can be identified, the potential significance of the distribution of Roman material within native society and the processes of exchange in operation cannot be appreciated. A steady increase in the use of independent dating methods, such as Carbon-14, is beginning to show that the distribution of Roman material is not uniform but differential (Macinnes 1980).

In the earlier period of Roman involvement in both Wales and Scotland, Roman artefacts have been recovered mainly from a few large settlements, like Traprain Law (Jobey 1976:198–203) and Braich y Ddinas (Davies 1974:39). Such sites would seem to have been of importance in the pre-Roman and Roman native settlement pattern; Traprain Law, for instance, is notable not only for its size and evidence of internal planning, but also for its domination of other settlements in the vicinity (Macinnes 1984b:193–5). In Scotland there does seem to be a differential distribution of Roman material in favour of sites distinguished within the settlement pattern either by size, like Traprain Law, or exotic form such as crannogs, like Hyndford, or the lowland brochs, like Torwoodlee (Macinnes 1984a). While the distribution of Roman material was wider in the 2nd century and encompassed a greater variety of sites, there nevertheless still seems to have been a concentration on the more unusual and possibly higher status sites. The indigenous social network seems to have remained a significant factor in the process of exchange between Roman and native.

That the principal medium of that exchange was the army itself is indicated by the influx of material into Scotland in the mid-2nd century when military occupation was most dense, for this was followed by a reduction in volume after the withdrawal of Roman forces from the Antonine Wall (Robertson 1970:212). The actual method of exchange is less clear, but presumably Roman goods were obtained from Roman forts, or more probably from the civilian settlements outside them, by purchase employing coin obtained from the requisition of foodstuffs (see above) or by barter. There is at least some support for a process of commercial exchange in the presence of native artefacts in Roman forts, though this material has never been comprehensively assembled largely because of the uncertainty in identifying it. Two types of personal ornament, glass bangles and button and loop fasteners, serve to illustrate the case. Both are probably of native manufacture, a mould for a fastener being recorded from Traprain Law, and are quite commonly found on Roman sites (Stevenson 1976; Kilbride-Jones 1980:159–67). An alternative method by which native communities acquired Roman goods was via diplomatic gifts or the payment of subsidies. The latter may have been paid either to friendly or hostile groups, as is attested at the end of the 2nd century when Virius Lupus was obliged to buy off the Maeatae (Cassius Dio 75, 5, 4), but there are indications in the archaeological record of favoured status for at least one tribe, the Votadini. Traprain Law, their capital, flourished throughout the Roman period, despite its proximity to the thriving *vicus* at Inveresk, and seems to have been the only site to have continued to acquire Roman goods in any quantity after the abandonment of the Antonine frontier (Jobey 1976:201–3).

Only in the initial period of Roman occupation in Wales does the distribution of Roman goods show much relation to the pre-Roman settlement pattern. Thereafter the picture is one of contrast between native and Romanised settlements – between rural farmsteads like Cefn Graeanog on the one hand and the urban sites and villas of the south and east on the other. It is surely significant that it is the agriculturally richer areas which supported the wealthier and more Romanised sites, a situation paralleled in Scotland, although there their architecture remains native in character. The development of villas from pre-Roman Iron Age settlement at Whitton and Cae Summerhouse suggest an increase in wealth amongst certain sectors of the native population, though even in the more Romanised areas other sites, like Biglis, display little evidence of contact with Rome.

The establishment of urban centres in the well settled areas of south and west Wales must have disrupted the native social network in a way unparalleled in Scotland. In north Wales, however, some pre-Roman hillforts like Treir Ceiri and Braich y Ddinas seem to have retained their importance, obtaining Roman goods throughout the occupation. Nevertheless, it is likely that even there the existing settlement pattern had begun to change by the 3rd century AD when new small and apparently wealthy settlements like Din Lligwy appeared. As already noted there is no evidence that these new settlements were anything other than local developments, but it is tempting to suggest that their wealth may have been related to the continued Roman exploration of minerals in the area.

The difference between Wales and Scotland seems to reflect the well-known pragmatic attitude shown by Rome to the annexation of provinces. In the early stages in both areas the emphasis seems to have been on continuity rather than disruption of the social order. Scotland never progressed beyond this stage, never becoming part of the province proper. In Wales, by contrast, integration did take place and the southern and eastern areas of the country assumed many traits of Romanisation, developing both new types of civilian settlement and wealthy native ones. The continued presence of sites with no Roman material confirms that contact with Rome continued to take place among a limited section of the native population only, though the process may have resulted in the creation of a new elite. All in all, the evidence emphasizes that the relations between Rome and the native population were not static, but evolving; not uniform, but variable.

References

Alcock L. 1960 Castell Odo: an embanked settlement on Mynydd Ystum, near Aberdaron, Caernarvonshire. *Archaeol. Cambrensis* 109:78–135.

A.W. Archaeology in Wales. Aberystwyth.

Baatz D. 1973 *Kastell Hesselbach.* Berlin.

Birley E., Dobson B. and Jarrett M.G. 1974 *Roman frontier studies 1969.* Cardiff.

Blagg T. and King A. (eds.) 1984 *Military and Civilian in Roman Britain: cultural relationships in a frontier province.* Oxford.

Boyd W.E. 1984 Environmental change and Iron Age land management in the area of the Antonine Wall, central Scotland: a summary. *Glasgow Archaeol. J.* 11:75–81.

Breeze D.J. 1982 *The Northern Frontiers of Roman Britain*. London.

Breeze D.J. 1984 Demand and supply on the northern frontier. In Miket and Burgess 1984:264–86.

Breeze D.J. and Dobson B. 1972 Hadrian's Wall: some problems. *Britannia* 3:182–208.

Clack P. and Haselgrove S. (eds.) 1982 *Rural Settlement in the Roman North*. Durham.

Clarke J. 1958 Roman and native, AD 80–122. In Richmond I.A. (ed.) *Roman and Native in North Britain*. Edinburgh:28–59.

Collingwood R.G. and Myres J.N.L. 1936 *Roman Britain and the English Settlements*. Oxford.

Davies J.L. 1974 Roman and native in Wales, first to fourth centuries AD. in Birley *et al* 1974:34–43.

Davies J.L. 1980 Roman military deployment in Wales and the Marches from Claudius to the Antonines. In Hanson W.S. and Keppie L.J.F. (eds.) *Roman Frontier Studies 1979*. Oxford:255–78.

Davies J.L. 1983 Coinage and settlement in Roman Wales and the Marches: some observations. *Archaeol. Cambrensis* 132:78–94.

Davies J.L. 1984 Soldiers, peasants and markets in Wales and the Marches. In Blagg and King 1984:93–127.

Davies R. 1971 The Roman military diet. *Britannia* 2:122–42.

Dobson B. and Mann J.C. 1973 The Roman army in Britain and Britons in the Roman army. *Britannia* 4:191–205.

Feachem R. 1966 The hillforts of northern Britain. In Rivet A.L.F. (ed.) *The Iron Age in Northern Britain*. Edinburgh:59–87.

Frere S.S. 1986 The use of Iron Age hillforts by the Roman army in Britain. In Unz 1986.

Fulford M. 1984 Demonstrating Britannia's economic dependence in the first and second centuries. In Blagg and King 1984:129–42.

Gates T. 1982 Farming on the frontier: Romano-British fields in Northumberland. In Clack and Haselgrove 1982:21–42.

Gillam J.P. 1984 A note on the *numeri Brittonum*. In Miket and Burgess 1984:287–94.

Halliday S.P. 1982 Later prehistoric farming in south-eastern Scotland. In Harding 1982:74–91.

Hanson W.S. 1978 The organisation of Roman military timber supply. *Britannia* 9:299–305.

Hanson W.S. 1986 Rome, the Cornovii and the Ordovices. In Unz 1986.

Hanson W.S. and Macinnes L. 1980 Forests, forts and fields: a discussion. *Scottish Archaeol. Forum* 12:98–113.

Hanson W.S. and Maxwell G.S. 1983 *Rome's north-west frontier: the Antonine Wall*. Edinburgh.

Harding D.W. (ed.) 1976 *Hillforts: later prehistoric earthworks in Britain and Ireland*. London.

Harding D.W. (ed.) 1982 *Later Prehistoric Settlement in Southeast Scotland*. Edinburgh.

Helbaek H. 1964 The Isca grain, a Roman plant introduction in Britain. *New Phytologist* 63:158–64.

Higham N.J. 1982 The Roman impact upon rural settlement in Cumbria. In Clark and Haselgrove 1982:105–122.

Hill P. 1982 Broxmouth hillfort excavations 1977–78. In Harding 1982 141–88.

Hogg A.H.A. 1966 Native settlement in Wales. In Thomas C. (ed.) *Rural Settlement in Roman Britain*. London:28–38.

Jarrett M.G. (ed.) 1969 *The Roman frontier in Wales*. Cardiff.

Jobey G. 1965 Hillforts and settlements in Northumberland. *Archaeol. Aeliana* 4, 43:21–64.

Jobey G. 1974 Notes on some population problems in the area between the two Roman Walls. *Archaeol. Aeliana* 5, 2:17–26.

Jobey G. 1976 Traprain Law: a summary. In Harding 1976:192–204.

Jobey G. 1978 Burnswark Hill. *Trans. Dumfriesshire Galloway Natur. Hist. Antiq. Soc.* 53:57–104.

Jones A.H.M. 1974 *The Roman economy*. Oxford.

Jones G.D.B. 1984 Becoming different without knowing. The role and development of *vici*. In Blagg and King 1984:75–91.

Jones M. 1981 The development of crop husbandry. In Jones and Dimbleby 1981:95–127.

Jones M. and Dimbleby G. (eds.) 1981 *The Environment of Man: the Iron Age to the Anglo-Saxon period*. London.

Kilbride-Jones H.E. 1980 *Celtic Craftmanship in Bronze*. London.

Knights B.A., Dickson C.A., Dickson J.H. and Breeze D.J. 1983 Evidence concerning the Roman military diet at Bearsden, Scotland, in the second century AD *J. Archaeol. Sci.* 10:139–52.

Lamb H.H. 1981 Climate from 1000 BC to 1000 AD. In Jones and Dimbleby 1981:53–65.

Macinnes L. 1982 Pattern and purpose: the settlement evidence. In Harding 1982:57–73.

Macinnes L. 1984 Brochs and the Roman occupation of Lowland Scotland, *Proc. Soc. Antiq. Scotland* 114:235–49.

MacKie E.W. 1982 The Leckie broch, Stirlingshire: an interim report. *Glasgow Archaeol. J.* 9:60–72.

Maltby M. 1981 Iron Age, Romano-British and Anglo-Saxon animal husbandry: a review of the faunal evidence. In Jones and Dimbleby 1981:155–203.

Manning W.H. 1975 Economic influences on land use in the military areas of the Highland zone during the Roman period. In Evans J.G., Limbrey S. and Cleere H. (eds.) *The Effect of Man on the Landscape of the Highland Zone*. London:112–116.

Maxwell G.S. 1983 Recent aerial discoveries in Roman Scotland: Drumquhassle, Elginhaugh and Woodhead. *Britannia* 14: 167–81.

Miket R. and Burgess C. 1984 *Between and Beyond the Walls: essays on the prehistory and history of north Britain in honour of George Jobey*. Edinburgh.

Musson C.R. 1976 Excavations at the Breiddin 1969–73. In Harding 1976:293–302.

Musson C.R. 1981 Prehistoric and Romano-British settlement in northern Powys and western Shropshire. *Archaeol. J.* 138:5–7.

O'Neil B.H. St J. 1937 Excavations at Breiddin Camp, Montgomeryshire, 1933–35. *Archaeol. Cambrensis.* 92:86–128.

Richmond I.A. 1951 Exploratory trenching at the Roman fort at Cappuck, Roxburghshire, in 1949. *Proc. Soc. Antiq. Scotland* 85:138–45.

Richmond I.A. and St. Joseph J.K.S. 1982 Excavations at Woden Law, 1950. *Proc. Soc. Antiq. Scotland* 112:277–84.

Rivet A.L.F. 1982 Brittones Anavionenses. *Britannia* 13:321–2.

Robertson A.S. 1970 Roman finds from non-Roman sites in Scotland. *Britannia* 1:198–213.

Robertson A.S. 1975 The Romans in north Britain: the coin evidence. In Temporini H. (ed.) *Aufstieg und Niedergang der römischen Welt II.3*. Berlin: 364–426.

Robertson A.S. 1978 The circulation of Roman coins in north Britain: the evidence of hoards and site finds from Scotland. In Carson R.A.G. and Kraay C.M. (eds.) *Scripta Nummaria Romana: essays presented to*

Humphrey Sutherland. London: 186–216.

Savory H.M. 1976 Welsh hillforts: a reappraisal of recent work. In Harding 1976:237–291.

Sekulla M.F. 1982 The Roman coins from Traprain Law. *Proc. Soc. Antiq. Scotland* 112:285–94.

Simpson G. 1964 *Britons and the Roman army*. London.

Smith C. 1980 The hut circles at Holyhead Mountain: an interim report on excavations in 1978 and 1979. *Archaeol. Cambrensis* 129:151–3.

Stanford S.C. 1974 Native and Roman in the central Welsh borderland. In Birley *et al* 1974:44–60.

Stevenson R.B.K. 1976 Romano-British glass bangles. *Glasgow Archaeol. J* 4:45–54.

Turner J. 1979 The environment of northeast England during Roman times as shown by pollen analysis. *J. Archaeol. Sci* 6:285–90.

Unz C. 1986 *Vorträdge des XIII Internationalen Limes-Kongresses*. Baden Württemberg.

Watkins T. 1980 Excavation of a settlement and souterrain at Newmill, near Bankfoot, Perthshire. *Proc. Soc. Antiq. Scot.* 110:165–208.

Webster G. 1953 The lead mining industry in north Wales in Roman times. *J. Flintshire Hist. Soc.* 13:5–33.

White R. forthcoming Cefn Graeanog.

13. Soldiers and Settlement in Northern England

N.J. Higham

At the conquest, northern England posed a challenge to Roman generals and administrators very different from that which they had experienced in southern, lowland Britain. The political epicentre of the north lay in Yorkshire. This was an unavoidable but crucial strategic weakness in the attempt by Venutius to resist the inevitable Roman invasion; by the time his troops reached Boroughbridge Cerealis had already neutralised the political and economic heartland of his opponents' territory. It is not known what relationship existed between the Brigantes in west Yorkshire and the Parisi on the Wolds in late prehistory (Hartley 1966; Stead 1977; Ramm 1978). The only ancient authority for the latter is Ptolemy (*Geogr.* II, 3, 10) and his passing mention by name of this separate tribal unit has generally been taken to reinforce archaeological evidence for the 'Arras Culture' (Stead 1965). The naming of the Parisi (vis-à-vis the Brigantes) by Ptolemy is neutral and neither denies or confirms that an intimate relationship existed between them. However, the close juxtaposition of these two relatively well-populated and prosperous communities implies that contact between them was both constant and intimate. There are indications that such contact may have contributed to the growing tension in Parisian society, identified in changing ritual and religious behaviour (Dent 1983). The siting by Ceriealis (or just possibly his predecessor (Wenham 1971)) of York on the main morainic ridge crossing the low-lying, wet vale that divided the Parisi from the Brigantes underlines the concern of the Roman administration to oversee the processes of contact between them and throttle any subsequent attempt at concerted, hostile action.

In general terms the region that confronted Ceriealis and Agricola was economically retarded and socially backward. The economic base of late prehistoric communities in Britain rested almost exclusively on the productivity of a numerous, low-status class practising agriculture and pastoralism. North of the Humber, alternative or supplementary economic strategies were less developed than in southern Britain; outside the nascent, putative entrepôt sites of North Ferriby and Stanwick elements of a market and proto-urban infrastructure are scarcely represented; no candidate has been identified between Stanwick and Traprain Law, or west of the Pennines. Nor was there a local tradition of minting; before the conquest small quantities of Corieltauvian coin reached Yorkshire; after AD 43, until the conquest, Roman coinage and provincial copies circulated in the same area but neither demonstrably penetrated beyond Stanwick. It is reasonable to assume that the agrarian base of the northern economy was more firmly entrenched even than that of lowland Britain.

Agricultural opportunity was not evenly distributed in northern England but was constrained by environmental factors and by the cumulative effects of economic activity both long past and recent. The greatest opportunities for agrarian land-use existed on lowland, calcareous soils in the rain shadow of the Pennines in south and east Yorkshire. It was no accident that these areas contained the political epicentre or epicentres of pre-conquest, northern society; on both the Wolds and the Jurassic Ridge there existed a tradition of intensive land division and management that predates the conquest, characterised by substantial field systems, a long tradition of both enclosed and unenclosed settlement and the presence of grain storage pits (Riley 1981; Faull and Moorhouse, 1981; Dent 1982, 1983). Other smaller areas shared some of the advantages of the Yorkshire Wolds – Wharfedale offered a range of calcareous soils between the river and the Moors, some of which were of adequate depth for cultivation and these supported a complex pattern of enclosures best seen around Grassington, numerous settlements and substantial land divisions. Similar systems have been identified in the western periphery of these calcareous soils at Eller Beck (Cumb.) and on the Lune-Eden watershed (Lowndes 1963, 1964; Higham 1978a, 1979, 1986a) but none certainly predate the conquest. Limited tracts of similarly advantaged, lowland soils exist around Bishop Middleham (County Durham) and Houghton-le-Spring (Tyne and Wear) and the former of these at least seems to have been extensively deforested at an early date (Bartley *et al.* 1975).

Evidence for large scale land management via dykes, linear earthworks of other kinds, substantial settlements and extensive field systems is currently to a large extent limited to these advantageous areas, north of the Humber. By the conquest, intensive land-use was also affecting other free-draining lowland soils (largely overlying sands and gravels) east of the Pennines. The identification of vast and highly organised field systems on Jurassic sandstone south of the Humber (Riley 1981) implies that similar terrain to the north may have attracted a comparable level of management. Catcote in County Durham remains the most significant example so far recorded (Challis and Harding 1975).

Elsewhere, wherever pre-conquest settlement has been identified, it is characterised by the isolated homestead from which a territory was exploited autonomously by pastoralism and less regularly by cereal cultivation, without any evidence for the integrated, enclosed landscapes typical of calcareous, lowland soils. No example of this form of settlement has yet been conclusively dated to the pre-Roman epoch in Lancashire or Cumbria.

In the northern and western periphery of the territory controlled by the Brigantes, agrarian development was retarded and deforestation was either incomplete or barely begun (e.g. the Lake District valleys – Pennington 1970). East of the

Pennines the upsurge of economic activity in late prehistory had resulted in the permanent deforestation of much at least of the lowlands and transhumance pressure had cleared parts of the more fragile upland woodlands (e.g. Turner 1981; Clack 1982). The available data is probably best explained by a climatically induced and long maintained rise in human population levels which originated in the ameliorating climate of the centuries after the mid-millennium BC (Lamb 1981; Harding 1982). Increasing population density within existing communities led inexorably to larger herds and in turn both to increased stocking ratios on existing pastures and to extensive expansion of traditional pasture lands. The result was deforestation and the replacement of trees by plant species typical of open ground. In parallel there occurred an increase in the extent and permanence of cereal cultivation. These economic activities probably spread concentrically from traditional areas of exploitation and the consequences for the natural vegetation reflected them. By the conquest, areas where population growth had occurred early were reaching saturation point – the Wolds remain the principal candidate (Dent 1983). Elsewhere, indigenous communities were displaying increasing territorial awareness at several levels. Even so, much of northern England resembled a 'Wild West' in which the principal concern of man was to maintain existing levels of activity and gradually to establish new settlements on the margins of existing, colonial archipelagoes, to build new homes, breech new ground and open up new grazing lands. West of the Pennines, this process was to continue throughout the 2nd and 3rd centuries. Only limited tracts were intensively managed before the conquest (Higham 1978a); Hadrianic occupation is not uncommon on well-drained soils in the Solway basin (Blake 1960; Higham and Jones 1983) but most rural settlements there betray 3rd century occupation and Inglewood Forest and the Central Lakeland Massif remained forested into the late Roman period or beyond (Walker 1966; Pennington 1970; Higham 1986b), offering a substantial reservoir of under-utilised land to subsequent generations.

That fundamental changes were occurring in the landscape of northern England before and after the conquest is not in serious doubt. The late arrival of symptoms characteristic of these changes in the wettest and most exposed parts of the region implies that it was principally climatic factors which constrained the mechanisms by which these changes occurred. Deforestation of the lowlands spread across the north as the agrarian implications of the oceanity of the prevailing climate receded as a consequence of a significant climatic amelioration (Lamb 1977; 1981).

Soldiers and Settlement

Immutable geographical factors determined that the initial occupation of England north of the Humber concentrated upon sites within or closely adjacent to the terrain defined above as offering the greatest economic opportunities. York henceforth acted as the pivot from which the frontier zone was administered – an arrangement that mirrors imprecisely the political structure of the region on the eve of the conquest, yet sheds no further light on that structure. However, the Agricolan advance carried the main garrison forces north, into and beyond the periphery of the territory over which the Brigantes had exercised some measure of control. The eventual stabilisation of the frontier on the Solway-Tyne isthmus established the greater part of the garrison of Britain in permanent forts north of the Mersey and the Tees. These areas were economically retarded and environmentally disadvantaged not only by comparison with southern Britain but also with the heartland of 'Brigantia'. It is a matter of reasonable inference that the army made substantial demands upon the environment in which it now found itself established and these demands were either channelled through the existing community or were additional to and replaced existing patterns of economic activity.

The huge scale of the military occupation requires that any assessment of settlement or economic activity during the Roman period in the frontier zone should give proper weight to the impact of the garrisons. If anything, the tendency has been to over- rather than undervalue that impact, particularly before the widespread presence of rural settlement was identified by aerial photography in the 1960s and after (Blake 1960; McCord and Jobey 1971; Higham and Jones 1975, 1985; Harding 1979; Higham 1979; Jobey 1981, 1982; Haselgrove 1981). In general, this impact has been presumed to be at least in some respects beneficial, providing economic stimuli and opportunities for the local population. In many cases such a view is implicit rather than explicit in modern accounts, or couched in non-specific terms such as the 'economic pressure and deliberate encouragement' as a result of which certain communities on the Wolds are thought to have expanded arable production (Ramm 1978). There have been oblique criticisms of the generally uncritical euphoria among commentators; we have all been gently chided by the irony in the comment: 'with peace came other 'benefits': taxation, slavery, forced labour, and so on' (Breeze 1982) and elsewhere doubt has been expressed whether the military impact was on balance of benefit to the indigenous community (Higham 1986a, 1989).

The Roman army affected local society both as a vast engine of demand and by the functions it performed. The latter is the simpler matter. The garrisons were present to guarantee the frontier, police adjacent areas and to oversee the passivity of the provincials. The imposition of peace had some potential economic value; where and when that was successfully established the local community was freed of the dangers posed by the raids of their neighbours near and far, the unpredictability of which may have been the cause of some economic dislocation. The need to participate in tribal warfare diverted resources and manpower for activities which were not strictly of economic benefit. An assessment of the impact of *pax Romana* on local communities depends on the balance that existed between various factors before and then after the conquest.

The cessation of raiding and tribal warfare reduced the risk of violent death among the indigenes excepting those who entered the army. However, the incidence of violence had not, as far as we can judge, seriously constrained population increase in the pre-Roman era and had had no more than a marginal impact on demographic trends.

The loss of livestock to raiders was balanced within that region by a net accretion elsewhere. The local impact of trading and warfare was probably variable; the activities of Venutius suggests that it focussed the military strength of the peripheral communities on to the lowlands of Yorkshire but the impact must depend on an evaluation of the normal strength and cohesiveness of the Brigantian state in the ultimate prehistoric.

One serious consequence of tribal warfare was possibly the retardation of the spread of cereal cultivation. Warfare absorbed considerable manpower during the harvest season and cultivation involved the immobilisation of the means of production resulting in an enhanced vulnerability to enemy attack. The pastoralist base of the densely populated Wolds in late prehistory has recently been emphasized (Dent 1983). The conquest may have relieved this community from that necessity to concentrate on pastoralism which escalating warfare had forced upon them. This release of productive capacity may have contributed to the substantial post-conquest increase in the acreage given over to cereal cultivation (Ramm 1978; Dent 1983) which arguably resulted in a substantial increase in gross food production. However, it should be emphasized that this is only one of several possible explanations for changes in land-use in the early Roman period and it may not have been the most important. Even if it were, there is less chance that it proved a significant factor outside the better arable lands of the Tees-Humber lowlands.

The provincial community was expected to fund the army and the *pax Romana* and to this effect were burdened with substantial taxes. There may have been some rudimentary taxation or tribute system within the pre-Roman tribal communities but it is likely that the post-conquest period witnessed a substantial increase in the compulsory outgoings of the rural population as taxation, rent or forced labour.

In economic terms, the benefits that directly derived from the police function of the Roman army and administration may have been considerable but must be balanced by the cost borne by the provincial community. It is not clear where the balance of advantage lay; in whichever direction it is unlikely to have been consistent across the whole region.

In demographic terms, the *pax Romana* has been deemed responsible for the visible expansion in size of many of the stone-built settlement sites in northern Northumberland (Jobey 1974; 1981) and signs of population expansion elsewhere. However, the conquest occurred against a background of existing economic and presumably demographic expansion. While it is important to note that this expansion

suffered no severe set-back as a result of the *pax Romana*, it is less than an adequate explanation to lay responsibility for that process at the door of events that occurred significantly after its inception. In practice, long-term demographic change can rarely be successfully attributed to the political climate and those that seek to establish such a causal relationship should be expected to construct a powerful case.

The pacification may have other implications for northern communities. Although the homestead-based settlement pattern throve north of the Tees, the most advantageous lowland soils witnessed changes in production and organisation that may have had major social implications. During the first two centuries of Roman rule, the network of livestock farms on some parts of the Wolds was replaced by fewer, larger units practising cereal cultivation (Dent 1983). The conquest allowed the abandonment of the long-established noble-retainer and noble-tenant relationships which had underpinned the late tribal society. In their place there emerged a landowner-unfree tenant/slave relationship centred on villa-based estates operating within a market economy (Branigan 1980). In the Brigantian and Parisian heartland, there are traces of a social revolution that occurred in the interests of a tenacious local aristocracy at the apex of a civilian hierarchy, to the detriment of the interests of large sections of their subordinates among the rural proletariat.

The economic needs of the Roman army dominated the markets and the commercial life of the frontier zone; the garrisons sucked into the region vast quantities of raw materials, manufactured goods of a perplexing variety and immigrants, presumably both skilled and unskilled, free and slave (Salway 1965; Casey 1981). These needs have recently been the subject of a brief but penetrating analysis (Breeze 1981) which sets out their main facets and establishes, where possible, the mechanisms by which it was met. Both demand and supply were complex and the latter in particular is not well understood. Within this economic system, the *vici* and their inhabitants arguably performed a variety of functions, marketing produce from near and far and acting as a convenient reservoir of human skills upon which the army units or individuals within them could call (Birley 1977; Casey 1981; Higham 1986a).

The majority of high value goods and many bulk products reached the army via lengthy lines of communication reaching out to southern Britain and the continent, or were manufactured by immigrant artificers in the extra-mural settlements. It is difficult to identify a substantial sector of this market in which the local rural community could successfully compete. One recent suggestion (Higham 1989) emphasizes the significance of local livestock in this respect but traces of a lucrative exchange economy are not prominent on farm sites in the frontier zone south of the Wall (Higham 1978b; 1981) and are conspicuously scarce in Northumberland (Jobey 1981). North of the Tees, it seems likely that the flow of goods was very largely in one direction, from the farming community to the forts and *vici*, and that most of this transfer occurred outside the exchange economy, via taxation or rent (Higham 1989).

Prior to the full publication of major excavations in the northern *vici*, it is pointless to reiterate the arguments that have already been presented. However, in one major respect the needs of the army were necessarily localised and arguably contentious in their impact. The army required land. Although in comparison to the total land surface of the military zone the needs of the army might appear modest, in practice many units were stationed in the strategic river valleys where lay the heartland of the scarce, free-draining lowland soils of the north and it was within these locations that the territorial needs of the Roman army were most acutely felt.

Pastoralism was by far the most widespread economic activity of the indigenes between the Tyne and the Tees in the first two centuries AD. The plethora of ditched or walled settlement sites on both sides of the Pennines implies that herd management was based upon a network of permanent settlements and concentrated within recognised territorial limits, with or without transhumance. Around these settlement sites was developing an increasing level of cereal cultivation; it is no accident that they were concentrated on well-drained sites below c. 280m above OD. Pastoralism is an extensive economic strategy. Only limited expansion of production (to compensate, for example, for demographic rise or taxation) was possible without increases in the land area available. By AD 100 it seems likely that herd density was already considerable in parts of the northeastern lowlands and rapidly developed thereafter in lowland Lancashire and Cumbria.

Into this expanding economic system was intruded the military requirements for land. There is some evidence to suggest that forts were sited on land that had been recently occupied, cultivated or grazed (Higham 1986a; Corder 1930; Ramm 1978; Wacher 1969) but the land on which to build garrison forts was only a small component of the territorial needs of the military which can be summarised as follows:

1. Land on which to construct military or quasi-military installations – garrison forts, fortlets, signal stations, ports, ... roads, possibly *vici*, cemeteries, etc.;

2. cleared space for surveillance needs around military installations; ... after the 2nd century this probably merges into:

3. the *territoria*, performing a variety of economic functions ... (R.I.B., 583, 1049) which probably included:

    a. extensive pastureland and meadows to provide for cavalry mounts, ... pack animals and perhaps to support livestock purchased or ... acquired via taxation, destined for the butcher or the leather ... worker;

    b. the cutting of timber for construction;

    c. the cutting of timber and peat for fuel.

4. stone quarries and mines for metal-ores.

The last of these were located where natural factors dictated; Roman mining of local deposits of iron ore is likely and working of lead ores on Alston Edge and elsewhere seems probable. These activities were concentrated in areas which offered little advantage to cultivators or pastoralists; unless local forced labour was used in their exploitation it seems unlikely that these seriously inconvenienced that local community and there was some possibility of gainful employment.

The remaining categories were concentrated at and around the forts, often in areas where indigenous occupation and more intensive land-use strategies were concentrated. Considerable potential existed for a conflict of interests and nowhere was this potential more marked than on the Tyne-Solway isthmus, where the permanent frontier was eventually established.

Tynedale

A by-product of the excavation of Roman military installations in the Tyne valley has been the recognition of plough or ard marks in sealed deposits with a *terminus ante quem* in the Hadrianic period or thereabouts. It seems likely that more examples might have been detected had pre- and immediately post-war excavation techniques been more sophisticated. As it is, it is much to the credit of recent excavators that these rarely-obvious traces have been recorded. Ridge and furrow was detected under a barrack block and beneath the *via quintana* at Rudchester (Gillam *et al.* 1973). Elsewhere plough or ard marks have been identified beneath the forts at Carrawburgh (Breeze 1974), Wallsend (Daniels 1976) and Halton Chesters, and under the military road at Walker (Jobey 1965a). At Wallhouses the *Vallum* was cut across an area which displayed traces of ploughing (Bennett *et al.* 1983a), and Turret 10A at Throckley was constructed on cultivated soil which sealed plough striations (Bennett *et al.* 1983b). If we extend westwards slightly along the Roman military corridor, ploughmarks were detected within a contemporary system of ditched enclosures at Tarraby Lane in a context that predated the Wall (Smith 1978), and carbonised material from one of the ditches, albeit one not directly associated with ploughing, was dated *c.* 130 BC.

With the exception of the Tarraby Lane evidence, objective dating has not yet become available for these plough or ard marks. Speculation as to their antiquity has resulted in the suggestion that they may belong within an early prehistoric context, in the 3rd, or more probably the 2nd millennium (Fowler 1981). This hypothesis has been strengthened by the opinions of those with specialist knowledge of plough technology, who have quite properly suggested that regular ploughing of a field does not result in the one or two directional plough striations which are generally identified, but these are more likely to have resulted from a single episode of deep 'rip' ploughing as part of the initial process of clearance (Reynolds 1981). However, the plough striations that have been identified display a regularity of spacing which is unlikely to have resulted from clearance ploughing. At Throckley, on relatively flat terrain, no fewer than six ploughing operations were detected; it is difficult to reconcile so many episodes with 'rip' ploughing, but far easier to accept that this evidence, like that from Tarraby Lane, is symptomatic of an intensification of land-use in a controlled and carefully managed landscape, characterised by frequent re-use of a designated cultivation area. The absence of more numerous striations may be due to surface soil drift as a result of cultivation rather than technological or functional peculiarities.

The problem of chronology is more difficult, setting aside temporarily the Tarraby Lane evidence. In practice the individual items of evidence could derive from a wide chronological spectrum, defined only by the *terminus ante quem* in the Hadrianic period. In general terms, the probability exists that most plough striations derive from one or other of the two major clearance episodes in the prehistoric period. An examination of the broad, regional characteristics of these leads to a mild preference for the late prehistoric episode. Clearance activity in the 2nd millennium BC tends not to display the same degree of permanence, of economic intensification or long-term spatial identity as that of the ultimate prehistoric (e.g. Davies and Turner 1979; Bartley *et al.* 1976).

This is, of course, a subjective evaluation, but where field systems of the earlier episode have been examined the unit size and layout has attracted the suggestion that spade cultivation was a normal strategy (e.g. Gates 1983). Compare this with the widespread evidence for field systems laid out in the ultimate prehistoric or Roman period, specifically designed to accommodate ploughing as a normal strategy (e.g. Gates 1981; Higham 1983). Plough striations outside the palisaded site of Belling Law (North Tynedale) were sealed under the bank and ditch of a later episode of occupation beginning probably in the 2nd century AD (Jobey 1977). The earliest house on the site was dated *c.* 160 BC. The spatial and directional relationship between the palisaded settlement and the plough lines creates a coincidence which invites the conclusion both that the two are contemporary, and that they are joint manifestations of the intensification of territoriality and of economic strategies typical of the colonisation process of the ultimate prehistoric.

While ploughing was probably an available strategy in the 2nd millennium BC (e.g. Gates 1983), there is comparatively little evidence that it was widely adopted. The plough or ard fragments identified in southern Scotland (Milton Loch and Lochmaben Crannog, Dumfriesshire; Traprain Law, East Lothian) belong exclusively within the last half millennium BC, or, possibly in the latter case, in the Roman period.

This brief survey of the circumstantial evidence does not demonstrate that the plough marks beneath

any one of the Tynedale forts should be assigned to the ultimate prehistoric in preference to earlier agricultural episodes. It does, however, create a pattern of probability by which many or most should be initially interpreted in the later context; it is up to those who would wish to transpose the evidence into an earlier context to justify their interpretation in individual instances. In general terms, that clearance episode that emerged in later prehistory and extended into and beyond the Roman period remains the one pre-Norman episode most commonly associated with palaeobotanical and archaeological evidence for cereal cultivation in the better terrains of the north, including Tynedale (Jobey 1981).

The one major objection to a late prehistoric date for the Tynedale plough marks has been the observed absence of settlement sites from which such intensive activity could have derived. With the exception of less than a handful of defensive sites (Jobey 1965a) the sole candidate was for long the stone-built undefended homestead or settlement at Milking Gap, High Shiel (Kilbride Jones 1938). There has, therefore, been a quite proper reluctance to interpret ploughing in a late prehistoric context where it had apparently occurred more than a few hundred metres from a settlement site.

Recent developments in settlement site excavation make possible an explanation of this evidence hiatus. The construction of the Kielder Dam and the subsequent flooding of parts of North Tynedale stimulated a series of excavations which have revealed a common tradition of settlement development (Jobey 1983). At each site, occupation was initially contained within a timber palisade, and utilised timber round houses. This large scale, even profligate, use of timber is typical of settlement development in a variety of colonising episodes throughout history as well as prehistory, where large reserves of forest existed on land that was being colonised and timber, therefore, provided a convenient local resource. The superimposition of three successive palisaded enclosures at Kennel Hall Knowe, Plashetts, demonstrates that this vernacular style was adopted by successive generations, within a community with an already well-developed sense of spatial identity and, therefore, most probably within a developing structure of territorial awareness (Jobey 1978). The third palisade (dated *c.* 20 BC and *c.* 30 AD) at Kennel Hall Knowe was eventually replaced by a bank and ditch defined enclosure, within which stood stone-founded houses, fronted by cobbled yards. This fourth phase was dated by two sherds of Roman coarse pottery (possibly 2nd century), and a single carbon date of *c.* 270 AD. Occupation of the site in phase IV probably occurred, therefore, in the Roman period; the changeover from phase III to phase IV need not have occurred before the occupation. The transfer from one style to another signifies the end of colonising activity characterised by active clearance, in favour of the maintenance of existing clearance. This is not to suggest that demand for structural timber and fuel were the major causes of deforestation. That most probably resulted from large-scale and long-term overstocking with beasts, and in particular with cattle, with a consequent reduction in the rate of forest rejuvenation below the level at which senile trees could be replaced. When the phase IV bank was erected at Kennel Hall Knowe, the hinterland had already suffered this fate, leaving impoverished woodland dominated by birch and alder interspersed with grassland, heathland and moorland peat. To reconstruct the settlement with a palisade was no longer a 'cheap' option.

At Belling Law a similar sequence has been detected, with an initial phase of timber post fencing (c. 160 BC) replaced by an entrenched palisade, and subsequently by a ditched and stone-built homestead which yielded 2nd century Roman pottery and may be associated with a carbon date of *c.* 280 AD (Jobey 1977). Similar sequences have been identified at Tower Knowe (Jobey 1973) and less certainly at Bridgehouse (Charlton and Day 1974). At Woolaw (Upper Redesdale) stone founded structures superseded timber round houses, in a broadly comparable chronological context (Charlton and Day 1978).

What has begun to emerge, therefore, is a sequential development from one architectural tradition to another, within circumstances in which human pressure on the local environment was resulting in deforestation. The consequent loss of forest cover offered substantial advantages to a community largely dependent on herding strategies, since the carrying capacity of the local environment was considerably raised. The community was thereby committed to the site, or at least the immediate vicinity and, therefore, eventually forced to adopt a structural form less profligate in the use of timber. The change over from one building strategy to another occurred within an ill-defined chronological framework which may have extended backwards into the ultimate prehistoric, but which centred on the 1st–2nd century AD. The pressures created by military demands for timber in the Flavian and Trajanic periods can only have hastened the demise of palisade-style construction among the indigenous community where their demands upon resources overlapped. This may well have been the situation which developed in parts of the Tyne valley on either side of *c.* 100 AD, at which stage stone construction emerges at the Milking Gap site. This may have been merely one, somewhat precocious manifestation of the new vernacular style, which appeared before the intensification of military activity (in the AD 120s) displaced the indigenous community in the Tyne-Irthing corridor. In contrast, the North Tyne communities were allowed to transform their settlements unmolested as the need arose in the Hadrianic and Antonine periods. Whether or not a palisaded site lies beneath the Milking Gap site is unknown; excavation occurred long before the recognition of small palisaded sites in the region, but it is worth noting that a simple reinterpretation of the report could easily support the presence of a primary phase of timber houses, preceding the stone-founded round houses.

If late prehistoric and early Roman palisaded sites are relatively widely distributed in the lower Tyne valley, it is not surprising that they have largely escaped detection since, away from the Cheviots (Ritchie 1970), the identification of northern palisades has relied heavily on chance discoveries, or on their location beneath a variety of other types of site with more easily identifiable features. Within the intensively utilised route corridor and the urban and even the agricultural development of Tyneside, little opportunity exists for site location, and the pattern of identification will remain one of chance. There is, however, a corpus of evidence already in existence that points to a scatter of such sites.

A putative palisaded settlement was identified, but not dated, beneath the successive Roman forts at Corbridge (Richmond and Gillam 1955). A possible timber round house was identified adjacent to the Agricolan base at Red House, Corbridge (Hanson *et al.* 1979). On Bishop Rigg, Corbridge, a two phase palisaded site of 'native' type was sealed by Roman pottery, and slighted by a rectangular, stockaded enclosure dated by pottery of *c.* 80–125 AD; the area had subsequently been seriously disturbed by Roman gravel extraction (Jobey 1979). A further possible site has been identified beneath Roman cremation burials on the west side of Dere Street (Jobey 1979). On the Irthing, Trajanic pottery was identified beneath the Hadrianic fort at Birdoswald (Simpson and Richmond 1934). In no one case can ultimate prehistoric or pre-Hadrianic occupation be demonstrated, but it seems likely that a handful, at least, of the farm sites of the Tyneside indigenes have already been located. The identification of traces of plough activity in a similar context might encourage us to anticipate the general vicinity of several more.

The choice of the Tyne-Irthing gap as the line of the fixed frontier in the period after AD 120 probably required the displacement of sections of the indigenous community. The military installations required land and the choice in many cases fell on well-drained relatively level tracts (viz. the temporary camp on Bishop Rigg, Corbridge). The wall and *Vallum* required a corridor free of indigenous settlement and disrupted local grazing lands. The fort garrisons needed grazing land, and were probably provided in the 2nd century with *territoria* which collectively excluded the indigenes from access to the bulk of the more hospitable terrain of the Tyne valley. The immediate consequence was probably the eviction of the rural community from the military corridor.

The observed distribution of enclosed settlements of possible Roman date is far more sparse throughout the valleys of the Irthing, South Tyne and Tyne than in the North Tyne, Rede, Wansbeck or Blyth (Jobey 1981). It is, however, worth noting that similar sites are common in the close environs of many lowland forts – obvious examples being Brougham, Old Penrith and Old Carlisle in Cumbria (Higham and Hones 1975; Higham 1981) – implying that in those areas at least *territoria* may have been leased or in some other way transferred to civilian use. Without more effective dating evidence, it seems unlikely that the chronology or mechanisms of this process can be known.

Conclusions

The Roman conquest occurred against a background of climatic, demographic and economic change. The establishment of substantial garrison forces in northern England had an impact upon the local community that was not always beneficial. Some sections occupying good agricultural land were able to take advantage of economic opportunities and switch production into cereal cultivation for the market. Some groups may have benefited from sales of livestock and grain via markets in the *vici*. In Yorkshire and northern Cumbria, the organisation of local civitates implies the presence of a Romanised section within the community and on the Wolds at least there are reasons to believe that these derive from indigenous landowners.

However, it is difficult to escape the conclusion that tax burdens and other obligatory outgoings were the most pervasive forms of economic contact between the Romanised sections of the community (army, administrators, merchants and the *civitas* aristocracies in Yorkshire) and the farming community. A one-sided competition for land between the military and the indigenes is illustrated by the extreme example of the Hadrianic frontier but existed elsewhere amid some of the best agricultural lands of the Tyne-Tees. Where local population levels were approaching the carrying capacity of this environment, military demands for land may have caused a loss of access that may have been both critical and traumatic. The permanent imposition of these demands fell disproportionately on the restricted, better terrain of an area that had been the periphery of the Brigantes of later prehistory where comparatively intransigent problems already derived from the economic inadequacies of a high proportion of the local environment.

Within the Tyne-Tees region and between the Pennines and the Irish Sea it seems unlikely that the set of stimuli consequent upon the presence of the army offset the burdens and dislocation that came in its wake. In contrast, the heartland of the pre-conquest Brigantes and the Parisi emerge as the most effectively Romanised, indigenous communities between the Humber and the Wall, supporting an identifiable local aristocracy and the trappings of the civilisation that they imported, albeit on a relatively modest scale (Stead 1971; Ramm 1978; Branigan 1980).

Richmond (1958) described 'Brigantia' on the eve of the conquest: 'Conditions among the Brigantes varied greatly, from primitive savagery at the barest subsistence level among scattered cow-herds inhabiting the bleak uplands, to a certain barbaric splendour among their chiefs'. Divested of the rhetoric, this view contains a kernel of truth. The extent of permanent occupation in the uplands at the time of Christ should not be overestimated but, where identified, the indigenous community on the periphery of 'Brigantia', in Cumbria, Tyne and Wear, Durham, parts of Cleveland and Lancashire, occupied late prehistoric and Roman period settlements to

which imports were few and where subsistence economics must have been paramount. Between the artifact deposition there and in the local forts and *vici* existed a gulf which no rhetoric can bridge. Far closer to the latter were the establishments occupied by the more affluent landowners and farmers of the middle Tees, the East Riding and the Jurassic Ridge, where the most splendid of Richmond's barbaric chiefs once roamed. There is no hint that those farming in these areas entertained any serious dissatisfaction at Roman rule after the first generation. A Brigantian revolt in the 2nd century still has its adherents (Hartley 1980); if any such episode occurred we should look for its architects and adherents to those who had been adversely affected by the ebb and flow of frontier policy (Higham 1981) and to those who had been dispossessed in the unequal struggle for land on the Hadrianic frontier and along the major route corridors. For many of them, at least, access to the opportunities that the occupation is supposed to have offered did not exist.

References

Bartley D.D., Chambers C. and Hart-Jones B. 1976 The vegetational history of parts of south and east Durham. *New Phytologist* 77:437–468.

Bennett J. and Turner R. with Bartlett D. and Andrea Kurlis 1983a The Vallum at Wallhouses, Northumberland: excavations in 1980 and 1981. *Archaeol. Aeliana* 5th Series, 11:61–78:

Bennett J., Keeley H. and Miller A. 1983b The pre-wall soil and ard marks. In Bennett J. The excavation of Turret 10A and the wall and vallum at Throckley, Tyne and Wear, 1980. *Archaeol. Aeliana* 5th Series, 11:27–60.

Birley R. 1977 *Vindolanda: a Roman frontier post on Hadrian's Wall*. London.

Blake B. 1960 Excavations of native (Iron Age) sites in Cumberland, 1956–58. *Trans. Cumberland and Westmorland Antiq. Archaeol. Soc.* N.S. 59:1–14.

Branigan K. 1980 Villas in the north: change in the rural landscape? In K. Branigan (ed.), *Rome and the Brigantes*. Sheffield, 18–27.

Breeze D.J. 1974 Ploughmarks at Carrawburgh on Hadrian's Wall. *Tools and Tillage* 2, 3:188–190.

Breeze D.J. 1981 Demand and supply on the northern Frontiers. In P. Clack and S. Haselgrove (eds.), *Rural Settlement in the Roman North*. Durham, 148–165.

Breeze D.J. 1982 *The Northern Frontiers of Roman Britain*. London.

Casey P.J. 1981 Civilians and Soldiers – Friends, Romans, Countrymen. In P. Clack and S. Haselgrove (eds.) *Rural Settlement in the Roman North*. Durham, 123–132.

Challis A.J. and Harding D.W. 1975 *Later Prehistory from the Trent to the Tyne*. Oxford.

Charlton D.B. and Day J.C. 1974 Bridge House re-examined. *Archaeol. Aeliana* 5th Series, 2:33.

Charlton D.B. and Day J.C. 1978 Excavation and field survey in Upper Redesdale. *Archaeol. Aeliana* 5th Series, 6:61–86.

Clack P.A.G. 1982 The northern frontiers: farmers in the military zone. In D. Miles (ed.), *The Romano-British Countryside*. BAR 103. Oxford, 377–402.

Corder P. 1930 *The Defences of the Roman Fort at Malton*. Malton.

Daniels C.M. 1976 Wallsend Roman fort, 1975

excavations. *Archaeol. News, CBA Group 3*:10–11.

Davies G. and Turner J. 1979 Pollen Diagrams from Northumberland. *New Phytologist* 82:783–804.

Dent J.S. 1982 Cemeteries and settlement patterns of the Iron Age on the Yorkshire Wolds. *Proc. Prehist. Soc.* 48:437–57.

Dent J.S. 1983 The impact of Roman rule on native society in the territory of the Parisi. *Britannia* 14:35–44.

Faull M.L. and Moorhouse S.A. 1981 *West Yorkshire: an archaeological survey to AD 1500*. Wakefield.

Gates T. 1981 Farming on the frontier: Romano-British fields in Northumberland. In P. Clack and S. Haselgrove (eds.) *Rural Settlement in the Roman North*. Durham, 21–42.

Gates T. 1983 Unenclosed settlements in Northumberland. In J.C. Chapman and H.C. Mytum (eds.) *Settlement in North Britain, 1000 BC–AD 1000*. BAR 118. Oxford, 103–48.

Gillam J.P., Harrison R.M. and Newman T.G. 1973 Interim report on excavations at the Roman fort of Rudchester. *Archaeol. Aeliana* 5th Series, 1:81–5.

Hanson W.S., Daniels C.M., Dore J.N. and Gillam J.P. 1979 The Agricolan supply base at Red House, Corbridge. *Archaeol. Aeliana* 5th Series, 7:1–88.

Harding A. 1982 Introduction: climatic change and archaeology. In A. Harding (ed.), *Climatic Change in Later Prehistory*. Edinburgh, 1–10.

Harding D.W. 1979 Air survey in the Tyne-Tees region, 1969–1979. In N.J. Higham (ed.), *The Changing Past*. Manchester, 21–30.

Hartley B.R. 1966 Some problems of the Roman military occupation of the north of England. *Northern History* 1:7–20.

Hartley B.R. 1980 The Brigantes and the Roman army. In K. Branigan (ed.), *Rome and the Brigantes*. Sheffield, 2–7.

Haselgrove C. 1981 Indigenous settlement patterns in the Tyne-Tees lowlands. In P. Clack and S. Haselgrove (eds.) *Rural Settlement in the Roman North*. Durham, 57–104.

Higham N.J. 1978a Dyke systems in north Cumbria. *Bull. Board Celtic Studs.* 28:142–155.

Higham N.J. 1978b Continuity studies in the 1st millennium AD in north Cumbria. *Northern History* 14:1–18.

Higham N.J. 1979 An aerial survey of the Upper Lune valley. In N.J. Higham (ed.) *The Changing Past*. Manchester, 31–8.

Higham N.J. 1981 The Roman impact upon rural settlement in Cumbria. In P. Clack and S. Haselgrove (eds.), *Rural Settlement in the Roman North*. Durham, 105–122.

Higham N.J 1983 A Romano-British field system at Yanwath Woodhouse. *Trans. Cumberland and Westmorland Antiq. Archaeol. Soc.* 83:49–58.

Higham N.J. 1986a *The Northern Counties to AD 1000*. Harlow, Essex.

Higham N.J. 1986b The origins of Inglewood Forest. *Trans. Cumberland and Westmorland Antiq. Archaeol. Soc.* 86.

Higham N.J. 1989 Roman and native in England north of the Tees: acculturation and its limitations. In J.C. Barrett, A.P. Fitzpatrick, L. Macinnes and M. Parker-Pearson (eds.) *Barbarians and Romans* BAR.

Higham N.J. and Jones G.D.B. 1975 Frontiers, forts and farmers, Cumbrian aerial survey, 1974–5. *Archaeol. J.* 132:16–53.

Higham N.J. and Jones G.D.B. 1983 The excavation of two Romano-British farm sites in north Cumbria. *Britannia* 14:45–72.

Higham N.J. and Jones G.D.B. 1985 *The Carvetti*.

Gloucester.

Jobey G. 1965a Stott's House 'Tumulus' and the military way, Walker. *Archaeol. Aeliana* 4th Series, 43:77–86.

Jobey G. 1965b Hill-forts and settlements in Northumberland. *Archaeol. Aeliana* 4th Series, 43:21–64.

Jobey G. 1966 Homesteads and settlements of the frontier area. In C. Thomas (ed.), *Rural Settlement in Roman Britain*. CBA, London, 1–13.

Jobey G. 1973 A Romano-British Settlement at Tower Knowe, Wellhaugh, Northumberland. *Archaeol. Aeliana* 5th Series, 1:55–79.

Jobey G. 1974 Notes on some population problems in the area between the two Roman Walls. *Archaeol. Aeliana* 5th Series, 2:17–26.

Jobey G. 1977 Iron Age and later farmsteads on Belling Law, Northumberland. *Archaeol. Aeliana* 5th Series, 5:1–38.

Jobey G. 1978 Iron Age and Romano-British settlements on Kennel Hall Knowe, North Tynedale, Northumberland. *Archaeol. Aeliana* 5th Series, 6:1–28.

Jobey G. 1979 Palisaded enclosures, a Roman temporary camp and Roman gravel quarries on Bishop Rigg, Corbridge. *Archaeol. Aeliana* 5th Series, 7:100.

Jobey G. 1981 Between Tyne and Forth: some problems. In P. Clack and S. Haselgrove (eds.), *Rural Settlement in the Roman North*. Durham, 7–20.

Jobey G. 1982 The settlement at Doubstead and Romano-British settlement on the coastal plain between Tyne and Forth. *Archaeol. Aeliana* 5th Series, 10:1–23.

Jobey G. 1983 A note on some northern palisaded sites. In A. O'Connor and D.V. Clarke (eds.), *From the Stone Age to the Forty Five*. Edinburgh, 197–205.

Kilbride-Jones H.E. 1938 The excavation of a native settlement at Milking Gap, High Shield, Northumberland. *Archaeol. Aeliana* 4th Series, 15:303–50.

Lamb H.H. 1977 *Climate: Present Past and Future. Volume 2 – Climatic History and the Future*. London.

Lamb H.H. 1981 Climate from 1000 BC to 1000 AD. In M. Jones and C. Dimbleby (eds.) *The Environment of Man: the Iron Age to the Anglo-Saxon Period*. BAR 87. Oxford, 53–65.

Lowndes R.A.C. 1963 'Celtic' fields, farms and burial mounds in the Lune valley. *Trans. Cumberland and Westmorland Antiq. Archaeol. Soc.* N.S. 63:77–95.

Lowndes R.A.C. 1964 Excavations of a Romano-British farmstead at Eller Beck. *Trans. Cumberland and Westmorland Antiq. Archaeol. Soc.* N.S. 64:6–13.

Manning W.H. 1975 Economic influence on land use in the military areas of the Highland Zone. In J.G. Evans, S. Limbrey and H. Cleere (eds.) *The Effect of Man on the Landscape: the Highland Zone*. CBA Research Report 11. London, 112–6.

McCord N. and Jobey G. 1971 Notes on air reconnaissance in Northumberland and Durham. *Archaeol. Aeliana* 4th Series, 49:119–30.

Pennington W. 1970 Vegetational history in the northwest of England – a regional study. In D. Walker and R. West (eds.), *Studies in the Vegetational History of the British Isles*. Cambridge, 41–80.

Ramm H. 1978 *The Parisi*. London.

Reynolds P. 1981 Deadstock and livestock. In R. Mercer (ed.), *Farming Practice in British Prehistory*. Edinburgh, 97–122.

Richmond I.A. 1958 *Roman and Native in North Britain*. Edinburgh and London.

Richmond I.A. and Gillam J.P. 1955 Some excavations at Corbridge 1952–4. *Archaeol. Aeliana* 4th Series, 33:218–20.

Ritchie A. 1970 Palisaded sites in north Britain: their context and affinities. *Scottish Archaeol. Forum* 2:48–67.

Salway P. 1965 *The Frontier People of Roman Britain.* Cambridge.

Simpson F.G. and Richmond I.A. 1934 Report of the Cumberland Excavation Committee for 1933: I. Birdoswald. *Trans. Cumberland and Westmorland Antiq. Archaeol. Soc.* N.S. 34:120–30.

Smith A.G. 1958 Tow lacustrine deposits in the south of the English Lake District. *New Phytologist* 57:363–86.

Smith G.H. 1978 Excavations near Hadrian's Wall at Tarraby Lane, 1976. *Britannia* 9:19–56.

Smith L.P. 1975 *Methods in Agricultural Metrology.* Amsterdam.

Stead I.M. 1965 *The La Tène Cultures of Eastern Yorkshire.* York.

Stead I.M. 1971 Beadlam Roman villa: an interim report. *Yorks. Archaeol. J.* 43:178.

Stead I.M. 1977 *The Arras Culture.* York.

Turner J. 1981 The Iron Age. In I. Simmons and M. Tooley (eds.) *The Environment in British Prehistory.* London, 250–281.

Wacher J.S. 1969 *Excavations at Brough on Humber 1958–61.* London.

Walker D. 1966 The late Quaternary history of the Cumberland lowlands. *Phil. Trans. Royal Soc.* B 251:1–210.

Wenham L.P. 1971 The beginnings of Roman York. In R.M. Butler (ed.) *Soldier and Civilian in Roman Yorkshire.* Leicester, 45–54.

14. Binchester - A Northern Fort and Vicus

I.M. Ferris and R.F.J. Jones

Forts are probably the most commonly investigated of all Roman period sites in Britain. Traditionally they have been seen as holding the keys to understanding the histories of the military campaigns which have so preoccupied many archaeologists of Roman Britain. There is therefore a very large set of excavation reports which have mostly been concerned with identifying structures related to the perceived historical sequence of political and military events. This has tended to discredit the study of military sites in the eyes of those more interested in broader issues of social and economic processes in Roman Britain, a tendency reinforced by the view that Roman forts all broadly conformed to the same stereotyped plan. However, to dismiss Roman forts in this way grossly undervalues the real importance of the Roman army as both an agent and a catalyst for change in the newly conquered province, and as the predominant institution in those frontier regions where there was a permanent military presence. To approach the issues of the role of the army and its forts in their regional environment, research has to be carried out on a wider plane than the traditional obsession with campaign histories. This is what we have tried to do at Binchester.

Binchester, Roman *Vinovia*, lies on a hilltop north of the modern town of Bishop Auckland, Co. Durham. The Roman fort controlled the bridge over the River Wear which carried Dere Street, the main Roman road north from York to Corbridge and beyond. It also lay at the node of a network of other roads leading to east and west. *Vinovia* was a large fort, about 3.6 ha. (9 acres). For part of its history at least it was garrisoned by cavalry, the *ala Vettonum*. It also housed a unit of Frisians and perhaps a detachment of the Sixth Legion. Around the fort grew up a very large civilian settlement, making the total Roman settlement area about 12 to 16 ha (30 to 40 acres).

The site has been recognised since the 16th century when it was mentioned by Leland and Camden, but was first substantially investigated in the late 19th (Hooppell 1891). Those excavations recovered traces of substantial internal buildings and a large civil settlement, where were recognised traces of both some very large individual structures and at least three consecutive major phases of stone building. For many years Binchester was the only example of a civilian settlement at a fort where any excavated details of buildings were available. Other limited investigations had taken place since, but there was little reliable evidence when the most recent research programme began in 1976 (Ferris and Jones 1980). The overall layout of the site, at least in the later Roman period, has now been revealed by resistivity survey, confirming some rather ephemeral details on air photographs (Figure 14.1). Our excavations have largely been confined to the area inside the fort around a very well preserved late

Roman bath-house, which had been exposed and placed in the guardianship of Durham County Council in the 1960s. Recent work has confirmed that the site has very well preserved stratification, to a depth of between two and three metres. Although the area we have been able to excavate represents only a small fraction of the interior of the fort, we are now able to suggest a much clearer framework for the development of the site.

Early military activity

The sequence of occupation discovered is long and complex; it can only be outlined here. Before Roman construction began, the ground was prepared by the removal of trees and bushes, deturfing and levelling. Four coins of Vespasian (69–79) were found in deposits associated with these activities. Also sherds of pre-Flavian fine pottery were recovered in later residual contexts. Nevertheless, the conventional date for the founding of Binchester assigned by previous authorities is AD 79, during Agricola's advance through northern England. The first buildings were of timber. Uprights were jointed into horizontal beams set into trenches or slots; floors were of puddled clay or planks. The building investigated may have been a barrack block, but it is hard to be certain from only fragmentary remains. It was substantially altered during its lifetime, then was systematically demolished down to ground level.

Subsequently, in the early 2nd century the area was used intensively for industrial activities, especially iron working. A series of hearths lay around a spoil heap of waste material, charcoal and slag. Some similar activities have been noted elsewhere inside the fort, over an area of at least 0.5 ha. This is important in showing that an evidently military site was also substantially involved in producing the goods needed by the army. It is a pattern to be found at other sites in northern Britain and in Wales at about the same period. The Roman army seems to have been managing the supply of its own specialised requirements, an intermediate stage between importing its own supplies into newly occupied territory and the full economic integration of the frontier region. Some forts at least were therefore not just fighting bases with their occupation determined by the need to contain hostile natives (c.f. Jones 1990).

Commandant's Houses

The industrial structures were cleared and the spoil heap was levelled to make way for a half-timbered courtyard house, built in the mid-2nd century. Only now was established the layout of the fort displayed through the geophysical survey, with a new line created for the *via principalis* on to which the courtyard building fronted. The building had *opus*

BINCHESTER

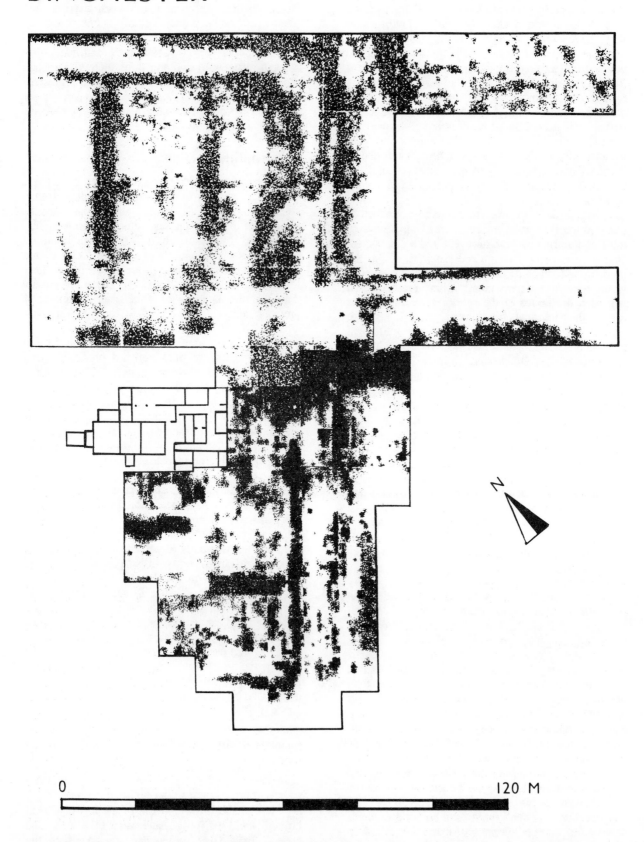

0   120 M

Figure 14.1   Binchester Roman fort: the resistivity survey of the south-eastern part of the fort, related to the excavated area.

signinum floors, plastered walls and a hypocaust system: it was clearly the fort commander's house (the *praetorium*). There were major changes made to the building later, and it remained in use until the mid- or late 3rd century. Then the timber superstructure was removed, but the stone wall-footings were incorporated into a new courtyard house, built completely of stone. The plan of this building included a bath-suite and other hypocausted rooms. The new parts of the building were constructed on massive foundations made of cobbles set in clay, from which came a coin, a 'barbarous radiate' dated 270–290.

Yet this substantial building was replaced in the mid-4th century by another on a much grander scale (Figure 14.2). Again it was a courtyard house with *opus signinum* floors and plastered walls, but it was provided with much larger rooms. Although we have been able to examine only a part of the building, we can reliably estimate from the results of resistivity survey that the whole building occupied a very large area, some 45 by 45 metres. Its construction is dated no earlier than 335–345 by a coin sealed beneath a primary *opus signinum* floor. This building had its own bathing facilities, but a much more impressive bath-suite was later added to the original plan, requiring some of the original structure to be demolished. The new bath-suite, which is today the centrepiece of the exposed remains, (Figure 14.3) originally had two furnaces, serving one warm and two main hot rooms, as well as two hot plunge baths. It was very solidly built, with walls a metre thick. It extended the area of the whole complex to about 65 by 45 metres. A terminus date for the addition of the bath-suite is given by a coin of 350–360 found in the foundation trench of its smaller furnace room.

From the construction of the first excavated stone house in the mid-2nd century, the structural evidence suggests a continuing occupation of the site. There is nothing in the observed record to support any significant phase of abandonment before the post-Roman period. Much effort and many resources were expended on the sequence of high quality buildings which presumably served the fort's commanding officers over perhaps two and a half centuries. This commitment reinforces the idea that Binchester held a high status among northern forts through most of the Roman period.

From Roman to post-Roman

Despite having been built so late in the Roman period, the bath-suite shows signs of long, heavy use. The thresholds at the doorways are badly worn and various repairs were made to the hypocausts. There were also more extensive changes in lay-out (Figure 14.4). The residential part of the building was replanned. Large rooms were divided into groups of much smaller rooms, but the constructional style of the new dividing walls remained the same as those of the original building, solid masonry 0.50 to 0.60 metres thick. The new rooms also still had concrete floors and plastered walls. Probably about the same time, the bath-suite was extended by new facilities around its entrance. Two cold plunge baths were built at the end of an exercise or entrance hall. The hall measured 12.50 by 4.50 metres and was floored with stone flags. The entrance from the hall to the main part of the baths was now through a massive triple archway. The changes made in the house and the baths seem inconsistent, with the baths extended and the house apparently being divided up. It appears that the whole complex was no longer a single private unit, the house being occupied by separate groups of people while the baths were given over to more public usage.

Eventually the bath-suite stopped being used as baths. The metal boiler and pipes were stripped out of the main furnace room. Meanwhile, or perhaps slightly later again, parts of what had been the house were turned to distinctly non-residential purposes. One room opening off the central courtyard was used as a smithy, with three successive blacksmithing furnaces and a thick accumulation of debris. Adjacent to that, the outer wall of another room next to the courtyard was partly knocked down. A rough platform was created on which cattle were slaughtered. From the quantities of animal bone found, it seems that they were slaughtered in great numbers. The slaughtering area itself was surrounded by deposits containing large amounts of butchered bone. Similar deposits containing butchering waste and other domestic rubbish were found at the rear of the bath-suite and in both the disused furnace rooms.

The site clearly remained a centre of significant activity. The chronology of these developments is less certain. The deposits characterised by butchery waste also contained large quantities of the latest recognisable Roman pottery, the products of the East Yorkshire industry, particularly Crambeck, as well as frequent finds of coins. These conform to the general pattern of coin finds at Binchester, with very few issued after 364. Superficially, there is no explicit dating evidence to fix the butchery and blacksmithing phase any later than the end of the 4th century. Such a date however stretches credulity too far in the face of the sequence of activities which followed the latest firm *terminus post quem*, the coin dated to 350–360 in the foundation trench of the bath-suite's smaller furnace room. Unless these activities were compressed into what would have to been an extremely short time, it is hard to avoid the conclusion that the butchery and blacksmithing took place in the 5th century – but equally hard to decide when exactly.

Overall our recent research has been specially revealing about late Roman and post-Roman Binchester. Geophysical survey has confirmed the indications from K.A. Steer's 1937 excavations that buildings spread over the filled-in ditch on the southeast side of the fort (Steer 1938). Since this had been a wide ditch, it had presumably been cut in the late Roman period. This sequence suggests that the community outside the fort was still thriving at a date apparently no earlier than the late 4th century, but there has been no modern excavation there to provide more reliable information.

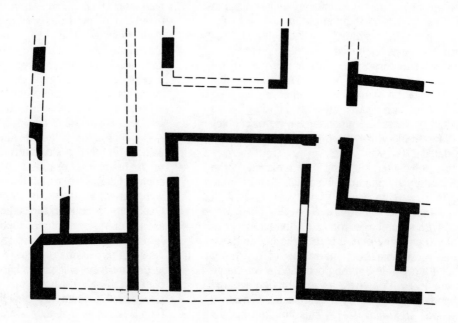

BINCHESTER Phase 8a

1
2
3

0 2 4 6 8 10 Metres

Figure 14.2   Binchester Roman fort: Phase 8a of the commander's house and bath suite. Mid-fourth century.

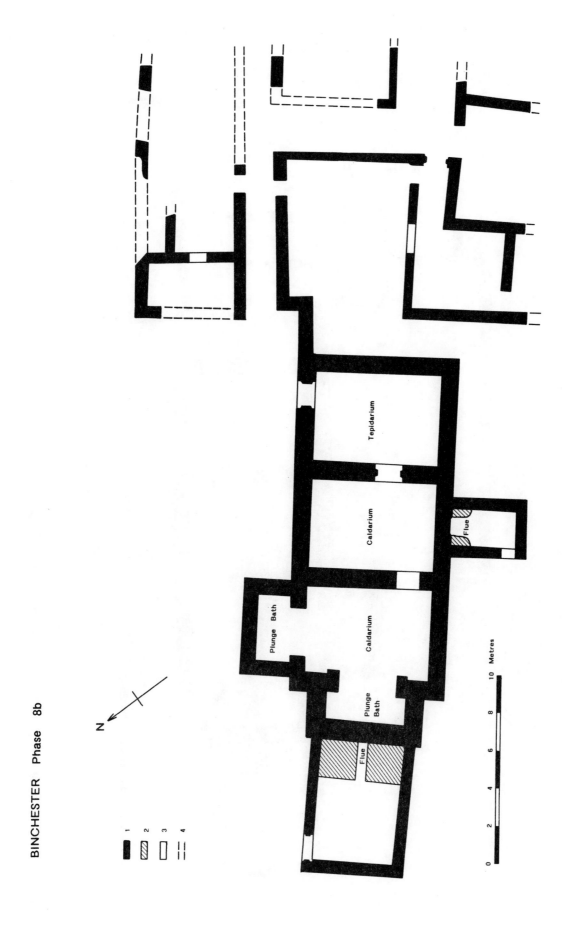

BINCHESTER Phase 8b

Figure 14.3   Binchester Roman fort: Phases 8b of the commander's house and bath-suite.

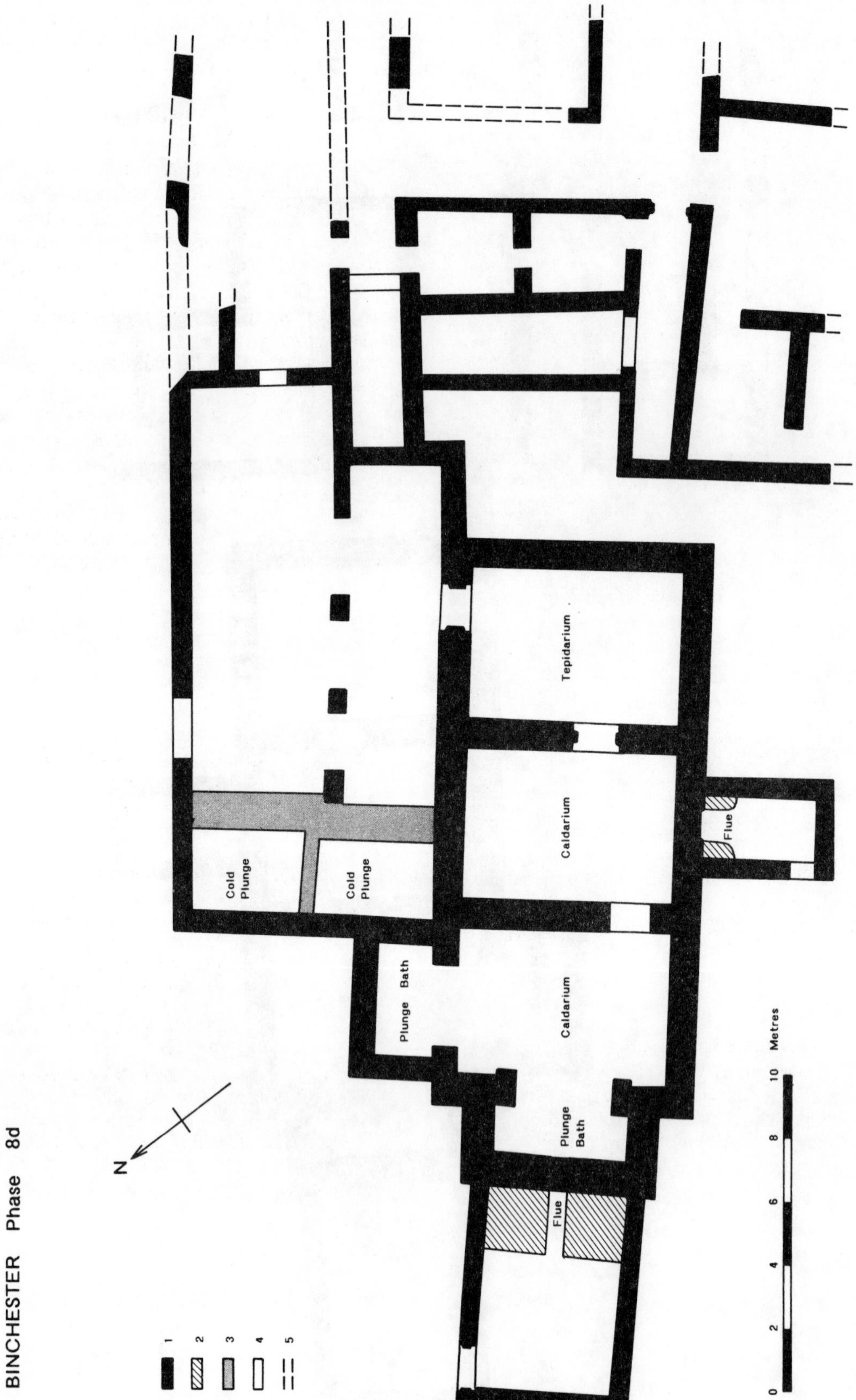

BINCHESTER   Phase   8d

Cold Plunge

Cold Plunge

Tepidarium

Caldarium

Flue

Plunge Bath

Caldarium

Plunge Bath

Flue

N

1
2
3
4
5

0   2   4   6   8   10   Metres

Figure 14.4   Binchester Roman fort: Phases 8d of the commander's house and bath-suite.

The Anglo-Saxon and medieval periods

Inside the defences, after the large furnace room of the bath-suite had been filled in with the dumps of butchery waste, a sequence of small workshops or sheds was built, perhaps for working bone and antler. The bath-suite itself was systematically robbed twice, first for brick and tile, later for stone. The stones taken were massive, necessitating some kind of crane or sheerleg mechanism to lift them out. They were removed at least from the arches between the main *caldarium* and the two hot plunge baths. The stones taken were of the same type used for the early Anglo-Saxon church at Escomb, some 3 km up the River Wear. It has long been argued that Escomb was built in the 7th century with stones taken from Binchester, because of the presence of some inscribed stones in the church's fabric and the interpretation that the chancel arch was simply a Roman arch brought to the site and reconstructed.

We know that the roof of the Binchester bath-suite had collapsed or been demolished when a woman's body was buried above the debris. The burial has been identified on the typology of the grave goods as mid-6th century and Anglo-Saxon. Other skeletons have been found in considerable numbers in the interior of the fort, suggesting a cemetery with interments numbered in hundreds. Carbon 14 determinations on four of these skeletons have given the following dates: ad 690±70, ad 740±80, ad 880±80, ad 930±90. The most recent calibrations would make those calendar dates between fifty and a hundred years later (Struiver and Pearson 1986). We can now therefore be confident that inside what had been the fort there was a large later Anglo-Saxon cemetery, dating perhaps from the 6th to the 11th centuries.

The ruins of the Roman buildings certainly remained apparent much later than this, as Camden's account of 1586 demonstrates. Our excavations have shown that Roman walls were re-used for another smithy in the later medieval period, probably the 13th or 14th century.

Conclusions

The structural sequence has been described in such extended detail to show that Binchester was a very complex site, which changed its character several times over centuries of occupation. The early military activities are not at all straightforward to interpret, but the size of the fort and its strategic location suggest that it was always an important base. It far exceeded in size other forts in the hinterland of the Hadrian's Wall frontier line, until it was matched in the later Roman period by Piercebridge on the River Tees to the south. Since very little is known of the contemporary rural settlement in the region, the relationships between Binchester and the neighbouring native population remain largely unknown. However, by the late Roman period the extent and intensity of the settlement outside the fort suggest that Binchester had become an important focus of settlement for lowland Durham, with at least some urban functions. We have also found that it retained some of that importance into the post-Roman period. These discoveries have much wider implications for the levels of social and economic development in the Roman frontier zone in the 4th century and beyond.

Binchester has more general lessons to offer for proto-historic archaeology. The only way to begin to understand the site's complexities has been to approach it as a settlement rather than a piece of military history, trying to establish the nature of activity at each stage rather than to perceive the hand of some general or emperor. Here there has been little room to discuss the implications of some of the structural changes, nor of the abundant finds, which include important assemblages of pottery, glass and animal bone. It is perhaps enough to stress that there is still a lot to be learned from asking the right questions of Roman forts.

Acknowledgements

We are grateful to Simon Clarke for drawing figures 14.2, 14.3 and 14.4.

References

Ferris I.M. and Jones R.F.J. 1980 Excavations at Binchester 1976–9. In W.S. Hanson & L.J.F. Keppie (eds.), *Roman Frontier Studies 1979*. BAR S71. Oxford, 233–254.

Hooppell R.E. 1891 *Vinovia, a buried Roman city*.

Jones R.F.J. 1990 Natives and the Roman army – three model relationships. In H. Vetters and M. Kandler (eds.), *Akten des 14. Internationalen Limeskongresses 1986*. Vienna:99–110..

Steer K.A. 1938 *The Archaeology of Roman Durham*. Unpubl. PhD thesis, University of Durham.

Struiver M. and Pearson G. 1986 High precision calibration of the Radiocarbon time scale, AD 1950–500 BC. *Radiocarbon* 22 (2B):805–838.

15. Hayling Island

Anthony King and Grahame Soffe

The archaeology of religion has experienced something of a revival in the past decade. Several temples have been excavated, notably Uley, Glos. (Ellison 1980); Bath, Avon (Cunliffe and Davenport 1985); Ivy Chimneys, Essex (Turner 1982); Harlow, Essex (Bartlett 1987); and Hayling Island, Hants (Downey, King and Soffe 1980). There have also been publications of earlier excavations (e.g. Harlow, France and Gobel 1985; Nettleton, Wedlake 1982; Hockwold, Gurney 1986), catalogues of religious artefacts (e.g. Green 1976; 1978; Johns and Potter 1983; Painter 1977; Pitts 1979; Toynbee 1986), studies of particular cults and themes (e.g. Bacchus, Hutchinson 1986; Christianity, Thomas 1981; Celtic religion, Green 1984, 1986a; King 1989; Webster 1986; epigraphy, Birley 1986; iconography Green 1986b), conference proceedings (Rodwell 1980; Henig and King 1986), a popular book (Green 1983) and a major synthesis (Henig 1984). This growth of interest has coincided with, and is partly explained by the general shift in archaeological theory away from primarily economic models, in which religion did not fit easily, towards models that allow for, and are sometimes even powered by, the influence of religion in ancient society.The contribution of Hayling Island to these developments is twofold. Firstly, it is one of the best examples so far excavated of an Iron Age temple that continues into the Roman period. Secondly, it has a wide range of artefacts that gives a valuable insight into the nature of votive offerings in Romano-Celtic religion.

The Iron Age Temple

The site lies on a slight rise in the middle of the northern part of the island, the island itself being one of a group that forms part of the coastline of southeast Hampshire. The first use of the site appears to be in the early to mid 1st century BC. The central building (Figure 15.1a) had a form resembling a round-house, c. 11m in diameter, with an entrance facing east on to a courtyard of roughly square plan. In the centre was a pit, 2.7 x 1.8m, which had been back-filled with brickearth and a variety of artefacts (pottery, bones, brooch fragments, Celtic coins and a piece of a mirror). Neither the shape of the pit nor its contents gave any obvious clue as to its function. There was no sign of it having held water, or that it was a *favissa*-type offering pit. It may possibly have been the foundation for some sort of cult-image, which had been deliberately removed when the Roman temple replaced the Iron Age building, presumably to be positioned on the floor of the Roman temple above the back-filled pit. Central pits are known from other Iron Age temples, e.g. Gournay-sur-Aronde, France (Brunaux *et al.* 1985:94ff), and, in the case of Hayling Island, it is the only feature apart from the associated finds assemblage that distinguishes the circular building

from its secular contemporaries. Just to the east of the porch structure of the circular shrine was an enclosure forming a rough trapezoidal shape. This seems to have been a fence made of squared posts and vertical planks set in a post-trench. Its purpose was probably to separate the entrance to the shrine from the rest of the courtyard, perhaps with a view to restricting access, for the ground inside it seemed less disturbed than in the courtyard generally. It is likely that different ritual activities took place within and without this enclosure. The main courtyard and its outer boundary contained a great many finds. Amongst these were pieces of binding, spearheads, horse harness, bridle bits, terret rings, nave hoops and other material that can be associated with the trappings of an Iron Age warrior and his chariot or cart. In addition there were brooches, some currency bars and c. 170 Celtic coins. The coins are of considerable interest, as the assemblage includes many continental issues and many relatively early types, which suggests a period of fairly prolific coin-offering in the mid 1st century BC, which tails off towards the early/mid 1st century AD. It is not known at present whether this reflects the general history of the temple, or simply a change in the pattern of votive offerings. An important feature of the coin group are some coins which are in silver or gold over bronze cores, i.e. non-standard or unofficial issues. An explanation for this may be that the more valuable solid gold or silver coins were not left in the ground as votive deposits, but were displayed. Their fate would thus have been to be dispersed when the temple site eventually lost its sanctity. The density of finds within the courtyard varied, with concentrations being found on the eastern side, particularly in the southeast corner, in the same area as amorphous groups of stake-holes and burnt patches that were probably part of the ritual activity. The finds assemblage demonstrates fairly clearly that the outer courtyard was the main area where votive offerings were made, and that objects and utensils were brought to the site to be left there, probably because they were deemed sacred once they had played their part in a sacrifice or ritual. A number of the artefacts were bent and broken, perhaps to prevent their reuse or to sacrifice them symbolically to the deity. In addition to the metal objects, the pottery and animal bone finds also represent the remains of offerings. Most of the pottery vessels were containers, and the bones were almost exclusively of sheep and pig, unlike contemporary local settlement sites. Surrounding the courtyard area was a boundary made up of a shallow ditch and postholes. It was of at least two phases, and probably took the form of a fence with a drainage ditch around it. In various places there were gaps, the most obvious being was the main entrance on the east side. The ditch on the south side of this entrance ended in a large rectangular hole, 1.5 x 1.2m, the

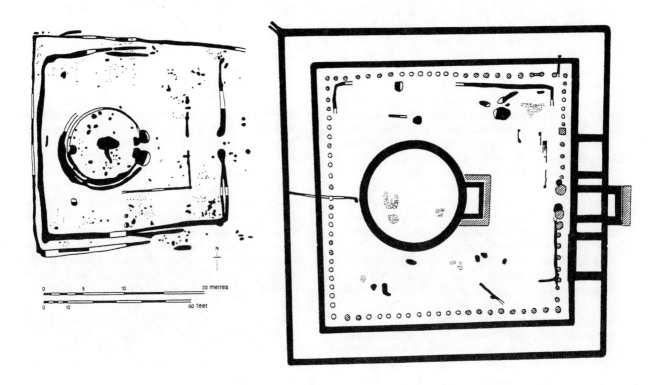

Figure 15.1   Hayling Island: the Iron Age temple (left) and the Roman temple (right).

profile of which is suggestive of a stonehole, possibly for one of the large sarsen boulders that are found as erratics in the region.   Large stones are known to have been held sacred in Celtic religion, most notably at Triguèbres, France (Horne and King 1980:482–3), where a small menhir entirely occupies the cella of a Romano-Celtic temple.   Outside the temple area traces of activity were very sparse.   The temple appears to have been isolated, and indeed the only signs of occupation known from the north part of the island are the shoreline hearths associated with salt production.

The Roman Temple

At the time of the Roman conquest of AD 43, the Iron Age temple was still in use.   Little appears to have changed, probably because the establishment of a client kingdom in the area under Cogidubnus ensured a peaceful transition to Roman rule.   In *c.* 60–70, however, a radical alteration took place, with the removal of the old structure and the setting up of a large stone temple in its place (Figure 15.1b).   This transformation, relatively soon after the conquest compared with other temples in Britain, reflects the rapid pace of Romanisation in the client kingdom, probably encouraged by the king himself. The proto-palace at Fishbourne, the Hayling Island temple and various other projects in the Chichester area were all begun at about the same time, and use similar, probably Gallic, expertise.   For the worshippers at Hayling, the large new temple, at least twice the

volume of the old, and in a different and very new building style, must have decisively altered the cult from one that was almost purely Celtic to one that was now Romano-Celtic.   The change marks an emphasis on the structure of the temple rather than on the votive offerings, which decline in variety and status. The new temple was not, however, a complete break with the past, since its plan was substantially the same as its predecessor.   A galleried temenos replaced the Iron Age courtyard area, and the open space thereby enclosed continued to be the main area of ritual depositional activity.   In the centre stood a circular cella, 13.8m in diameter, with a porch on the east side.   It was plastered red externally, and had a tiled roof.   Inside there was probably some polychrome wall-painting, and a flagged floor, in the centre of which may have stood the cult-image over the Iron Age central pit. Further information on the general appearance of the cella can be gained by looking at three surviving temples in southwest France: Périgueux, Villetoureix and Eysses (Horne and King 1980:409, 446, 490–1).   Each has a cylindrical tower-like shape higher than the overall diameter, an eastern entrance and a blank windowless wall.   The only possible position for windows is above the entrance, since the masonry does not survive in this sector at any of the three.   The temple at Hayling was probably like these – an austere, tall, dimly-lit shrine.   The existence of these parallels in Gaul is of some interest, for it appears that Hayling Island is the only British representative of a distinctive group of large circular temples set in rectilinear courtyards. They are mostly located in western Gaul, and one, Allonnes, has yielded inscriptions to Mars Mullo and a suite of votive offerings that is very similar to that at Hayling (Horne and King 1980:374–5). It is therefore suggested that the latter was also dedicated to a Romano-Celtic Mars. Allonnes also has evidence for a pre-Roman phase, and it is likely that the others, too, had similar origins. Hayling Island Iron Age temple may provide the exemplar for their form. The votive deposits within the Roman courtyard follow the same pattern as that set in the Iron Age, with one important exception. Metalwork was less common than previously, and the wealthy warrior element almost entirely absent. This is probably due to the rapid decline of warrior 'culture' after the Roman conquest, and its replacement by new forms of status display that included the construction of conspicuously Roman-style buildings, of which the Roman phase at Hayling Island itself is a testament.

Conclusion

Although the temple discussed here is not of the classic Romano-Celtic form, since it has no cella ambulatory and is circular rather than square, there are some general points arising from the excavation that are applicable to Romano-Celtic temple studies as a whole. Firstly, the finds assemblage is essential to the understanding of the cult. Temples vary greatly in the composition of their assemblages, and it will only be after many more excavations that the full significance of these differences will become apparent. For the moment, it is a reasonable working hypothesis to suggest that the finds from a temple site provide a clearer guide to the deity worshipped than does its plan. In this respect, the continental evidence, from Gaul in particular, deserves close examination. The reconstruction of the Roman phase as a tower cella is of interest when put in juxtaposition with the Iron Age plan, since the evidence from the latter would suggest a structure no more substantial than a typical Iron Age round-house. Superficially, this may be suggestive of a difference in approach between the two phases, with solely the ground-plan providing the continuity between them. However, it is more likely that there was some formal element in Celtic religion that made tower-like structures desirable, which could only be properly realised when Roman construction methods became available. This may account for the relatively early reconstruction in stone of many Romano-Celtic temples. If this is the case, Celtic religion only reached its fruition in structural terms in the Roman period, and it can be argued that the Roman element in Romano-Celtic religion is no mere veneer over a conservative Celtic base, but marks a decisive stage of development. The change in the complexion of the votive offerings may also be a reflection of a similar process.

References

Bartlett R. 1987 *Harlow Temple Excavations 1985–86: an interim report*. Harlow Museum Occasional Paper 1: Harlow.

Birley E. 1986 The deities of Roman Britain. In W. Haase (ed.) *Aufsteig und Niedergang der Römischen Welt*. Berlin. II 18:3–112.

Brunaux J.L., Meniel P. and Poplin F. 1985 *Gournay I: les fouilles sur le sanctuaire et l'oppidum (1975–1984)*. Amiens.

Cunliffe B.W. and Davenport P. 1985 *The Temple of Sulis Minerva at Bath. I: the site*. Oxford University Committee for Archaeology Monograph 7. Oxford.

Downey R., King A. and Soffe G. 1980 The Hayling Island temple and religious connections across the Channel. In Rodwell 1980:289–304.

Ellison A. 1980 Natives, Romans and Christians on West Hill, Uley: an interim report on the excavation of a ritual complex of the first millennium AD. In Rodwell 1980:305–328.

France N.E. and Gobel B.M. 1985 *The Romano-British Temple at Harlow, Essex*. Gloucester.

Green M.J. 1976 *A Corpus of Religious Material from the Civilian Areas of Roman Britain*. BAR 24. Oxford.

Green M.J. 1978 *Small Cult Objects from the Military Areas of Roman Britain*. BAR 52. Oxford.

Green M.J. 1983 *The Gods of Roman Britain*. Princes Risborough.

Green M.J. 1984 *The Wheel as a Cult Symbol in the Romano-Celtic World*. Collection Latomus, Brussels.

Green M.J. 1986a *The Gods of the Celts*. Gloucester.

Green M.J. 1986b The iconography and archaeology of Romano-British religion. In W. Haase (ed.), *Aufsteig und Niedergang der Römischen Welt*. Berlin. II 18, 1:113–162.

Gurney D. 1986 Settlement, Religion and Industry on the Fen-edge: three Romano-British sites in Norfolk. *East Anglian Archaeol*. 31. Gressenhall, 49–92.

Henig M.E. 1984 *Religion in Roman Britain*. London.

Henig M.E. and King A.C. 1986 (ed.) *Pagan Gods and Shrines of the Roman Empire*. Oxford University Committee for Archaeology Monograph 8. Oxford.

Horne P.D. and King A.C. 1980 Romano-Celtic temples in continental Europe: a gazetteer of those with known plans. In Rodwell 1980:369–555.

Hutchinson V.J. 1986 *Bacchus in Roman Britain: the evidence for his cult*. BAR 151. Oxford.

Johns C.M. and Potter T.W. 1983 *The Thetford Treasure: Roman jewellery and silver*. London.

Painter K. 1977 *The Water Newton Early Christian Silver*. London.

Pitts L.F. 1979 *Roman Bronze Figurines from the Civitates of the Catuvellauni and Trinovantes*. BAR 60. Oxford.

Rodwell W. 1980 (ed.) *Temples, Churches and Religion: recent research in Roman Britain*. BAR 77. Oxford.

Thomas C. 1981 *Christianity in Roman Britain to AD 500*. London.

Toynbee J.M.C. 1986 The Roman Art Treasures from the Temple of Mithras. *London and Middlesex Archaeol. Soc.* Special Paper 7. London.

Turner R. 1982 *Ivy Chimneys, Witham: an interim report*. Essex County Council Archaeology Section Occasional Paper 2. Chelmsford.

Webster G. 1986 *The British Celts and their Gods under Rome*. London.

Wedlake W.J. 1982 The Excavation of the Shrine of Apollo at Nettleton, Wiltshire, 1956–1971. Soc. Antiq. Res. Rep. 40. London.

16. Cultural Change in Roman Britain

R.F.J. Jones

The central issue in the study of the Roman period in Britain is the nature of the interaction between native British customs, values and social, political and economic systems and those of the intrusive Roman Empire. Whether formulated as Romanisation, acculturation, or cultural change, the issue subsumes all patterns of culture as learned behaviour, whether expressed in house types, pottery forms, or religious and political systems. The topic has been much discussed since Haverfield's fundamental study (1915; cf. Millett 1990). Haverfield relied heavily on written sources and archaeological material from elsewhere, which he used as analogies to explain the archaeological data from Roman Britain itself. In that approach he has largely been followed by more recent writers. However, the growth of modern archaeological evidence means that the topic can now be examined in terms of material from Roman Britain itself. Such material must now be seen as indisputably the prime source of information for dealing with the question. This requires a change of attitude in the use of the sources, since the archaeology must be used on its own terms and not as a deficient written source. Assertions of interpretations of the archaeology based on scant written material will simply no longer do.

The archaeological data must be rigorously assessed in ways that are common to all archaeological data of whatever period. There is a frequent misconception that the Roman period is somehow special and different from the rest of the human past, a view put about by classically-trained specialists and too often meekly accepted by other archaeologists. Prehistorians sometimes see in historical periods opportunities to substantiate theories of complex systems which can be demonstrated in the written sources but only inferred from archaeological data. The written sources provide a resource of incomparable value for the general picture of ancient life and patterns of thought. They cannot normally validate directly what we find through archaeology. The whole trend of modern work has moved against the idea that it is possible to excavate with a trowel in one hand and a copy of Tacitus in the other: only very rarely can specifically attested historical events be identified in the archaeological record. The particular value of Roman period archaeology therefore lies only partly in the generalised support provided by the written sources. Roman archaeology should be strong because of the quality and quantity of its archaeological data as archaeology. Site and artefactual evidence is abundant, it has been intensely studied and classified, and the chronologies are tight, derived ultimately from the written sources. This all gives Roman period data a quality in archaeological terms that has the highest potential.

Clearly some framework of understanding is necessary to synthesise the varied archaeological material into useful statements on cultural change (cf. Van der Leeuw 1983). In our pots and postholes different levels of change and continuity can be found. Whilst it is relatively easy to document changes in artefacts like pottery, it becomes progressively more difficult to deal with more abstract concepts such as exchange systems or social structure. It is therefore necessary to be clear about the ways in which our data can be applied to achieve the desired result. There is still a need to link social and political theory satisfactorily with observable archaeological evidence. The extensive literature on social and political evolution which addresses itself to periods where the main evidence is archaeological has too often failed to define hypotheses which are testable in that archaeological evidence. The most productive way forward is to define explicit archaeologically testable correlates of social organisation, and then to test them (cf. Peebles and Kus 1977).

With the specific character of the evidence for Roman Britain in mind, three levels of approach can be defined: cultural forms, economic base and social structure. These can be described further as follows:

Cultural Forms (Things you can excavate) e.g. house forms, movable material culture, burial forms, diet.

Economic Base (Direct relationships between the things you can excavate) e.g. mode of production, trade and exchange systems, settlement hierarchy.

Social Structure (Inferences drawn) e.g. political legitimation, kinship structures, religion.

Cultural forms are the simplest levels of analysis. We are all familiar with work describing and classifying artefacts or food remains, buildings or burial types. It is the essential basis of doing archaeology. There is no substitute for establishing what the evidence actually is. Once we have worked out patterns of change in for example building types, we are left to interpret them. In Roman Britain we can readily observe that more and more houses were built in stone to a rectangular plan and with specialised rooms like baths and dining rooms. We must ask how far does a change in plan and organisation represent fashion, function, wealth, or social organisation (cf. Smith 1978). The question of the process involved takes us beyond the form into more complex areas, where cultural forms connect with the economic base and social structure.

The *economic base* of a community or social group is something which archaeologists feel competent to tackle, since archaeological remains are by definition material. Pots were made and moved around, settlements were constructed. Thus the manufacture of pots can be described, the distribution of defined types can be plotted, and the range of settlement forms in a region can be displayed. It is only one further step to talk of the mode of production, exchange systems and settlement hierarchy. These are terms that archaeologists have become familiar with, where we can feel that solid progress to understanding has been made and can be continued. Here our abstract constructs remain closely related to material things.

With *social structure* our abstract constructs have to approximate to ancient abstractions and are therefore most difficult of all. Although archaeologists have long sought enlightenment on the workings of societies from other areas of the human sciences, there has been a tendency to prefer theories of economic structure, social evolution and ranking. Yet issues of kinship, political legitimation, and religion lie at the heart of modern anthropological thought on the dynamics of a society (cf. Claessen 1983). Any full assessment of cultural change in Roman Britain must take account of whether British systems of kinship links persisted, how far new sources of political power took over, and whether traditional religious structures retained their hold.

Most of the papers in this volume address themselves to these problems in one way or another. However this framework of analysis offers a wider perspective on an agenda different from that outlined by Haverfield three-quarters of a century ago (Haverfield 1915). Haverfield's work has been fundamental to the development of our patterns of thought on Roman Britain (cf. Jones 1987a). Yet through the course of this century we have accumulated a massive new base of archaeological information, which must now be utilised to create new perspectives. Such a new analysis on a full scale is beyond the scope of this essay. My aim here is no more than to sketch an outline of how research may proceed in the future. I will try to illustrate the possibilities by discussing two important areas, burial and religion.

Burial Archaeology and Romano-British Society

The study of burial practice should provide one of the best indicators of patterns of learned behaviour and cultural rules. Every society has rules and conventions about the proper way to dispose of its dead. They set the parameters within which the arrangements for any specific funeral can be made. Therefore a general study of a community's burial practice should reveal the underlying common rules which may be obscured by the peculiarities of individual cases. This should apply even to that fraction of the funerary process which is left for the archaeologist in an excavated grave. To be effective, such an approach requires large, systematically collected archaeological samples, whether within an individual cemetery or a region.

Unfortunately, the cemeteries of Roman Britain have received scant attention. Regional studies are very few, and in some areas virtually impossible. A recent exception has dealt with the southeast (Black 1986). Although his account is essentially descriptive, Black argues that a continuous tradition existed from the change to cremation in the pre-Roman period in the mid-first century BC to the adoption of inhumation in the late Roman period. This generalisation is broadly unexceptionable, but it masks a much more complex, multi-level pattern of variability in burial practice.

That variability can be defined at three levels: the local individual community, the region, and the Roman Empire as a whole (cf. Jones 1987b). Much of the interest in studying Roman cemetery archaeology lies in trying to understand the interplay of these different influences. There can be no single 'right answer' to so complicated a question as the social meaning of burial practice. However significant light can be shed on the articulation of these social forces in the Roman provinces through funerary archaeology.

Burial traditions that are in detail specific to communities are best seen in Britain in urban contexts, although there are clear examples of the phenomenon occurring more widely in Continental Europe. It is apparent that within the extensive cemeteries that surrounded Roman towns there were zones where different conventions were followed. At York, the best known Roman cemetery of Trentholme Drive was characterised by the very intensive cutting of inhumation graves into slightly earlier burials. Yet at the same time other York cemeteries were receiving inhumations in an orderly fashion, respecting earlier burials (cf. Jones 1984a). It seems very likely that different social groups were using the different areas.

Links between apparently defined communities and burial areas can also be found in contexts away from the major cities. At Skeleton Green in Hertfordshire the funerary enclosure contained graves in a quite homogenous burial tradition, with notably richer grave goods than neighbouring sites (Partridge 1981). There are few examples known of the burial places of the majority of the Romano-British population, the rural people. At Bradley Hill and Lynch Farm cemeteries serving small farmsteads of later Roman date have been found (Leech 1981; Jones 1975). Again the burial rite was internally consistent at each site, and broadly conformed to the norm of unaccompanied inhumation found throughout the province.

Traditions are more difficult to define at a regional level, given our present state of knowledge. Only in the southeast of England have there been enough investigations for a confident picture to be created, and that material has not been systematically brought together. Yet what we tend to think of as 'normal' Romano-British burials in fact betray standard features which are not exactly reproduced in neighbouring parts of northern Gaul, from where models for the British to follow might have been expected to have originated. Most Romano-British cremations are found as groups of ashes collected from a pyre and deposited in the ground in some sort of container with a selection of grave goods. *Bustum* graves are rare, where the cremation has taken place in situ in a grave pit. Also unusual in Britain are *Brandschüttungsgräber* or *Brandgrubengräber*, where the grave pits have been filled with the remains of the pyre itself, which are common in the Rhineland and northern Gaul (cf. Van Doorselaer 1969; Bechert 1980). The types of object used as grave goods tend to reflect the material culture assemblage available at the time, at least as much as conscious funerary choices. So oil lamps are rare in the northern provinces in both domestic and funerary contexts, but are common in both in the Mediterranean. However, also unusual in Britain are the large iron nails found in Roman graves from modern Belgium, which are apparently not just the only remaining trace of a wooden object. They seem to have been put there for their own sakes, as ritual objects, *clous magiques* (e.g. at Blicquy, de Laet *et al.* 1972). With inhumations, simple grave goods are more common in continental Europe than in Britain.

Overall, there is a degree of standardisation within Roman Britain compared to practices in adjacent provinces. The present state of knowledge does not however allow the confident definition of regional styles within Britain, even at the limited level offered by Whimster (1981) for the Iron Age.

Empire-wide influences seem more obvious. The style of cremation defined above is broadly consistent with practices that can be observed throughout the western provinces of the Roman Empire. Its prevalence and its origins are not quite so clear. Assessing prevalence is made difficult by the bias in the evidence of excavated graves towards those from towns or smaller urban centres. Military cemeteries have hardly been examined (Jones 1984b). More importantly, our knowledge of rural burial is still very poor, especially for the first and second centuries AD. We simply do not know how most Romano-Britons were buried at that time. We cannot therefore pretend that the evidence we do have is representative of the province's population as a whole and so we cannot judge whether or not any style was followed. Equally the relationship is unclear between the pre-conquest cremation tradition in southeastern Britain and the succeeding Roman one. Quantified comparisons are hard to achieve without substantial samples of pre-conquest graves. The most important such set comes from King Harry Lane, Verulamium, recently published by Stead and Rigby (1989). For some Roman settlements there is a different obstacle. At Chichester St Pancras the cemetery began in use in the last quarter of the first century, with the growth of the Romanised town (Down and Rule 1971). The cemetery is therefore Roman in date, without predecessors for direct comparison. At the rural site of Owslebury there is some continuity of use of a cemetery area, but changes take place in the actual practice and probably the graves of only a part of the living population were found (Collis 1977). Nevertheless it does seem that overall the two cremation traditions were similar. Thus it is hard to distinguish at present whether Romano-British cremation was more influenced by insular or Empire-wide traditions.

Indeed the distinction may be a false one.

A more illuminating manifestation of common influences across the Empire lies in the change in practice from cremation to inhumation. This was a widespread phenomenon throughout the western provinces, taking place during the third century (Jones 1981). Modern excavations have shown that the change was usually gradual, with both practices often co-existing in the same cemetery for some time, as at Chichester and York. The common linking of this change directly with the spread of Christianity has long been discredited. This view is now reinforced by the evidence of excavation which has shown that the change in burial practice was common long before there is any comparable evidence for widespread Christianity. Explaining the change is more difficult. We have no written evidence for why any individuals chose inhumation when generations of their ancestors had been cremated. Whatever the intellectual and spiritual climate that may have influenced such choices (cf. Brown 1981), the archaeological evidence makes it clear that the same choices were being made by people from peasants to aristocrats, from North Africa to Britain. The outcome was the same for them all. By the end of the third century most people in the Roman West were inhumed, when a century earlier most had been cremated. The mechanisms remain mysterious by which such common perceptions spread so widely. That common perceptions existed on that scale seems unquestionable.

The patterns of burial archaeology can be related to the framework of analysis set out earlier. Some changes in burial practice are best related to the development of cultural forms. For example the choice of objects to place in graves as grave goods was closely related to the range of objects in general use at the time. As a wider range of pottery forms became available, they were more likely to be incorporated into the burial habit. Such changes may give the appearance of richer grave provision, but may be no more than a reflection of wider change in the availability of goods in the market. Similarly, the appearance of cemeteries serving new settlements tells us more about settlement history than about anything specifically funerary.

However the levels of variability in defining funerary behaviour relate to patterns by which people defined themselves in communities. The connection between such communities defined in burial practice and those recognisable to those living at the time is more problematic, but they are no less real a reflection of what those people were doing. How far patterns of funerary behaviour can be fixed precisely to identifiable ethnic groups is highly questionable. The claims made for the apparently anomalous graves in the Winchester Lankhills cemetery have yet to be substantiated by rigorous quantified analysis either of the Lankhills cemetery itself or of the continental traditions proposed as parallels (Clarke 1979; Baldwin 1985). Yet the tracing of such anomalies is less important than the general picture. In Roman Britain the interaction between different levels of community seems to have been similar to that elsewhere in the Roman west. In terms of burial at least, it seems that people followed cultural patterns of shared and learned behaviour at the levels of their immediate community, of some regional grouping, and of the whole Roman west. This suggests a society more integrated across long distances than is commonly perceived. It implies a widespread participation in common cultural forms, which may be termed acculturation, or perhaps Romanisation. Within that network of integration, the local face-to-face communities remained the basic units. It seems most likely that those communities showed a continuity from pre-conquest social forms, since they can be observed from a time very soon after the conquest. The ties binding such groupings are therefore most likely to have rested on traditional Celtic kinship systems. Their survival through the Roman period points to minimal discontinuity in basic social organisation, although gradual change must have happened.

Social Implications of Religion in Roman Britain

Romano-British religion has been a field ripe for antiquarian interest, collecting curiosities of ancient behaviour, whether reflections of the Greco-Roman pantheon or of darker Celtic mysteries. However, new finds of religious objects and excavations at a number of temple sites have woken much fresh interest in the topic. Major reviews have recently been published by Henig (1984) and Thomas (1981), to set alongside a host of more specialised studies (e.g. Green 1986; Henig and King 1986). What most of these works have in common is that they are predominantly concerned with the iconography, theology and popularity of the cults discussed. They generally give little attention to the anthropological perspective on religion which sees there a central element of social organisation and political legitimation (cf. Claessen 1983). That perspective has successfully been applied to the Roman Imperial Cult, in a study based on written evidence (Price 1984). It has also now been used to inform our view of archaeological evidence in northern Gaul (Roymans 1988).

Roymans' work is of fundamental importance to advancing ideas on religion in Roman Britain. It applies the social perspective to a set of evidence drawn from northern Gaul, where we might expect a situation most closely parallel to that in Britain. Roymans suggests that cults and cult-places were directly identified with the various structural elements of Celtic society, both tribes and smaller sets such as *pagi*. Such a structure is proposed on the basis of a variety of sources for northern Gaul. The social groups are essentially defined through kinship and lineages. The recognition of these associations between cult-places and the structures of Celtic society offers a new range of interpretative possibilities. It is necessary to appreciate the social significance of temples as the cult-centres of a tribe or a *pagus* or another social unit. We can then expect to trace archaeologically the histories of those

temples – and thereby of the cults themselves and of the social organisation that was intertwined with them.

Certain major temples immediately suggest themselves as probable cult-centres for a whole tribe. The Romano-Celtic temple with its precinct and adjacent theatre at the centre of Verulamium is one obvious case (Frere 1983, 10). Others are the temples at Hayling Island (King and Soffe, this vol.) and at Gosbecks, Colchester, also with a theatre next to it (Hull 1958:259–71). These were major monumental buildings. They needed substantial support simply for continuing maintenance, which inevitably implies some degree of collective action by the participating community, or at least large private donations in the interests of that community. The case to see them as the religious centres of their respective tribes is convincing. At Hayling Island there is good evidence for continuity of the cult from the pre-Roman Iron Age into the Roman period, but the temple did not survive into the late Roman period (cf. King and Soffe, this vol.). This might suggest a weakening of traditional structures, but Hayling Island contrasts with Verulamium in being situated at a distance from the tribal capital. At Verulamium the temple and its precinct remained in use until the end of the fourth century (Frere 1983:21). However the survival of the actual buildings cannot simplistically be taken as meaning that they were still being used in the same ways after two or three centuries. There is less evidence for the details of the cult practices carried out, except at Hayling Island where some continuation in what was being done can be seen even when the form of the structure was transformed from Iron Age timber to Roman stone. We are far from having enough detail of cult practices to reach confident conclusions, but the retention of such prominent temples implies that changes in their use were evolutionary rather than dramatic. If changes in the forms and processes of religious practice were gradual, it is likely that the related social structures changed only gradually too. This suggests that social relationships at the tribal level remained recognisably descendants of their pre-conquest forms.

There is a consistent pattern at the level of the smaller temples. Modern excavations are producing examples of sites such as Uley (Ellison 1980) or Springhead (Harker 1980), where a temple in unequivocally Roman materials had been built over an earlier cult-place. These more modest sites were provided with buildings in Roman forms which endured into the late Roman period, and in some cases into the sub-Roman (cf. Rahtz and Watts 1979). Such strength in the Celtic religious tradition at the routine local level lends impressive support to the idea that Celtic social structures persisted to underpin it.

The political importance of religious practices is particularly clearly demonstrated in the one area where the Roman Empire required observance, the Imperial cult. Here political allegiance was explicitly expressed through religious ceremonies. The extent of observance in Roman Britain is poorly represented in the archaeological record, except in the Temple of

Claudius at Colchester. There the most dramatic stories surround its origins and its place in the Boudiccan revolt in the first century. What is less well appreciated is that like the Romano-Celtic temple precinct in the centre of Verulamium it enjoyed prolonged use (Drury 1984). For the greater part of the Roman period it must be presumed that it was a major centre of the Imperial cult in the province, and that it was appropriately funded by the people of the province. However there need have been no threat here to the proposed linkages between Celtic religion and social structures. The recent studies by Price (1984) on the social role of the Imperial cult in Asia Minor show that it could easily have been accommodated as the topmost layer on the stratified scheme of Celtic social and religious relationships. It would have acted as the common cult to everyone in the province.

It seems likely the other intrusive cults that appeared in Britain from elsewhere in the Empire had little effect on the fundamental structures of Celtic religion. The association of Classical deities such as Mercury with Celtic equivalents seems to have enriched the existing cults rather than changed them significantly, as the cult-places and the recognition of the original deity seem to have been retained. Oriental religions like Mithraism might have been more disruptive to the traditional order. They have attracted much archaeological interest. This is no doubt partly explained by the thrill of the exotic, partly by the relative ease of identifying a temple with a cult. That is to some extent accounted for by the presence of high quality objects like inscriptions or sculpture which are clearly portraying or are associated with a known deity. The identified temples of Mithras in Britain are characterised by smallness of internal area and the presence of expensive objects inside, particularly stone sculptures (cf. Henig 1984:95–109). That pattern is consistent with what we know of the cult from elsewhere, that participation was restricted by various levels of initiation and that the relatively small groups of followers were often drawn from the wealthier and more cosmopolitan parts of society. The distribution of known Romano-British Mithraea in London, York and on military sites, particularly on Hadrian's Wall, argues for a cult associated with soldiers and traders. It is unlikely that such cults had much impact on the hold exercised over most of Celtic society by traditional religion.

The real threat to Celtic religion came from Christianity. It could not be freely accommodated within a polytheistic system. Widespread conversion to Christianity would have meant the inevitable end of the socio-religious scheme evolved from pre-Roman times. Social power and authority would have needed new forms of expression. Yet perhaps they had already developed by the fourth century. There is no space here for a full assessment of the extent of Christian conversion in Roman Britain. It should be noted however that whilst it might be expected that the Temple of Claudius at Colchester be turned in the fourth century to the new official religion of the Empire (cf. Drury 1984), many temples in town and country seem to have continued much as usual (Rahtz and Watts 1979). Even so prominent a site as the Temple of Sulis Minerva at Bath continued to have similar patterns of use until the mid-fourth century (Cunliffe and Davenport 1985:184). Overall there is little evidence that the mass of the Romano-British population had adopted Christianity, even quite late in the fourth century, although a substantial and influential minority may have done.

This section obviously gives only a superficial sketch of the possible social implications of religious observances in Roman Britain. It is intended to do no more than to expose the interpretational possibilities of work on cult sites. The investigation of temples offers unequalled potential for reconstructing not so much the details of a particular liturgy, but the history of observances, with the implications for the development of ideologies and the legitimation of social power. An extended study of the archaeology of religion in Roman Britain should allow the explicit testing of models of change on archaeological data at the most complex of three levels of social inference defined above.

Conclusions

Both burial and religious practices provide evidence of communities at various scales in the Roman world defining themselves by their common traditions. Although both areas of study at present lack large-scale systematic treatments that ask questions of this kind, they suggest a model of a society structured in a similarly stratified way to that envisaged by Roymans (1988) for northern Gaul. Such stratification may have been the key to social change in Roman Britain. It allowed the development of a native élite that was quickly integrated into the Roman system to become the link between the mass of the provincial population and the Empire. That élite both maintained the traditions of an earlier social order and collaborated in the creation of a new one (cf. Robinson 1976; Bloemers 1988).

The problem we have in examining such hypotheses is how to link them with evidence that is predominantly archaeological. A differentiated framework of analysis, as proposed above, can provide ways of testing cultural change operating at different levels. Clearly house structures are easier than social structures to assess archaeologically. Archaeological data has recently been successfully used to demonstrate aspects of cultural interaction in diet by King (1984) and in language by Evans (1987). Both studies produced similar pictures of a gradient of the degree of assimilation to Roman practices from the Roman legionary base to the British peasant farm. Yet it is only in the more complex areas of social and political organisation that any judgements can be made on how substantial change actually may have been. We now have large quantities of reliable archaeological information. They connect with new perspectives on such matters as burial and religion to open exciting prospects of a more mature understanding of how change operated in the Roman period in Britain.

References

Baldwin R. 1985 Intrusive burial groups in the late Roman cemetery at Lankhills, Winchester – a re-assessment of the evidence. *Oxford J. Archaeol.* 4(1):93–104.

Bechert T. 1980 Zur Terminologie provinzialrömischer Brandgräber. *Archäologisches Korrespondenzblatt* 10:253ff.

Black E.W. 1986 Romano-British burial customs and religious beliefs in South-East England. *Archaeol. J.* 143:201–39.

Bloemers J.H.F. 1988 Periphery in pre- and protohistory. In *First Millennium Papers*, R.F.J. Jones *et al.* (eds.), pp.11–35. Oxford: Brit. Archaeol. Rep., Inter Ser 401.

Brown P. 1981 *The Cult of the Saints*. SCM Press.

Claessen H. 1983 Kinship, chiefdom and reciprocity – on the use of anthropological concepts in archaeology. In *Roman and Native in the Low Countries*, R.W. Brandt and J. Slofstra (eds.), pp.211–22. Oxford: Brit. Archaeol. Rep., Inter Ser 184.

Clarke G. 1979 *The Roman Cemetery at Lankhills*. Winchester Studies 3: Pre-Roman and Roman Winchester, part II.

Collis J. 1977 Owslebury (Hants) and the problem of burials on rural settlements. In *Burial in the Roman World*, R. Reece (ed.), pp.26–34. CBA Res. Rep. 22.

Cunliffe B. and Davenport P. 1985 *The Temple of Sulis Minerva at Bath*, volume 1. Oxford Univ. Comm. Archaeol. Mono. 7.

Van Doorselaer A. 1967 *Les Nécropoles d'époque romaine en Gaule septentrionale*. Brugge: Dissertationes Archaeologicae Gandenses 10.

Down A. and Rule M. 1971 *Chichester Excavations I*.

Drury P.J. 1984 The Temple of Claudius at Colchester reconsidered. *Britannia* 15:7–50.

Ellison A. 1980 Natives, Romans and Christians on West Hill, Uley. In *Temples, Churches and Religion in Roman Britain*, W. Rodwell (ed.), pp.305–28. Oxford: Brit. Archaeol. Rep. 77.

Evans J. 1987 Graffiti and the evidence of literacy and pottery use in Roman Britain. *Archaeol. J.* 44:191-204.

Frere S.S. 1983 Verulamium Excavations II. *Soc. Antiq. London Res. Rep.* 41.

Harker, S. 1980 Springhead, a brief reappraisal. In *Temples, Churches and Religion in Roman Britain*, W. Rodwell (ed.), pp.285–88. Oxford: Brit. Archaeol. Rep. 77.

Haverfield, F. 1915 *The Romanization of Roman Britain* 3rd ed. Oxford.

Henig M. 1984 *Religion in Roman Britain*. London: Batsford.

Henig M. and King A.C. (eds.) 1986 *Pagan Gods and Shrines of the Roman Empire*. Oxford Univ. Comm. Archaeol. Mono. 8.

Hull M.R. 1958 *Roman Colchester*. Oxford: Soc. Antiq. London.

Jones R.F.J. 1975 The Romano-British farmstead and its cemetery at Lynch Farm, near Peterborough. *Northants. Archaeol.* 10:94–137.

Jones R.F.J. 1981 Cremation and inhumation – change in the third century. In *The Roman West in the Third Century*, A.C. King and M. Henig (eds.), pp.15–19. Oxford: Brit. Archaeol. Rep., Inter. Ser. 109.

Jones R.F.J. 1984a The cemeteries of Roman York. In *Archaeological Papers from York presented to M.W. Barley*, P.V. Addyman and V.E. Black (eds.), pp.34–42. York Archaeological Trust.

Jones R.F.J. 1984b Death and distinction. In *Military and Civilian in Roman Britain*, T.F.C. Blagg and A.C. King (eds.), pp.219–25. Oxford: Brit. Archaeol. Rep. 136.

Jones R.F.J. 1987a The archaeologists of Roman Britain. *Bull. Inst. Archaeol. Univ. London* 24:85–97.

Jones R.F.J. 1987b Burial in Rome and the western provinces. In *The Roman World*, J. Wacher (ed.), pp.812–37. London: Routledge Kegan Paul.

King A.C. 1984 Animal bones and the dietary identity of military and civilian groups in Roman Britain, Germany and Gaul. In *Military and Civilian in Roman Britain*, T.F.C. Blagg and A.C. King (eds.), pp.187–217. Oxford: Brit. Archaeol. Rep. 136.

de Laet S.J. *et al.* 1972 *La Nécropole Gallo-Romaine de Blicquy*. Brugge: Dissertationes Archaeologicae Gandenses 14.

Leech R. 1981 The excavation of a Romano-British farmstead and cemetery on Bradley Hill, Somerton, Somerset. *Britannia* 12:177–252.

van der Leeuw S.E. 1983 Acculturation as information processing. In *Roman and Native in the Low Countries*, R.W. Brandt and J. Slofstra (eds.), pp.11–41. Oxford: Brit. Archaeol. Rep., Inter Ser 184.

Millett, M. 1990 *The Romanization of Britain*. Cambridge: Cambridge University Press.

Partridge C. 1981 *Skeleton Green: a Late Iron Age and Romano-British Site*. Britannia Mono.

Peebles C.S. and Kus, S. 1977 Some archaeological correlates of ranked societies. *Amer. Antiq.* 42(3):421–48.

Price S.R.F. 1984 *Rituals and Power. The Roman Imperial Cult in Asia Minor*. Cambridge: Cambridge University Press.

Rahtz P. and Watts L. 1979 The end of Roman temples in the west of Britain. In *The End of Roman Britain*, P.J. Casey (ed.), pp.183–201. Oxford: Brit. Archaeol. Rep. 71.

Robinson R. 1976 Non-European foundations of European Imperialism: sketch for a theory of collaboration. In *Imperialism, the Robinson and Gallagher Controversy*, W.R. Louis (ed.), pp.128–51.

Roymans N. 1988 Religion and society in Late Iron Age northern Gaul. In *First Millennium Papers*, R.F.J. Jones *et al.* (eds.), pp.55–71. Oxford: Brit. Archaeol. Rep., Inter. Ser. 401.

Smith J.T. 1978 Villas as a key to social structure. In *Studies in the Romano-British Villa*, M. Todd (ed.), pp.149–85. Leicester: Leicester University Press.

Stead I.M. and Rigby V. 1989 *Verulamium: the King Harry Lane Site*. London: English Heritage Archaeol. Rep. 12..

Thomas C. 1981 *Christianity in Roman Britain*. London: Batsford.

Whimster R. 1981 *Burial Practices in Iron Age Britain*. Oxford: Brit. Archaeol. Rep. 90.